NARROW-LOT
HOME PLANS

Design Q482, page 75

250 Designs For Houses 17' To 50' Wide

HOME PLANNERS, LLC
Wholly owned by Hanley-Wood, Inc.
Tucson, Arizona

NARROW-LOT HOME PLANS

Published by Home Planners, LLC
Wholly owned by Hanley-Wood, Inc.
Editorial and Corporate Offices:
3275 West Ina Road, Suite 110
Tucson, Arizona 85741

Distribution Center:
29333 Lorie Lane
Wixom, Michigan 48393

Rickard D. Bailey, *CEO and Publisher*
Cindy Coatsworth Lewis, *Director of Publishing*
Jan Prideaux, *Senior Editor*
Carlene Tejada, *Editor*
Paul Fitzgerald, *Senior Graphic Designer*
Joan Simmons, *Book Design/Production*

Design/Photography Credits
Front Cover: Design Q482
    Photo by Raef Grohne Photography
    Builder: Harald Koehn Construction, Ltd.
    Designer: Select Home Designs
Back Cover: Design 8001
    Photo courtesy of Larry E. Belk Designs
    Photo by Karen Stuthard

First Printing, July 1999
10 9 8 7 6 5 4 3 2 1

Printed in the United States of America

Library of Congress Catalog Card Number: 99-073183

ISBN softcover: 1-881955-58-3

TABLE OF CONTENTS

Design 7469, page 69

3

THE DESIGNERS

Blue Ribbon Designers

Alan Mascord Design Associates, Inc.
Design Basics
Stephen Fuller
Donald A. Gardner Architects, Inc.
Frank Betz Associates, Inc.
Home Planners
Larry E. Belk Designs
Living Concepts Home Planning
The Sater Design Collection

New Discovery Designers

Ahmann Design, Inc.
Andy McDonald Design Group
Archival Designs, Inc.
Authentic Historical Designs, Inc.
Chatham Home Planning, Inc.
Drummond Designs, Inc.
Fillmore Design Group
Greg Marquis & Associates
Home Design Services
James Fahy Design
Jannis Vann & Associates, Inc.
Lucia Custom Home Designers, Inc.
Nelson Design Group, LLC
Piercy & Barclay Designers, Inc.
R.L. Pfotenhauer
Select Home Designs
Studer Residential Designs, Inc.
TAG Architects
United Design Associates, Inc.

INTRODUCTION

Diversity in Narrow Design

Living in narrow spaces is not new to the human race, but never have narrow spaces offered so much comfort and so many amenities! A narrow house doesn't mean deprived design. A look at the plans on the following pages will show you the wealth of advanced designs available for building on narrow lots. Open floor plans in many designs create spacious livability absent in wider homes, and square footage ranges from 1,008 to 3,045 square feet. A home that looks no wider than a 20-foot room can extend to the back of property as far as 120 feet. Or the home can include three or even four floors, or be a split level with rooms spinning off like the striations on a spider's web.

The designers of these remarkable homes have included everything from grand scale dimensions to delicate details: high ceilings, two-story living rooms, decorative columns, bay windows, walk-in closets, garden tubs, balconies and verandas, fireplaces, porches and patios, breakfast nooks, ample storage space, often a two- or three-car garage, and master suites that are true homeowners' retreats.

Just because the home is built on a narrow lot doesn't limit the size of the family— many plans have three or even four bedrooms and most provide two or three baths. In these homes, parents can raise a growing family, a career-minded couple can create sophisticated surroundings, or empty-nesters can retire to the peaceful pursuits they've dreamed of for a lifetime.

Italian-style villas fit as well on a narrow lot as quaint Cape Cod homes and Caribbean cottages. Many designs have been adapted from historical houses and European and Mediterranean styles. You'll also find regional designs from New England, the South and the Southwest. For city living, "zero-lot-line" homes can be constructed as condominiums or multi-family units. For country life, choose from a myriad of farmhouses and cottages.

This collection presents a range of widths, styles and designs for various lifestyles. After the "Wide Diversity in Narrow Designs" section, the plans are divided by width, beginning with the most narrow—from 17 to 37 feet—in "Affordable Dream Homes." The next section, "Designs for Family Living," introduces plans from 37 to 41 feet, while "At Home in the City or Country" offers designs from 41 to 45 feet. "Grand Traditions in Small Spaces" contains plans from 45 to 48 feet, and "Spacious Designs for Narrow Lots" includes homes from 48 to 50 feet.

For those plans accompanied by the Quote One® logo, Home Planners offers their estimating service for the cost of building the home in your zip-code area. The Quote One® system is available in two stages: The Summary Cost Report and The Materials Cost Report. See page 246 for details—and here's to a happy building experience!

WIDE DIVERSITY IN NARROW DESIGNS

Design 3316

First Floor: 1,111 square feet
Second Floor: 886 square feet
Total: 1,997 square feet

L

DESIGN BY
© **Home Planners**

◆ Don't be fooled by the small-looking exterior. This plan offers three bedrooms and plenty of living space. Notice that the screened porch leads to a rear terrace with access to the breakfast room. A living room/dining room combination adds spaciousness to the floor plan. Other welcome amenities include box-bay windows in the breakfast room and dining room, a fireplace in the living room, a planning desk and pass-through snack bar in the kitchen, a whirlpool tub in the master bath and an open two-story foyer. The thoughtfully placed flower box, beyond the kitchen window above the sink, adds a homespun touch to this already comfortable design.

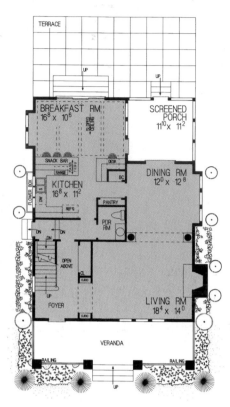

Width: 34'-1"
Depth: 50'-0"

QUOTE ONE®

Cost to build? See page 246 to order complete cost estimate to build this house in your area!

This home, as shown in the photograph, may differ from the actual blueprints. For more detailed information, please check the floor plans carefully.

Photo by Andrew D. Lautman

*This home, as shown in the photograph, may differ from the actual blueprints.
For more detailed information, please check the floor plans carefully.*

Photo by Bob Greenspan

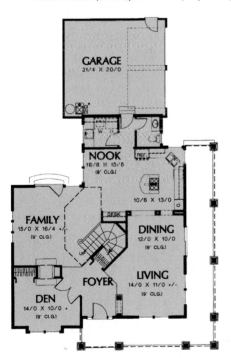

GARAGE
21/4 X 20/0

NOOK
10/8 X 15/6
(9' CLG.)

10/6 X 13/0

FAMILY
15/0 X 16/4 +/-
(9' CLG.)

DINING
12/0 X 10/0
(9' CLG.)

DESK

FOYER

LIVING
14/0 X 11/0 +/-
(9' CLG.)

DEN
14/0 X 10/0 +
(9' CLG.)

DESIGN BY
© Alan Mascord
Design Associates, Inc.

Design 9557

**First Floor: 1,371 square feet
Second Floor: 916 square feet
Total: 2,287 square feet**

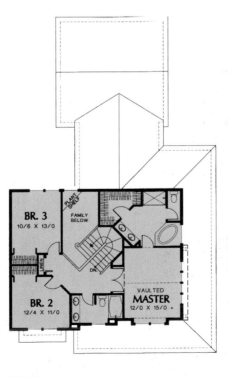

BR. 3
10/6 X 13/0

PLANT SHELF

FAMILY BELOW

LINEN

DN.

BR. 2
12/4 X 11/0

VAULTED
MASTER
12/0 X 15/0

◆ The decorative pillars and the wraparound porch are just the beginning of this comfortable home. Inside, an angled, U-shaped stairway leads to the second-floor sleeping zone. On the first floor, French doors lead to a den that has a box-bay window and shares a see-through fireplace with the two-story family room. The large kitchen includes a work island, a planning desk, a corner sink, a breakfast nook and access to the laundry room, powder room and two-car garage. The master suite provides ultimate relaxation with its French-door access, vaulted ceiling and luxurious bath. Two other bedrooms and a full bath complete the second floor.

Width: 43'-0"
Depth: 69'-0"

7

Design 7253

First Floor: 976 square feet
Second Floor: 823 square feet
Total: 1,799 square feet

DESIGN BY
©Design Basics, Inc.

◆ Arch-top windows and a front covered porch with a balustrade add charm to this country-style exterior. Inside, the formal parlor offers a ten-foot ceiling and a dining room option. The tiled entry opens through French doors to a well-lit breakfast area with a patio door to a covered deck. The gourmet kitchen offers a food preparation island, a pantry and convenient access to the large family room, which boasts a fireplace. Upstairs, two secondary bedrooms feature built-in desks and open to a gallery hall that leads to a full bath. The light-filled master suite, also on this floor, enjoys a private dressing area set off by French doors, a whirlpool spa tub, twin vanities and a compartmented area with linen storage.

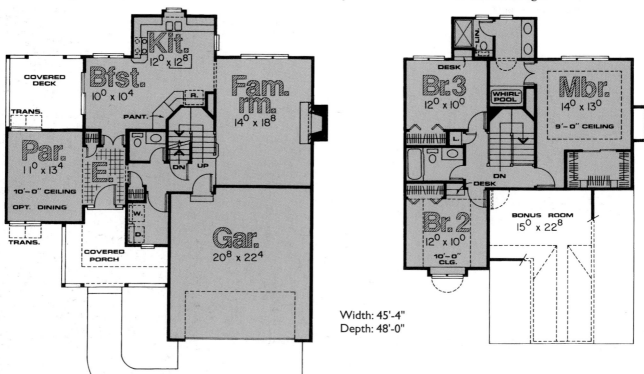

Width: 45'-4"
Depth: 48'-0"

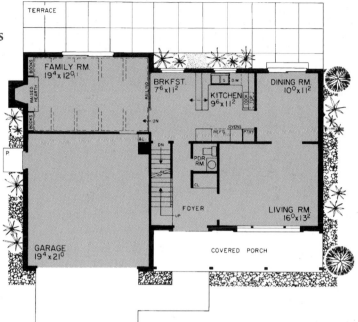

DESIGN BY
© Home Planners

Design 1956

First Floor: 990 square feet
Second Floor: 728 square feet
Total: 1,718 square feet

D

Width: 48'-0"
Depth: 34'-10"

◆ Simple, functional, and loaded with Colonial appeal, this versatile two-story plan features the finest in family floor plans. The entry foyer offers a powder room for guests and a staircase to the second floor. A large formal living room connects to the dining room, allowing adequate space for entertaining in style. The U-shaped kitchen features a pass-through counter to the breakfast room. Step down to the family room, which is enhanced by a beam ceiling, a raised-hearth fireplace, and built-in bookshelves. Two plans are available for the second floor: one with three bedrooms and one with four. Either option allows for a master bedroom with a private bath. Other highlights of the plan include a full-length rear terrace and extra storage space.

QUOTE ONE®
Cost to build? See page 246
to order complete cost estimate
to build this house in your area!

Optional 3-Bedroom Plan

This home, as shown in the photograph, may differ from the actual blueprints. For more detailed information, please check the floor plans carefully.

Photo by Andrew D. Lautman

9

This home, as shown in the photograph, may differ from the actual blueprints. For more detailed information, please check the floor plans carefully.

Photo courtesy of Living Concepts Home Planning

Design A153

First Floor: 1,200 square feet
Second Floor: 1,039 square feet
Total: 2,239 square feet
Bonus Room: 309 square feet

DESIGN BY
©**Living Concepts Home Planning**

◆ A bay window accents the brick and siding facade of this handsome three-bedroom, contemporary design. An angled staircase in the foyer leads to the second floor. A formal dining room is to the left of the foyer and the living room is to the right. A large family room features a fireplace and direct access to the rear deck. The U-shaped kitchen provides lots of room for a breakfast nook. The master suite on the second floor has two walk-in closets and a separate sitting area. Two secondary bedrooms, a hall bath and a large bonus room are also on this floor.

Width: 50'-0"
Depth: 40'-5"

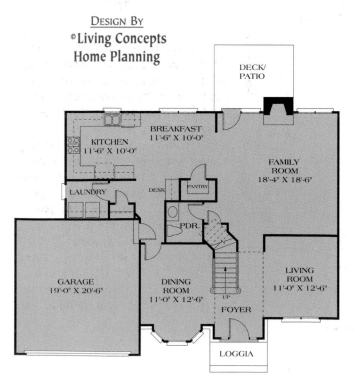

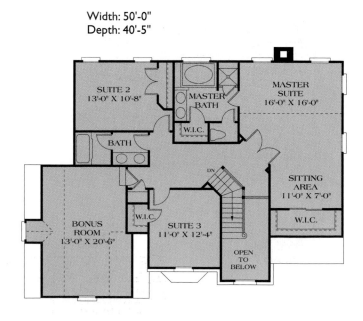

This home, as shown in the photograph, may differ from the actual blueprints. For more detailed information, please check the floor plans carefully.

Photo by Bob Greenspan

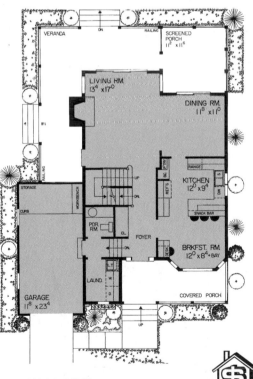

Width: 38'-0"
Depth: 52'-0"

Design 2974

First Floor: 911 square feet
Second Floor: 861 square feet
Total: 1,772 square feet

L

◆ Victorian houses are well known for their orientation on narrow building sites. This house is 38 feet wide, but the livability is tremendous. From the front covered porch, the foyer directs traffic to the back of the house with its open living and dining rooms. The U-shaped kitchen conveniently services both the dining room and the front breakfast room. High-lighting the outdoor livability presented in this plan, the rear living area contains a veranda and a screened porch. Three bedrooms and two baths account for the second floor; the third floor provides ample storage space and a fourth bedroom.

Design 9525

First Floor: 1,396 square feet
Second Floor: 523 square feet
Total: 1,919 square feet

DESIGN BY
© Alan Mascord
Design Associates, Inc.

◆ Double pillars herald the entry to this charming design. They are offset from the front door and introduce a porch that leads to the den (or make it a fourth bedroom). Living areas center on the casual life and include a great room that has a fireplace and opens directly to the dining room. The kitchen is L-shaped for convenience and features an island cooktop. The master suite is on the first floor and sports a vaulted ceiling and bath with spa tub and separate shower. The upper floor holds two secondary bedrooms and a full bath. The open staircase is decorated with a plant shelf that receives light from double windows over the foyer.

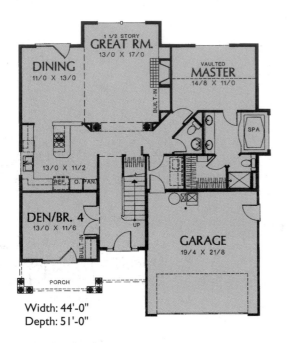

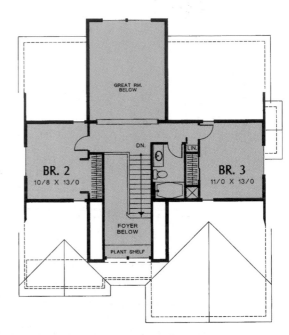

Width: 44'-0"
Depth: 51'-0"

© 1989 Donald A. Gardner Architects, Inc.

NATHAN

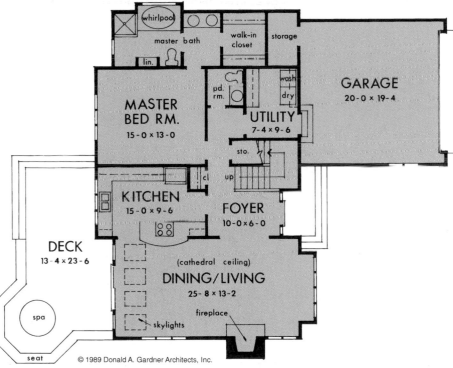

whirlpool

master bath

walk-in closet

storage

lin.

MASTER BED RM.
15-0 x 13-0

pd. rm.

wash
dry

GARAGE
20-0 x 19-4

UTILITY
7-4 x 9-6

sto.

up

cl

KITCHEN
15-0 x 9-6

FOYER
10-0 x 6-0

DECK
13-4 x 23-6

(cathedral ceiling)

DINING/LIVING
25-8 x 13-2

fireplace

skylights

spa

seat

© 1989 Donald A. Gardner Architects, Inc.

Width: 49'-0"
Depth: 48'-6"

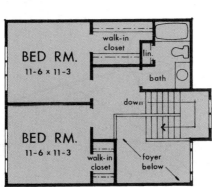

BED RM.
11-6 x 11-3

walk-in closet

lin.

bath

down

BED RM.
11-6 x 11-3

walk-in closet

foyer below

Design 9610

First Floor: 1,209 square feet
Second Floor: 525 square feet
Total: 1,734 square feet

DESIGN BY
Donald A. Gardner
Architects, Inc.

◆ A well-proportioned, compact house such as this never feels cramped, and the special floor plan makes it seem larger than it really is. From the two-story entrance foyer, move to the living/dining area with a cathedral ceiling and sky-lights. The master suite features its own bath with a double-bowl vanity, whirlpool tub and separate shower. Look for walk-in closets here as well as in the two family bedrooms upstairs. A large deck off the living area allows space for a hot tub.

Design Q620

First Floor: 995 square feet
Second Floor: 484 square feet
Total: 1,479 square feet

◆ What an appealing plan! Its rustic character is defined by cedar lattice, covered columned porches, exposed rafters and multi-paned double-hung windows. The great room/dining room combination is reached through double doors off the veranda and features a fireplace towering two stories to the lofty ceiling. A U-shaped kitchen has an angled snack counter and loads of space for a breakfast table—or use the handy side porch for alfresco dining. To the rear is the master bedroom with a full bath and double doors to the veranda. An additional half-bath sits just beyond the laundry room. Upstairs there are two family bedrooms and a full bath.

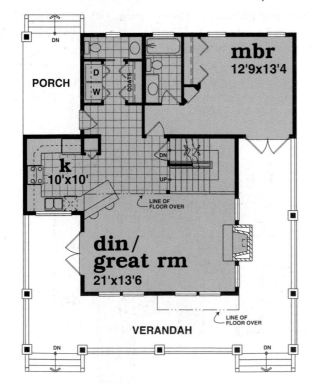

PORCH

mbr
12'9x13'4

k
10'x10'

LINE OF
FLOOR OVER

UP

DN

**din/
great rm**
21'x13'6

LINE OF
FLOOR OVER

VERANDAH

DN   DN

Width: 38'-0"
Depth: 44'-0"

DESIGN BY
©Select Home Designs

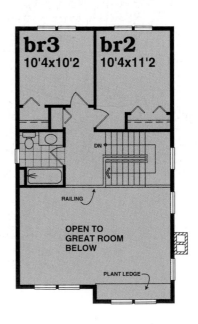

br3
10'4x10'2

br2
10'4x11'2

DN

RAILING

OPEN TO
GREAT ROOM
BELOW

PLANT LEDGE

This home, as shown in the photograph, may differ from the actual blueprints. For more detailed information, please check the floor plans carefully.

Design 9711

DESIGN BY
Donald A. Gardner
Architects, Inc.

First Floor: 1,271 square feet
Second Floor: 665 square feet
Total: 1,936 square feet

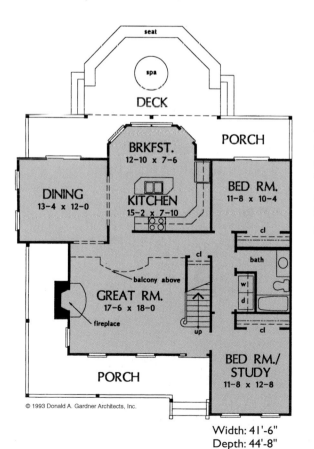

◆ This gabled and dormered country home with an L-shaped wrapping porch fits unexpected luxury into a compact plan. A balcony adds drama to the vaulted great room that offers a fireplace. The large kitchen—with a center island—opens to rear porches and a deck with a spa area for outdoor entertaining. The second-floor master bedroom features a bath with all of the extras. Also on this floor is a fourth bedroom with a private bath.

DECK

PORCH

seat

spa

BRKFST.
12-10 x 7-6

DINING
13-4 x 12-0

KITCHEN
15-2 x 7-10

BED RM.
11-8 x 10-4

cl

bath

balcony above

cl

GREAT RM.
17-6 x 18-0

w
d

fireplace

up

cl

**BED RM./
STUDY**
11-8 x 12-8

PORCH

© 1993 Donald A. Gardner Architects, Inc.

Width: 41'-6"
Depth: 44'-8"

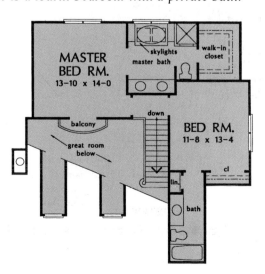

**MASTER
BED RM.**
13-10 x 14-0

skylights
master bath

walk-in
closet

balcony

down

great room
below

BED RM.
11-8 x 13-4

cl

lin.

bath

Design Z018

First Floor: 1,274 square feet
Second Floor: 983 square feet
Total: 2,257 square feet

DESIGN BY
©Drummond Designs, Inc.

◆ Three porches make outdoor living easy. The foyer opens to a home office on the left and the formal living area on the right. A large arched window and a cathedral ceiling highlight the living room. The family room is enhanced by a fireplace. The kitchen includes an unusual round snack bar and access to the rear porch. A walk-in closet and a bath with twin sinks highlight the second-floor master suite. Also on the second floor, two secondary bedrooms share a bath. This home is designed with a basement foundation.

Width: 50'-0"
Depth: 46'-0"

© American Home Gallery, Ltd.

◆ This home is a true Southern original. Inside, the spacious foyer leads directly to a large vaulted great room with its handsome fireplace. The dining room, just off the foyer, features a dramatic vaulted ceiling. The spacious kitchen offers both storage and large work areas opening up to the breakfast room. At the rear of the home, you will find the master suite with its garden bath, His and Hers vanities and oversized closet. The second floor provides two additional bedrooms with a shared bath and a balcony overlook to the foyer below. Storage space or a fourth bedroom may be placed over the garage area. This home is designed with a basement foundation.

DESIGN BY
Stephen Fuller

Design T013

First Floor: 1,580 square feet
Second Floor: 595 square feet
Total: 2,175 square feet

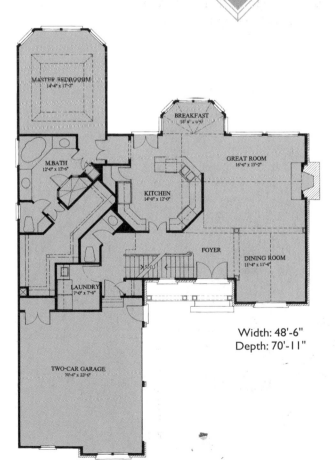

Width: 48'-6"
Depth: 70'-11"

Design 6655

First Floor: 1,586 square feet
Second Floor: 601 square feet
Total: 2,187 square feet

DESIGN BY
©**The Sater
Design Collection**

◆ Lattice walls, pickets and horizontal siding complement a relaxed Key West, island-style design. Sunburst transoms lend a romantic spirit to this seaside plan, perfect for waterfront properties. Inside, an elegant interior offers an open foyer that leads to an expansive great room, made cozy by a warming hearth. Just right for entertaining, the living and dining rooms open to the veranda, which invites a moonlit after-dinner dance. A gallery hall leads to two secondary bedrooms, one with French doors to the veranda. The upper level is dedicated to the master suite—a perfect homeowner's retreat. French doors reveal a vestibule open to both bedroom and bath. A walk-in closet and a morning kitchen complement lavish amenities in the bath. Enclosed storage plus bonus space is tucked away on the lower level.

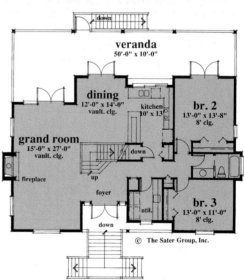

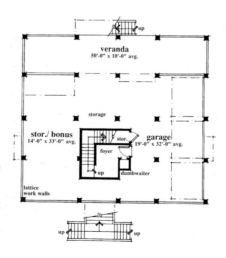

Width: 50'-0"
Depth: 44'-0"

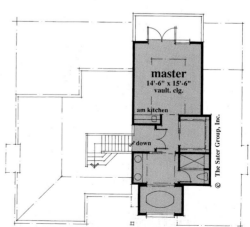

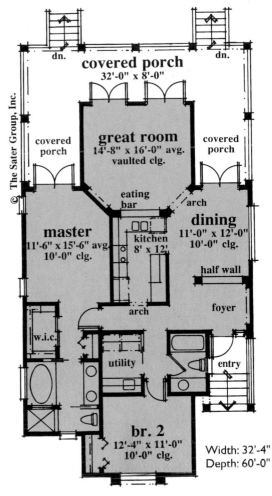

covered porch
32'-0" x 8'-0"

dn.   dn.

© The Sater Group, Inc.

covered porch   **great room**   covered porch
                       14'-8" x 16'-0" avg.
                       vaulted clg.

eating bar   arch

master   kitchen   **dining**
11'-6" x 15'-6" avg.   8' x 12'   11'-0" x 12'-0"
10'-0" clg.   10'-0" clg.

                                          half wall

                       arch   **foyer**

w.i.c.

            utility   entry

br. 2
12'-4" x 11'-0"
10'-0" clg.

Width: 32'-4"
Depth: 60'-0"

DESIGN BY
© The Sater
Design Collection

Design 6691
Square Footage: 1,288

◆ This Tidewater design offers casual living in modest square footage. Asymmetrical lines celebrate the turn of the century and blend with elements of Gulf-Coast style. The heart of the home is the great room, which features two sets of double French doors to the covered porch at the rear. Both the master suite and the dining room also have French doors to the porch. The kitchen is centrally located and provides a snack-bar pass-through to the great room. A second bedroom at the front of the plan has its own bath.

Rear View

Design M533

Square Footage: 2,048

<small>DESIGN BY</small>
© Andy McDonald
Design Group

◆ Presenting a narrow frontage, this plan extends back 75 feet and provides spacious rooms for a family. Entry is through a front corner porch or through a side courtyard that opens into the dining room. A fireplace warms the family room, which accesses the rear yard through French doors. A bright corner breakfast nook highlights the kitchen, which provides a cooktop island and laundry-room access. The master suite features a walk-in closet and separate vanities in the compartmented bath. Two family bedrooms share a bath.

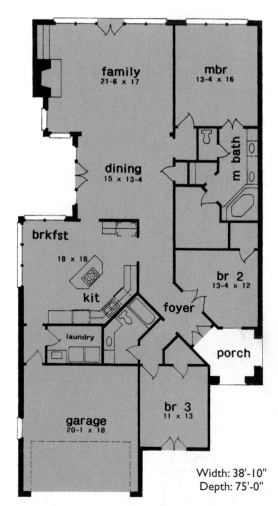

family
21-6 x 17

mbr
13-4 x 16

m bath

dining
15 x 13-4

brkfst

18 x 16

kit

laundry

foyer

br 2
13-4 x 12

porch

br 3
11 x 13

garage
20-1 x 18

Width: 38'-10"
Depth: 75'-0"

This home, as shown in the photograph, may differ from the actual blueprints.
For more detailed information, please check the floor plans carefully.

Photos by Andrew D. Lautman

◆ This shingle-and-stone Nantucket Cape design caters to the casual lifestyle. The side entrance gives direct access to the wonderfully open living areas: the gathering room with a fireplace and an abundance of windows; an island kitchen with an angled, pass-through snack bar; and a dining area with sliding glass doors to a covered porch. A large terrace further extends the outdoor living potential. Also on the first floor is the master suite with a compartmented bath, private dressing room and walk-in closet. Upstairs you'll find three family bedrooms and two baths. One bedroom features a private deck.

Design 2493

First Floor: 1,387 square feet
Second Floor: 929 square feet
Total: 2,316 square feet

QUOTE ONE®

Cost to build? See page 246
to order complete cost estimate
to build this house in your area!

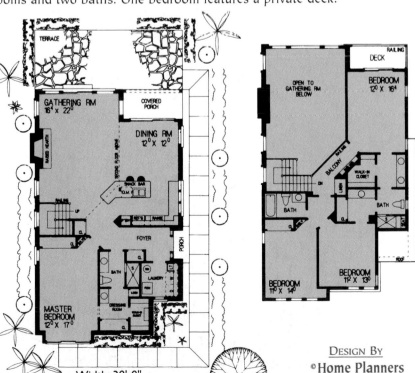

Width: 30'-0"
Depth: 51'-8"

DESIGN BY
© Home Planners

Rear View

23

Design 9553

First Floor: 1,466 square feet
Second Floor: 1,369 square feet
Total: 2,835 square feet

◆ Multi-pane windows and keystones enhance the beauty of this impressive two-story home. From the bay-windowed living room to the casual family room, this plan caters to the active lifestyle of today's family. The large, U-shaped kitchen contains an island cooktop and a sunny nook nearby that accesses a covered porch. Upstairs, the master suite is designed for the ultimate in luxury. Three family bedrooms, a full bath and a den complete the second floor.

DESIGN BY
©Alan Mascord
Design Associates, Inc.

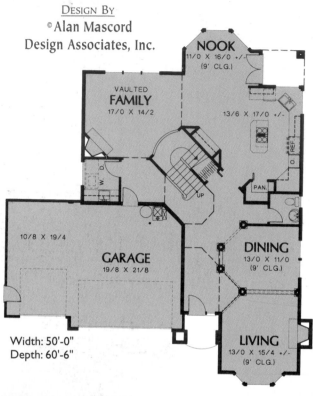

NOOK
11/0 X 16/0 +/-
(9' CLG.)

VAULTED
FAMILY
17/0 X 14/2

13/6 X 17/0 +/-

PAN.

10/8 X 19/4

GARAGE
19/8 X 21/8

DINING
13/0 X 11/0
(9' CLG.)

UP

LIVING
13/0 X 15/4 +/-
(9' CLG.)

Width: 50'-0"
Depth: 60'-6"

DECK

MASTER
13/0 X 16/0 +/-
(9'-4" CLG.)

SPA

FAMILY
BELOW
(8' CLG.)

BR. 2
11/2 X 12/2

DN.

NICHE

LIN.

LIN.

LIN.

BR. 3
11/6 X 12/8 +/-

FOYER
BELOW

DEN
9/6 X 11/0

BR. 4
13/0 X 11/0

24

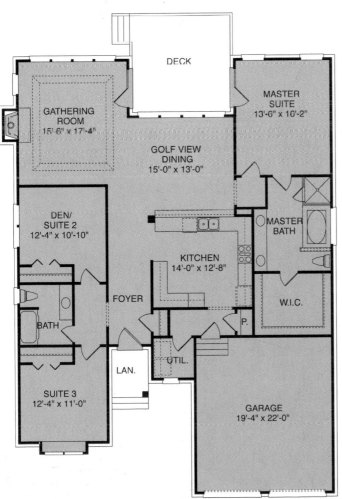

Design A149

Square Footage: 1,915

DESIGN BY
©**Living Concepts
Home Planning**

◆ Choose three bedrooms or two bedrooms plus a den in this compact, single-level, contemporary design. The well-equipped kitchen is open to a large dining room that overlooks the deck and golf course or lake. The gathering room—with a sloped ceiling—features a wall of windows across the back and a fireplace in the side wall. The master suite offers a double-bowl vanity, a separate tub and shower and a walk-in closet. Two other bedrooms with an adjoining bath are off the entry foyer, one of which may be used as a den.

Width: 45'-10"
Depth: 62'-6"

Design 9246

First Floor: 891 square feet
Second Floor: 885 square feet
Total: 1,776 square feet

DESIGN BY
©Design Basics, Inc.

◆ The inviting wraparound front porch of this home leads to a gracious entry with an interesting staircase. Immediately to the right is the formal dining room, featuring a box-bay window. Straight ahead, the great room—with a raised-hearth fireplace—opens to the breakfast room and kitchen. Windows over the sink and sliding glass doors to the rear yard open up this area. Four bedrooms upstairs include a master suite with a boxed ceiling and generous closets. The master bath has a double vanity, a whirlpool tub and a compartmented toilet. Note such special features as the the powder room, the coat closet in the entry hall and the planning desk in the kitchen.

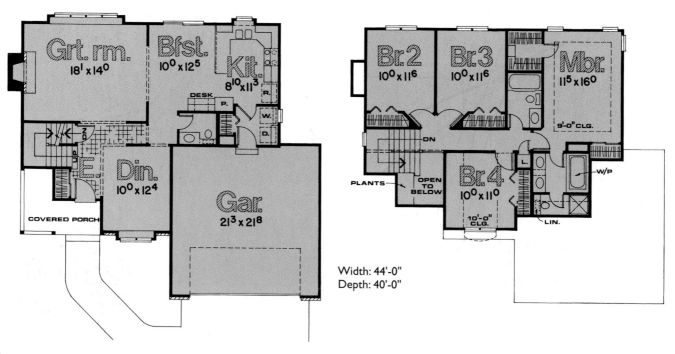

Width: 44'-0"
Depth: 40'-0"

◆ Yesterday's simpler lifestyle is reflected throughout this plan. From the tiled entrance hall with coat closet and powder room, through the large bayed parlor with its sloped ceiling, to the sunken gathering room with a fireplace, there's plenty to appreciate about this floor plan. The formal dining room opens to the parlor for convenient entertaining. An L-shaped kitchen with an attached breakfast room is nearby. Upstairs quarters include a master suite with a private dressing area and whirlpool tub. On this floor there are also three family bedrooms and a shared bath.

Design 9252

First Floor: 1,113 square feet
Second Floor: 965 square feet
Total: 2,078 square feet

DESIGN BY
©Design Basics, Inc.

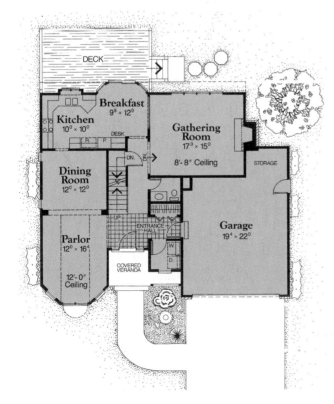

Width: 46'-0"
Depth: 41'-5"

Design 9256

Square Footage: 1,347

DESIGN BY
©Design Basics, Inc.

◆ From the ten-foot ceiling in the entry to the spacious great room with a fireplace, this plan expresses an open feeling. A snack bar and pantry in the kitchen complement the work area. Bright windows light up the breakfast room. To the left side of the plan are three bedrooms—two share a full bath. The master suite offers a box-bay window, built-in bookcase and tiered ceiling. The skylit dressing area features a double vanity, and there is a whirlpool spa in the bath. The two-car garage is reached through the service entrance, which has a laundry room. Extra storage space in the garage makes it even more handy.

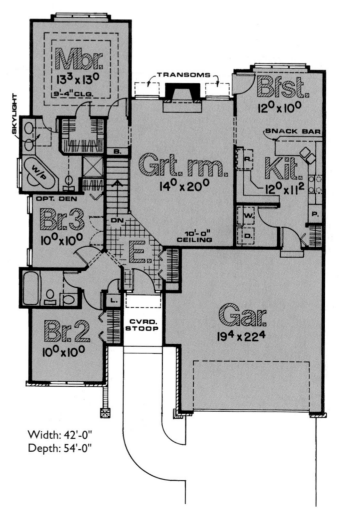

Width: 42'-0"
Depth: 54'-0"

Width: 49'-0"
Depth: 53'-0"

Breakfast

PLANT SHELF ABOVE

VAULT

FPL.

Master Suite
12⁰ x 15⁷
TRAY CLG.

RANGE

DW.

Kitchen

REF.

Vaulted Family Room
16² x 17⁵
15'-3" HIGH CLG.

SERVING BAR

Bedroom 3
11⁰ x 10²

Bath

L/L

Vaulted M.Bath

PLANT SHELF ABOVE

CTS.

WET BAR

W.

D.

Laun.

Foyer
12' - 0" HIGH CLG.

SHWR.

W.i.c.

Dining Room
10¹ x 11¹⁰
14'-0" HIGH CLG.

Covered Porch

Bedroom 2
11⁰ x 10¹

Storage

OPT. STAIRS TO BASEMENT

Garage
19⁵ x 19⁷

copyright ©1992 frank betz associates,inc.

QUOTE ONE®
Cost to build? See page 246
to order complete cost estimate
to build this house in your area!

Design P110

Square Footage: 1,429

DESIGN BY
© Frank Betz
Associates, Inc.

◆ This home's gracious exterior is indicative of the elegant, yet extremely livable, floor plan inside. Volume ceilings that crown the family living areas combine with an open floor plan to give the modest square footage a more spacious feel. The formal dining room is set off from the foyer and vaulted family room with stately columns. The spacious family room has a corner fireplace, rear-yard access and a serving bar from the galley kitchen. A breakfast nook with a bay window flanks the kitchen on one end while a laundry center and wet-bar lead to the dining room on the other. The split-bedroom plan allows the amenity-rich master suite maximum privacy. A pocket door off the family room leads to a hall and two family bedrooms that share a bath. Please specify basement, crawlspace or slab foundation when ordering.

Design T075

First Floor: 1,720 square feet
Second Floor: 545 square feet
Total: 2,265 square feet

◆ The foyer opens to the living and dining rooms, providing a spectacular entrance to this English country cottage. A gourmet kitchen offers a work island and a food bar opening to the breakfast room. Accented by a fireplace and built-in bookcases, the family room is an excellent setting for family gatherings. The master bedroom includes a rectangular ceiling detail and access to the rear deck, while the master bath features His and Hers vanities, a garden tub and a spacious walk-in closet. The central stairway leads to the balcony overlook and three bedrooms sharing two baths. This home is designed with a basement foundation.

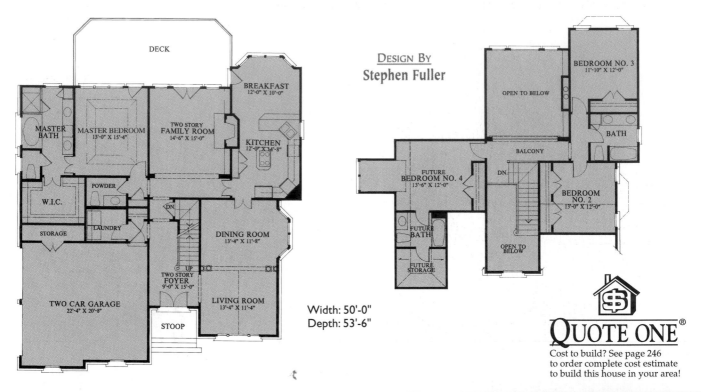

DESIGN BY
Stephen Fuller

Width: 50'-0"
Depth: 53'-6"

QUOTE ONE ®
Cost to build? See page 246
to order complete cost estimate
to build this house in your area!

◆ This French country cottage is a charming example of European architecture. Stucco and stone blend with multiple gables and hipped roof lines to establish the character of the design. A two-story foyer opens to an even more impressive two-story family room with a fireplace. To the right, a formal living area opens to a dining room through decorative columns. This room is easily served by a generous kitchen with an island cooktop counter. A bright breakfast nook with a bay window and access to the rear deck is nearby. The well-appointed master suite is located on the first floor. The second floor holds two family bedrooms, a full bath, space for an additional bedroom and future bath, and bonus storage space. This home is designed with a basement foundation.

Design T102

First Floor: 1,720 square feet
Second Floor: 545 square feet
Total: 2,265 square feet

DESIGN BY
Stephen Fuller

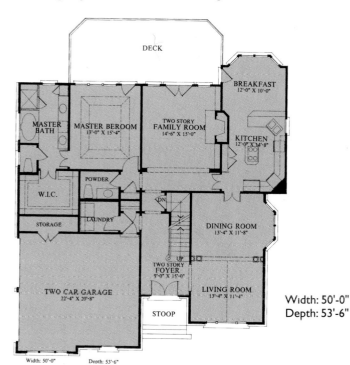

Width: 50'-0"
Depth: 53'-6"

© American Home Gallery, Ltd.

This home, as shown in the photograph, may differ from the actual blueprints. For more detailed information, please check the floor plans carefully.

Photo courtesy of Larry E. Belk Designs
Photo by Karen Stuthard

Design 8001

First Floor: 1,309 square feet
Second Floor: 1,343 square feet
Total: 2,652 square feet

◆ Clean, contemporary lines set this home apart and make it a stand-out in any location. The metal roof and rooftop cupola rotated on a 45-degree angle add interest to this stunning home. Remote control transoms in the cupola open automatically to increase ventilation. Originally designed for a sloping site, the home incorporates multiple levels. Additionally, there is access to a series of multi-level outside decks from the dining room, sun room and great room. All these areas have at least one glass wall overlooking the rear. The master bedroom and bath upstairs are bridged by a pipe rail balcony that accesses a rear deck. The master suite includes a huge closet. Additional storage is located off the hallway to the office. The open, spacious layout and emphasis on the views to the rear make this home a winner for harbor, golf course, lake or wooded sites.

DESIGN BY
©Larry E. Belk
Designs

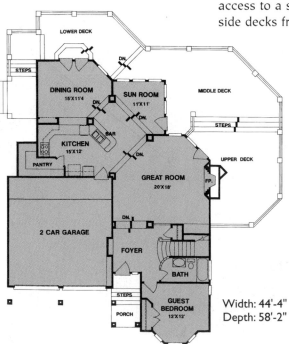

Width: 44'-4"
Depth: 58'-2"

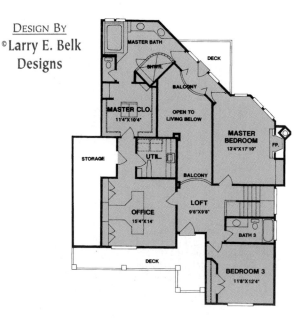

Design 8277

First Floor: 1,181 square feet
Second Floor: 446 square feet
Total: 1,627 square feet

DESIGN BY
©Larry E. Belk
Designs

◆ Soaring heights in the foyer, great room and dining room set this plan apart. The open dining room and great room area invites easy entertaining. The kitchen connects to the dining room with a snack-bar pass-through. The master suite, on the first floor, displays two walk-in closets and separate vanities. The master bath also connects to the laundry room, which has a service entrance to the two-car garage. Two secondary bedrooms, located on the second floor, share a bath. One bedroom offers a romantic window seat in the dormer.

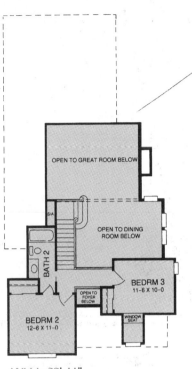

Width: 32'-11"
Depth: 65'-3"

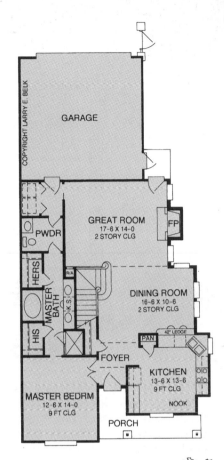

Design X050

First Floor: 850 square feet
Second Floor: 901 square feet
Total: 1,751 square feet

◆ Outdoor-living possibilities on the wide sun deck draw attention to this stucco design that has European flair. The deck is accessed from the dining-room bay and from the breakfast room, which is framed in windows that flood the entire kitchen area with natural light. The living area boasts an extended-hearth fireplace and a box-bay window. The foyer provides a powder room and a U-shaped staircase that leads to the second floor. Here, the master suite includes a volume ceiling and a luxurious bath with separate vanities, a walk-in closet and a garden tub. Two family bedrooms share a bath that also has separate vanities.

DESIGN BY
©Jannis Vann &
Associates, Inc.

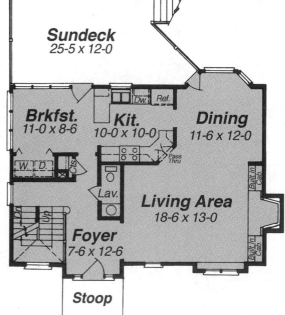

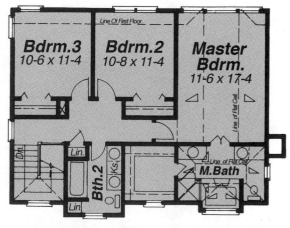

Width: 34'-0"
Depth: 37'-6"

◆ French doors and a walk-on balcony enhance this European-style brick exterior. The living and dining areas are open to each other and are easily served by the kitchen, which offers a service entrance from the garage. A powder room off the kitchen leads to the laundry room. Stairs from the foyer lead up to the second floor where the master suite includes a walk-through closet, French doors to the balcony and a bath with a corner tub. Two additional bedrooms share a bath and a lounge area, which could be used as a fourth bedroom. This home is designed with a basement foundation.

Design Z013

First Floor: 844 square feet
Second Floor: 1,104 square feet
Total: 1,948 square feet

DESIGN BY
©Drummond Designs, Inc.

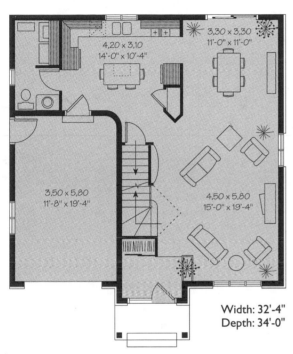

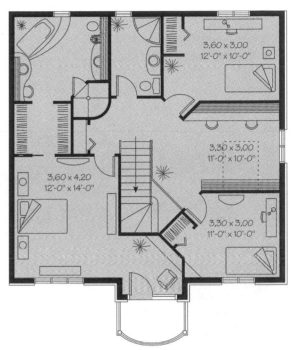

Width: 32'-4"
Depth: 34'-0"

35

Enhanced Plan

Design 3721

Square Footage: 1,648

DESIGN BY
© Home Planners

◆ Narrow and affordable, this ranch design provides enhancements you can add later. These are shown by the highlighted areas of the floor plan. The master bedroom includes a full bath and a walk-in closet, while a second full bath serves the remaining three bedrooms. A galley kitchen with an eat-in nook opens up to a huge great room. The house may be built with or without the two-car garage, rear deck, bay windows and fireplace. Blueprints include details for both the basic and the enhanced version.

BEDROOM
10⁴ x 10⁴

BEDROOM
10⁴ x 10⁴

RAILING   DN   DECK
13² x 9⁸

GREAT RM
13² X 33⁴

OPT. FIREPLACE

BEDROOM
11⁴ x 10⁴

BATH

KITCHEN
9² x 17¹⁰

OPT. BAY WINDOW

BATH

OPT. BAY WINDOW

WALK-IN CLOSET

LIN

MASTER BEDROOM
11⁴ x 16⁰

FOYER

DN

COVERED PORCH

Width: 35'-0"
Depth: 76'-0"

GARAGE
20¹⁰ X 21⁸

Basic Plan

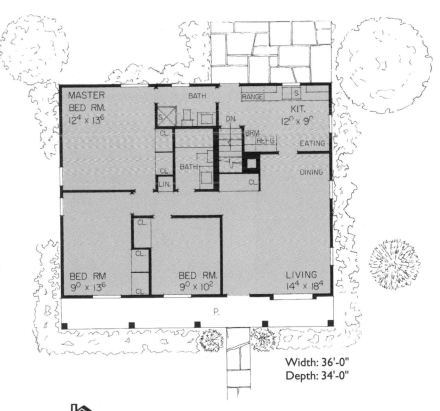

Width: 36'-0"
Depth: 34'-0"

Design 1113

Square Footage: 1,080

L D

DESIGN BY
©Home Planners

◆ A cozy plan that's just right for a small family or empty-nesters. A covered front porch shelters visitors from inclement weather. An ample living/dining area leads the way to a rear kitchen overlooking a terrace. Two full baths serve three bedrooms—one is the master suite. The kitchen includes informal eating space and a window sink. Stairs lead to a full basement that may be developed as desired. Multi-lite windows with quaint shutters add a touch of charm to this design.

Design 5527

Design 5527/5529

First Floor: 1,228 square feet
Second Floor: 1,285 square feet
Total: 2,513 square feet

DESIGN BY
©Home Planners

◆ Light and warmth envelop this two-story traditional home, beginning with a Palladian window above the foyer. Separated by decorative columns, the living and dining rooms are also bathed in light via the glass-door entry to the backyard. An island kitchen with a writing desk, a pantry and ample counter space leads to the dining area, breakfast nook and family room with its central fireplace. Upstairs, the master bedroom features a fireplace and a massive bath with a walk-in closet. The full bath shared by three family bedrooms has a double-bowl vanity, which is separate from the tub and toilet area. This allows room for more than one family member to get ready on busy mornings. A deck completes the second floor.

Width: 36'-8"
Depth: 66'-2"

Design 5529

Design 5525

◆ A fine starter home for a young family, this plan will also please empty-nesters who require a guest room or office space. The expansive first floor allows guests to mingle in any room with ease, whether it be in the combination living/dining room with backyard access, in the amenity-filled kitchen and breakfast nook or in the family room with its warming fireplace. The upstairs sleeping zone promotes privacy. The master bedroom, with its cozy fireplace, will become a favorite haven. The master bath separates the bedrooms and features a walk-in closet, a vanity sink, a separate shower and a corner whirlpool tub. The second bedroom can be a child's room, a guest room or a corner office. It includes a built-in writing desk and easy access to a hall bath with dual basins.

Design 5525/5526

First Floor: 1,228 square feet
Second Floor: 924 square feet
Total: 2,152 square feet

DESIGN BY
©Home Planners

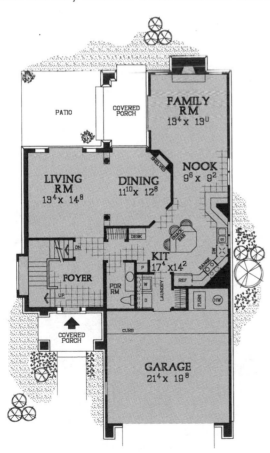

Width: 36'-8"
Depth: 66'-2"

Design 5526

Design M184

Square Footage: 1,943

DESIGN BY
©Fillmore
Design Group

◆ A covered front porch at the side of the plan leads to an entry with two closets. Through double French doors, the study with a box-bay window offers a private retreat. On the other side of the entry, the living room is open to the dining area, which shares a skylight with the U-shaped kitchen. Access to the garage is from the kitchen through the utility room. Two bedrooms at the rear of the plan include a master suite with two walk-in closets and a secondary bedroom with access to a hall bath that has a skylight.

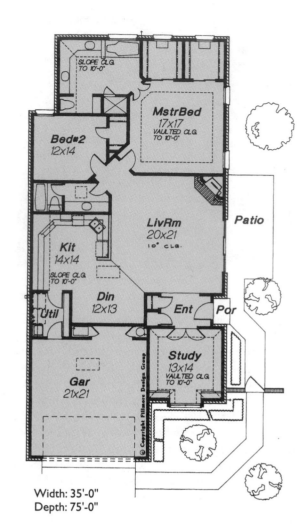

MstrBed
17x17
VAULTED CLG
TO 10'-0"

SLOPE CLG
TO 10'-0"

Bed#2
12x14

LivRm
20x21
10' CLG.

Patio

Kit
14x14
SLOPE CLG
TO 10'-0"

Din
12x13

Ent

Por

Util

Study
13x14
VAULTED CLG
TO 10'-0"

Gar
21x21

Width: 35'-0"
Depth: 75'-0"

Design M187

First Floor: 1,689 square feet
Second Floor: 672 square feet
Total: 2,361 square feet

<small>DESIGN BY</small>
©Fillmore
Design Group

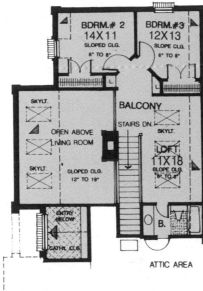

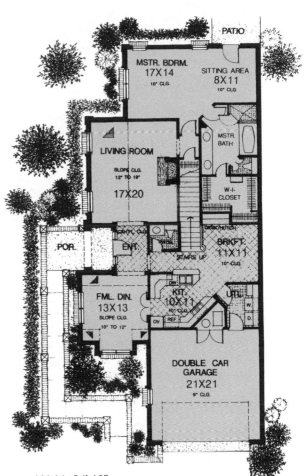

Width: 34'-10"
Depth: 75'-0"

◆ Surrounded by garden areas for expressing yourself with rose bushes and herbs, this home is a delight from every angle. The side entry leads to a living room on the left and a formal dining room on the right. The dining room has two sets of windows that look out to the garden, while the living room displays windows, a fireplace and three skylights in the sloped ceiling. The master suite is on the first floor with a sitting area that opens to the garden. Two bedrooms, a bath and a skylit loft are on the second floor.

Design B140

First Floor: 1,040 square feet
Second Floor: 503 square feet
Total: 1,543 square feet

DESIGN BY
©Greg Marquis
& Associates

◆ With its simplified floor plan, this home is ideal as a vacation or second home, but complete enough to live in year-round. The covered front porch invites you to sit and relax a while—rocking chairs or a porch swing will be enjoyed by all ages. Inside, the family room offers a nine-foot ceiling and a cheery fireplace. The efficient island kitchen and dining area form one large room, making it easy to serve family and guests. Completing the ground floor, the master suite offers views of the backyard and a bath with a walk-in closet and double-bowl vanity. Upstairs, two family bedrooms have large closets and share a full hall bath. There is also ample attic storage.

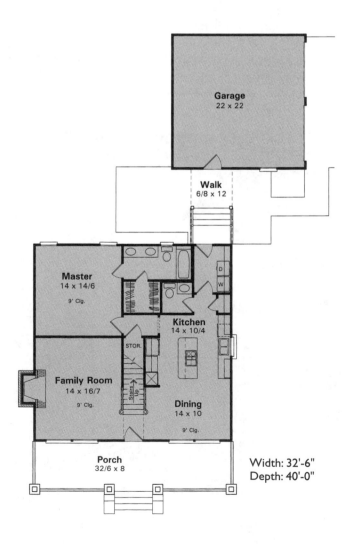

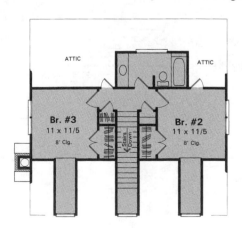

© 1994 Donald A. Gardner Architects, Inc.

DESIGN BY
Donald A. Gardner
Architects, Inc.

Design 9769

First Floor: 966 square feet
Second Floor: 584 square feet
Total: 1,550 square feet

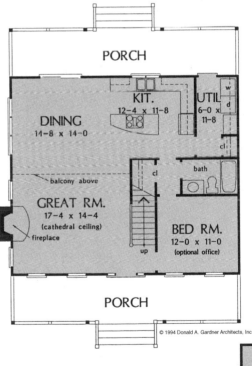

PORCH

KIT.
12-4 x 11-8

UTIL
6-0 x
11-8

w
d

DINING
14-8 x 14-0

cl

balcony above

bath

GREAT RM.
17-4 x 14-4
(cathedral ceiling)
fireplace

cl

up

BED RM.
12-0 x 11-0
(optional office)

PORCH

© 1994 Donald A. Gardner Architects, Inc.

Width: 35'-9"
Depth: 43'-0"

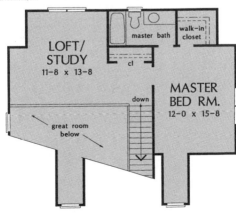

LOFT/
STUDY
11-8 x 13-8

master bath

walk-in
closet

cl

down

great room
below

MASTER
BED RM.
12-0 x 15-8

Quote One®

Cost to build? See page 246
to order complete cost estimate
to build this house in your area!

◆ A country farmhouse exterior combined with an open floor plan creates a comfortable home or vacation getaway. The great room, warmed by a fireplace and opened by a cathedral ceiling, combines well with the dining room and the kitchen for casual gatherings. Flexibility is offered with a front bedroom that easily doubles as a home office. The second floor contains the master bedroom with a walk-in closet and a private bath. Overlooking the great room below is the loft/study. Front and rear porches provide plenty of room for outdoor enjoyment.

Design Z025

Square Footage: 972

DESIGN BY
©Drummond Designs, Inc.

◆ Eye-catching exterior details distinguish this small Victorian design. Inside, natural light flows through the living area from the turret's windows, where there's a sitting bay. The living room and dining room make one open space, which is helpful for entertaining. A sliding door in the dining room leads to the backyard. An angled kitchen provides plenty of workspace. The master bedroom and a secondary bedroom share a full bath. This home is designed with a basement foundation.

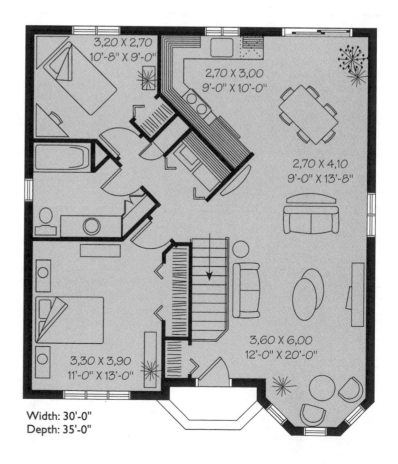

3,20 X 2,70
10'-8" X 9'-0"

2,70 X 3,00
9'-0" X 10'-0"

2,70 X 4,10
9'-0" X 13'-8"

3,30 X 3,90
11'-0" X 13'-0"

3,60 X 6,00
12'-0" X 20'-0"

Width: 30'-0"
Depth: 35'-0"

◆ The two-story turret houses the living room on the first floor and the master bedroom on the second floor. The dining room is open to the living room and provides a box-bay window. The L-shaped kitchen features a window sink, a breakfast room and access to the rear property. Natural light floods the kitchen through the breakfast room window wall. A curved staircase beside the powder room leads upstairs to three bedrooms and a bath. Each family bedroom has a walk-in closet. This home is designed with a basement foundation.

Design Z039

First Floor: 759 square feet
Second Floor: 735 square feet
Total: 1,494 square feet

Width: 22'-0"
Depth: 36'-0"

DESIGN BY
©Drummond Designs, Inc.

Design V039

First Floor: 648 square feet
Second Floor: 608 square feet
Total: 1,256 square feet

DESIGN BY
©United Design
Associates, Inc.

◆ Country-style porches sur-round three full sides of this quaint home, providing the per-fect environment for entertain-ing family and friends. The main floor contains the living areas, which include a great room and dining area. There's also a powder room and a laundry room. The upstairs is allocated to the sleeping zone, with three bedrooms (including a master suite), two baths and a small deck, which is accessed from two of the bedrooms.

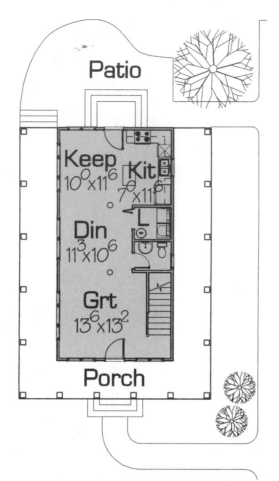

Patio

Keep
10^0x11^6

Kit
7^6x11^6

L

Din
11^3x10^6

Grt
13^6x13^2

Porch

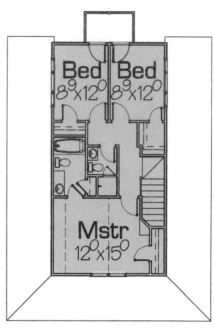

Bed
8^9x12^0

Bed
8^9x12^0

Mstr
12^0x15^0

Width: 30'-0"
Depth: 42'-0"

◆ Designed for one person or a couple, a vacation retreat or a year-round home, this plan presents simple living with maximum comfort. The porch is big enough for a pair of rocking chairs, and the two-story living room is cozy with a fireplace flanked by windows. There's a washer-dryer closet and a tiled kitchen with a bumped-out breakfast nook surrounded by windows. In addition to the master bath on the second floor, there's a bath with a shower on the main floor.

Design 8739

First Floor: 512 square feet
Second Floor: 255 square feet
Total: 767 square feet

DESIGN BY
© Home Design
Services, Inc.

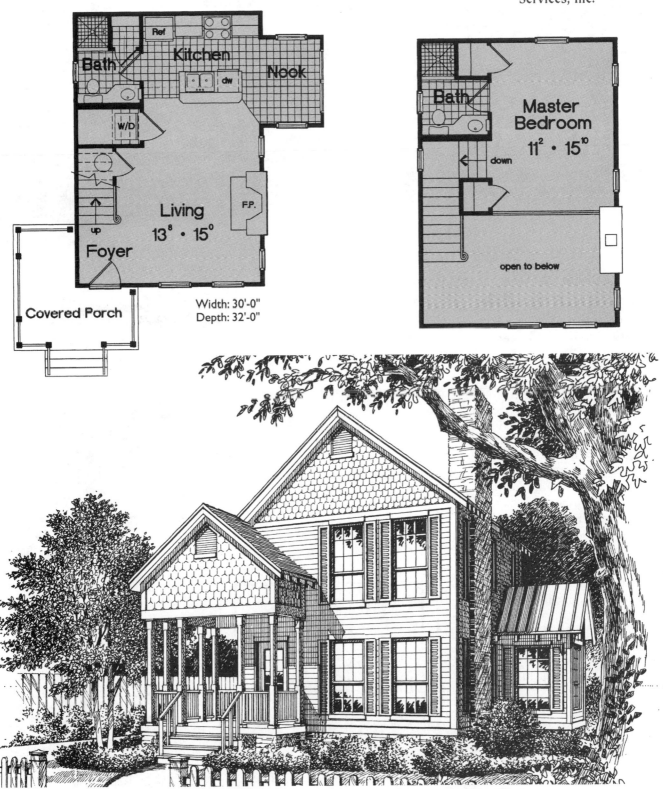

Bath

Kitchen

Ref

Nook

dw

W/D

Living
13⁸ • 15⁰

F.P.

up

Foyer

Covered Porch

Width: 30'-0"
Depth: 32'-0"

Bath

Master
Bedroom
11² • 15¹⁰

down

open to below

Design 2661

First Floor: 1,100 square feet
Second Floor: 808 square feet
Total: 1,908 square feet
LD

DESIGN BY
© Home Planners

◆ It would be difficult to find a starter or retirement home with more charm than this. Inside, it contains a very livable floor plan. An outstanding first floor centers around the huge country kitchen which includes a beam ceiling, a raised-hearth fireplace, a window seat and rear-yard access. The living room, with its warming corner fireplace, and a private study are to the front of the plan. Upstairs are three bedrooms and two full baths. Built-in shelves and a linen closet in the upstairs hallway provide excellent storage.

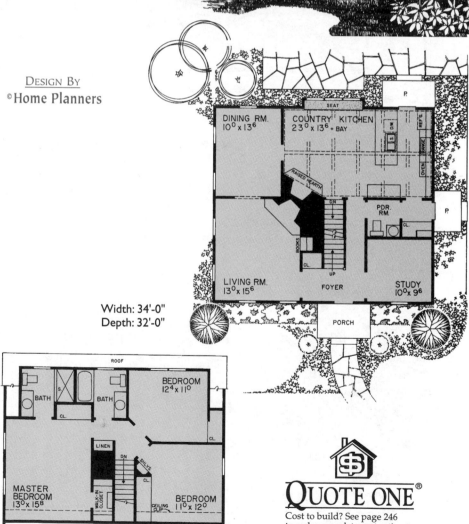

Width: 34'-0"
Depth: 32'-0"

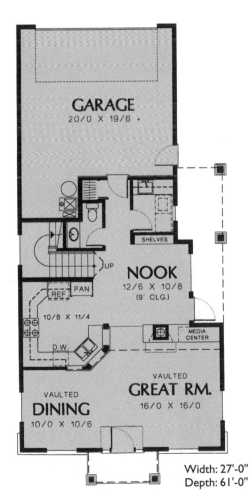

GARAGE
20/0 X 19/6 +

SHELVES

UP

NOOK
12/6 X 10/8
(9' CLG.)

PAN

REF

10/8 X 11/4

MEDIA
CENTER

D.W.

VAULTED
GREAT RM.
16/0 X 16/0

VAULTED
DINING
10/0 X 10/6

Width: 27'-0"
Depth: 61'-0"

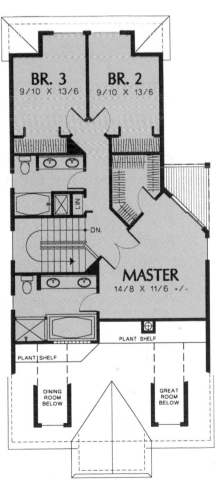

BR. 3
9/10 X 13/6

BR. 2
9/10 X 13/6

LIN

DN.

MASTER
14/8 X 11/6 +/-

PLANT SHELF

PLANT SHELF

DINING
ROOM
BELOW

GREAT
ROOM
BELOW

Design 7464
First Floor: 847 square feet
Second Floor: 845 square feet
Total: 1,692 square feet

DESIGN BY
© Alan Mascord
Design Associates, Inc.

◆ This petite bungalow provides amenities for the active family. The great room is warmed by a wood stove and features built-ins. Adjacent to the kitchen, the nook offers outdoor access. A curved staircase leads upstairs where a private balcony and a pampering bath highlight the master suite. The pentagon-shaped master bedroom boasts a walk-in closet. Two secondary bedrooms share a full hall bath. The two-car garage enters from the back of the property, hiding it effectively from the road.

Design 8051

First Floor: 1,078 square feet
Second Floor: 921 square feet
Total: 1,999 square feet

DESIGN BY
©Larry E. Belk
Designs

Width: 24'-11"
Depth: 73'-10"

◆ This charming clapboard home is loaded with character and is perfect for a narrow lot. High ceilings throughout give the home an open, spacious feeling. The great room and the dining room are separated by columns with connecting arches. The efficient, U-shaped kitchen features a corner sink with a window view and a breakfast bay with access to the rear porch. A bedroom and a bath (with a shower tucked under the stair) are conveniently located for guests on the first floor. Upstairs, the master bedroom features a vaulted ceiling and a luxurious master bath with dual vanities, a whirlpool tub and a separate shower. Access to a covered patio from the master bedroom provides a relaxing outdoor retreat. A secondary bedroom and full bath are also on the second floor. A large rear balcony completes this compact, highly livable plan. Please specify crawlspace or slab foundation when ordering.

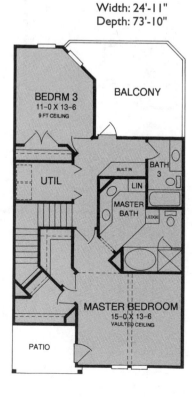

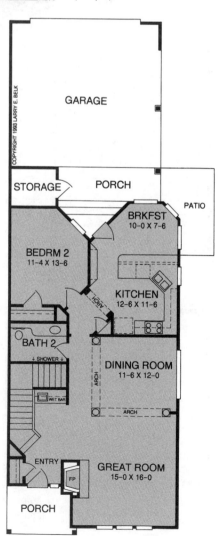

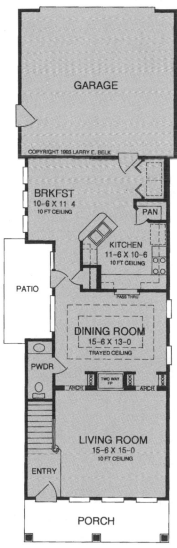

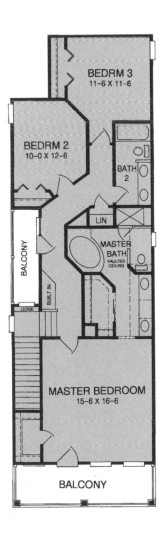

GARAGE

COPYRIGHT 1993 LARRY E. BELK

BRKFST
10-6 X 11 4
10 FT CEILING

PAN

KITCHEN
11-6 X 10-6
10 FT CEILING

PATIO

PASS THRU

DINING ROOM
15-6 X 13-0
TRAYED CEILING

PWDR

TWO WAY
FP

ARCH   ARCH

LIVING ROOM
15-6 X 15-0
10 FT CEILING

ENTRY

PORCH

BEDRM 3
11-6 X 11-6

BEDRM 2
10-0 X 12-6

BATH 2

BALCONY

LIN

BUILT IN

MASTER BATH
VAULTED CEILING

LEDGE

MASTER BEDROOM
15-6 X 16-6

BALCONY

Design 8052

First Floor: 904 square feet
Second Floor: 1,058 square feet
Total: 1,962 square feet

DESIGN BY
©Larry E. Belk
Designs

◆ Reminiscent of the popular "shotgun" homes of the past, this fine clapboard home is perfect for urban or riverfront living. Two balconies grace the second floor—one at the front and one on the side. A two-way fireplace between the formal living room and dining room provides visual impact. Built-in bookcases flank an arched opening between these rooms. A pass-through from the kitchen to the dining room simplifies serving, and a walk-in pantry provides storage. On the second floor, the master bedroom opens to a large balcony, and the relaxing master bath is designed with a separate shower and an angled whirlpool tub. Two secondary bedrooms and a full bath are located at the rear of the plan. Please specify crawlspace or slab foundation when ordering.

Width: 22'-0"
Depth: 74'-0"

Design 8278

First Floor: 1,233 square feet
Second Floor: 824 square feet
Total: 2,057 square feet

DESIGN BY
©Larry E. Belk
Designs

◆ Stately columns add grace to the entry of this clapboard home. From the foyer, you can enter the two-story living room, step into the study or take the stairs to the second floor. Adjacent to the downstairs bath, which contains a shower, the study could be a third bedroom. The living room is open to the dining room and a step through a pair of columns reveals a bright breakfast room and a U-shaped kitchen. This area offers a pass-through to the living room, a walk-in pantry, a laundry area and access to a covered porch. The second-floor balcony leads to two bedrooms, each with its own bath. The master suite includes two walk-in closets and access to a covered porch.

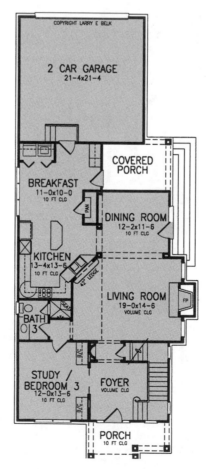

Width: 31'-10"
Depth: 77'-10"

Design 6686

First Floor: 1,046 square feet
Second Floor: 638 square feet
Total: 1,684 square feet

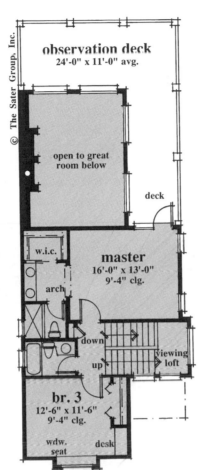

covered porch
24'-0" x 11'-0" avg.

© The Sater Group, Inc.

built ins

great room
15'-0" x 19'-0"
19'-0" clg.

tv niche

fireplace

covered porch

built ins

eating bar

arch

arch

kitchen

dining
11'-8" x 13'-0"
9'-4" clg.

arch

util.

arch

railing

up

mid level foyer

up

br. 2
12'-6" x 11'-6"
9'-4" clg.

wdw. seat

desk

down

Width: 25'-0"
Depth: 65'-6"

DESIGN BY
© The Sater
Design Collection

© The Sater Group, Inc.

observation deck
24'-0" x 11'-0" avg.

open to great room below

deck

w.i.c.

arch

master
16'-0" x 13'-0"
9'-4" clg.

down

up

viewing loft

br. 3
12'-6" x 11'-6"
9'-4" clg.

wdw. seat

desk

◆ A Key West design can be built anywhere and this cozy three-bedroom home has plenty to offer. The observation deck and covered porch provide enjoyable outdoor living areas both above and below. Indoors, the main attraction is the two-story great room with double doors to the porch, a fireplace flanked by built-in shelves and a pass-through to the kitchen, which is graced by archways and a large prep island. The downstairs bedroom, with its window seat and built-in desk, could be an office or a study. On the second floor, Bedroom 3 enjoys the same amenities as the downstairs bedroom, while the master bedroom has exclusive access to the observation deck. The compartmented master bath is accented by an arched vanity area.

Rear View

53

Design 6701

First Floor: 876 square feet
Second Floor: 1,245 square feet
Total: 2,121 square feet

DESIGN BY
©The Sater
Design Collection

◆ Key West conch style blends Old World charm with New World comfort in this picturesque design. A glass-paneled entry lends a warm welcome and complements a captivating front balcony. Two sets of French doors open the great room to wide views and extend the living areas to the back covered porch. A gourmet kitchen is prepared for any occasion with a prep sink, plenty of counter space, an ample pantry and an eating bar. The mid-level landing leads to two additional bedrooms, a full bath and a windowed art niche. Double French doors open the upper-level master suite to a sun deck and offer views from the bedroom. Circle-head windows and a vaulted ceiling maintain a light and airy atmosphere. The master bath has a windowed soaking tub and a glass-enclosed walk-in shower. Sunsets may be viewed from the privacy of the deck, a remarkable vantage point in moonlight as well. The plan offers the option of a fourth bedroom.

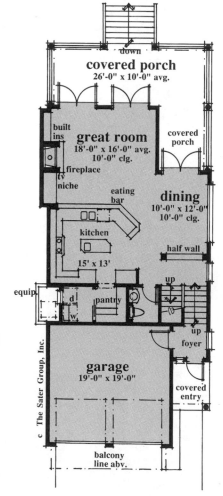

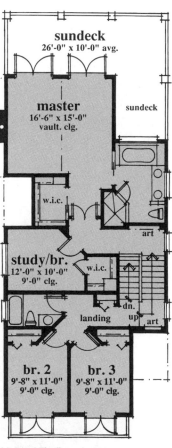

Width: 27'-6"
Depth: 64'-0"

Design 6700

First Floor: 1,305 square feet
Second Floor: 1,215 square feet
Total: 2,520 square feet
Bonus Space: 935 square feet

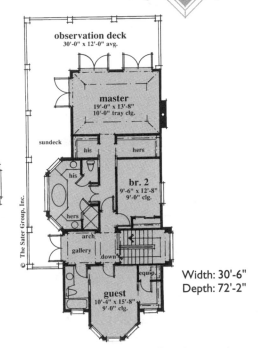

covered porch
30'-0" x 12'-0" avg.

bonus space
19'-0" x 19'-0" avg.
8'-0" clg.

optional fireplace

arch

bonus space
24'-6" x 14'-0" avg.
8'-0" clg.

garden courtyard

covered porch

entry

foyer

up!

privacy wall

entry gate

garage
21'-4" x 21'-0"

DESIGN BY
©**The Sater Design Collection**

covered porch
30'-0" x 12'-0" avg.

great room
10'-0" x 19'-0"
10'-0" clg.

built ins

fireplace

built ins

eating bar

covered porch

arch   arch

dining
11'-4" x 14'-0"
10'-0" clg.

kitchen

arch

arch

gallery

arch

down

up!

util.

study
10'-4" x 11'-4"
10'-0" clg.

© The Sater Group, Inc.

observation deck
30'-0" x 12'-0" avg.

master
19'-0" x 13'-8"
10'-0" tray clg.

sundeck

his   hers

his

br. 2
9'-6" x 12'-8"
9'-0" clg.

hers

arch

gallery   down

equip.

guest
10'-4" x 15'-8"
9'-0" clg.

© The Sater Group, Inc.

Width: 30'-6"
Depth: 72'-2"

Rear View

◆ Louvered shutters, balustered railings and a slate-style roof complement a stucco-and-siding blend on this three-story design. Entry stairs lead to the main-level living areas, defined by arches and columns. A wall of built-ins and a warming fireplace add coziness to the open, contemporary great room, while four sets of French doors expand the living area to the wraparound porch. Upper-level sleeping quarters include a guest suite with a sitting bay, an additional bedroom and a full bath. The master suite features two walk-in closets and French doors to a private observation deck. The lower level offers bonus space for future use—perhaps a home office—and another porch.

Design 9509

First Floor: 1,022 square feet
Second Floor: 813 square feet
Total: 1,835 square feet

DESIGN BY
©Alan Mascord
Design Associates, Inc.

◆ This house accommodates not only a narrow lot, but also fits a sloping site. Notice how the two-car garage is tucked away under the first level of the house. The angled corner entry gives way to a two-story living room with a tiled hearth. The dining room shares an interesting angled space with this area and enjoys easy service from the efficient kitchen. A large pantry and an angled corner sink add character to this area. The family room offers double doors to the balcony. A powder room and a laundry room complete the main level. Upstairs, three bedrooms include a vaulted master suite with a private bath. Bedrooms 2 and 3 each take advantage of direct access to a full bath.

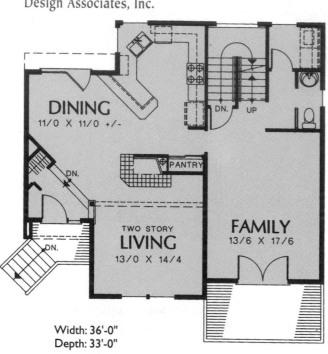

DINING
11/0 X 11/0 +/-

PANTRY

TWO STORY
LIVING
13/0 X 14/4

FAMILY
13/6 X 17/6

DN.   UP

DN.

DN.

Width: 36'-0"
Depth: 33'-0"

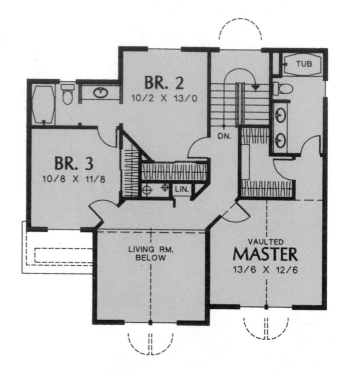

BR. 2
10/2 X 13/0

BR. 3
10/8 X 11/8

TUB

LIN.

DN.

LIVING RM.
BELOW

VAULTED
MASTER
13/6 X 12/6

56

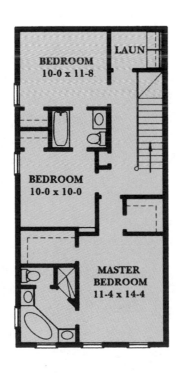

GARAGE
19-0 x 21-6

STOR.

STORAGE

DINING ROOM
10-10 x 11-0

GREAT ROOM
13-0 x 19-0

BEDROOM
10-0 x 11-8

LAUN

BEDROOM
10-0 x 10-0

MASTER
BEDROOM
11-4 x 14-4

Width: 20'-0"
Depth: 64'-0"

Design J500

First Floor: 680 square feet
Second Floor: 795 square feet
Total: 1,475 square feet

DESIGN BY
© Authentic Historical
Designs, Inc.

◆ Subdued and dignified, this ageless Federal residence will have lasting appeal. The inviting front door is accentuated by a curved transom and topped by a pediment. Inside, the great room connects to a formal dining area, giving the impression of a house much larger than its actual square footage. The kitchen opens directly to the courtyard to facilitate outdoor grilling and gardening. A breakfast bar provides additional dining space for a quick snack. The roomy kitchen also has space for a sitting area, table or computer center tucked up next to the open stairway. Two separate garage storage areas are available for alternative uses, such as a walk-in pantry or first-floor laundry. On the second floor, the master suite contains separate vanities and two walk-in closets. The other two bedrooms enjoy private entrances to their shared bath.

Design J510

First Floor: 1,190 square feet
Second Floor: 1,220 square feet
Total: 2,410 square feet

DESIGN BY
© Authentic Historical
Designs, Inc.

◆ This stately home is striking in its simplicity, dignity and strength. The facade is balanced with a deep entablature, which displays dentil blocks, modillions or brackets. These enduring classical components have been adapted to a narrow urban site. Inside, the high-ceiling rooms retain the grandeur of the original homes of the late 19th Century. An expansive great room flows into a formal dining room, separated by a pair of elegant columns. Beyond, a spacious kitchen features an informal snack bar and a light-filled breakfast area that overlooks the secluded courtyard. A downstairs bedroom can also function as an office or cozy den. Three bedrooms—each with its own bath—share the second floor and a sitting area.

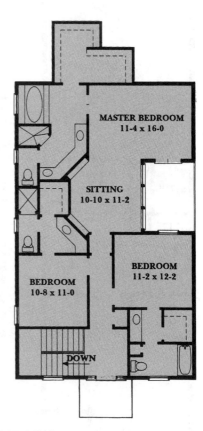

Width: 30'-0"
Depth: 72'-0"

Design J506

First Floor: 1,340 square feet
Second Floor: 651 square feet
Total: 1,991 square feet

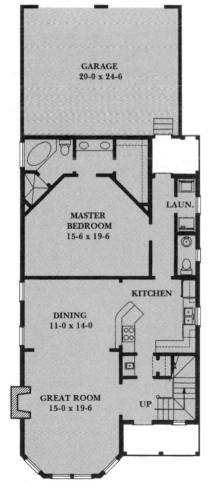

Width: 30'-0"
Depth: 74'-0"

GARAGE
20-0 x 24-6

LAUN.

MASTER
BEDROOM
15-6 x 19-6

KITCHEN

DINING
11-0 x 14-0

GREAT ROOM
15-0 x 19-6   UP

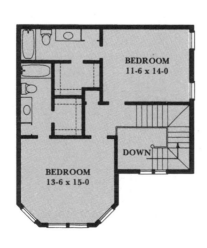

BEDROOM
11-6 x 14-0

DOWN

BEDROOM
13-6 x 15-0

◆ The resurgence in urban revival has dictated a style of residential architecture that preserves the charm of the past. This pleasing Victorian, with its double-stacked front bay, responds to that need. A multitude of windows admits the sun into this glittering home, drenching the house with light. The handsome great room showcases an old-fashioned fireplace and leads into the dining room. Between the great room and dining room, a large cased opening deserves special treatment—perhaps an interior transom, an arch or fret-work. The kitchen is partially separated from the dining area by a raised breakfast bar. A wet bar off the foyer assists in entertaining and could open to the great room, if desired. The master bedroom displays intriguing angles and is near the laundry room. A graceful, open stairway rises to the two bedrooms and their private baths on the second floor.

Design J505

First Floor: 900 square feet
Second Floor: 1,081 square feet
Total: 1,981 square feet

DESIGN BY
©Authentic Historical
Designs, Inc.

◆ A classic Greek Revival design would be at home in any region. The friendly front-facing gable with a spiderweb window accentuates the openness of the front facade. The double tier of galleries proclaims a house that will play a strong role in a vibrant urban streetscape. Inside, transom-topped windows lend additional grandeur to the ample great room. The bayed dining room can be handled with as much or as little formality as you desire. An adjacent breakfast bar provides a more casual setting for sandwiches and snacks. A covered porch is accessible for a summer barbecue. The large walk-in laundry has a separate sink and a pantry. The master bedroom, with its walk-in closet and private bath, is on the second floor. Two additional bedrooms share a bath but have private vanities.

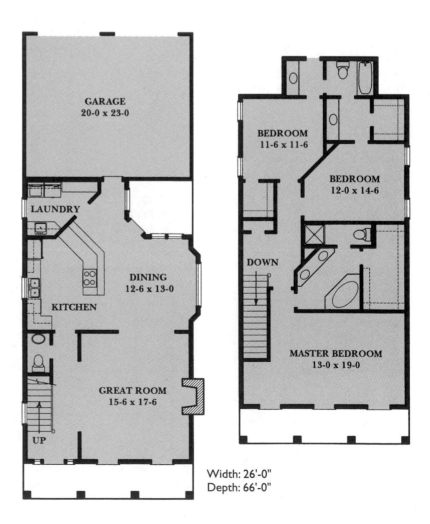

GARAGE
20-0 x 23-0

LAUNDRY

KITCHEN

DINING
12-6 x 13-0

GREAT ROOM
15-6 x 17-6

UP

BEDROOM
11-6 x 11-6

BEDROOM
12-0 x 14-6

DOWN

MASTER BEDROOM
13-0 x 19-0

Width: 26'-0"
Depth: 66'-0"

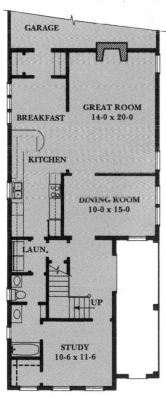

GARAGE

GREAT ROOM
14-0 x 20-0

BREAKFAST

KITCHEN

DINING ROOM
10-0 x 15-0

LAUN.

UP

STUDY
10-6 x 11-6

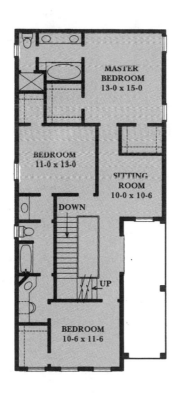

MASTER
BEDROOM
13-0 x 15-0

BEDROOM
11-0 x 13-0

SITTING
ROOM
10-0 x 10-6

DOWN

UP

BEDROOM
10-6 x 11-6

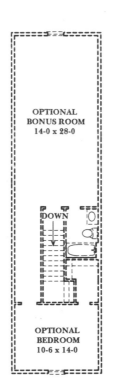

OPTIONAL
BONUS ROOM
14-0 x 28-0

DOWN

OPTIONAL
BEDROOM
10-6 x 14-0

Design J509

First Floor: 1,227 square feet
Second Floor: 1,133 square feet
Total: 2,360 square feet
Optional Bonus Space:
792 square feet

Design By
© Authentic Historical
Designs, Inc.

Width: 25'-0"
Depth: 77'-0"

◆ The distinctive design of the Charleston single house makes it a perfect candidate for the narrow urban lot. Since its narrow side faces the street and its two-story piazza faces the side yard, the single house affords optimum privacy. The street entry leads, not into the foyer, but onto a porch that provides a graceful transition from the urban setting. A grand foyer with an open stairwell greets the visitor.

Beyond, a formal dining room can be glimpsed, carefully planned so foot traffic will bypass the table and chairs. The study, at the front of the house, could serve as a home office or guest room. The adjacent breakfast area and galley kitchen will please the family cook. Three bedrooms and a sitting room are on the second floor. The third floor provides an optional bedroom, bath and bonus room.

Design 3734

First Floor: 523 square feet
Second Floor: 544 square feet
Total: 1,067 square feet

DESIGN BY
©Home Planners

◆ Designed to be part of a multi-family dwelling, this town-house could also be used as a single home on a small lot—perfect for a vacation or retirement home. You can select either the basic version or the enhanced version with a box-bay window and gables. Inside, the great room, kitchen and deck are on the first floor and two bedrooms plus a bath are on the second. The garage is tucked under the rear of the house.

Front View Basic Version

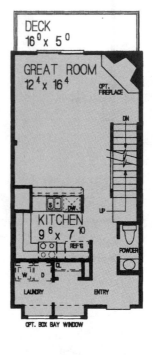

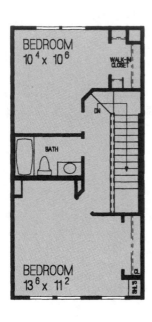

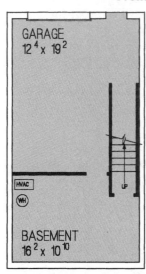

Width: 17'-0"
Depth: 34'-0"

Front View Enhanced Version

Rear View Enhanced Version

Front View Basic Version

◆ Perfect on a narrow, front-sloped lot, or joined to two or more similar dwellings to form a set of townhouses, this plan offers efficiency and comfort. You even have a choice of elevations: a simpler, basic version or an enhanced version with gables and a box-bay window. The first floor features an efficient U-shaped kitchen with a snack bar, a powder room and a great room with an optional corner fireplace and rear deck. Upstairs are two bedrooms—one with a walk-in closet and one with built-in shelves—sharing a bath. The garage is tucked up under the first floor at the front of the house.

Design 3735

First Floor: 523 square feet
Second Floor: 544 square feet
Total: 1,067 square feet

DESIGN BY
© Home Planners

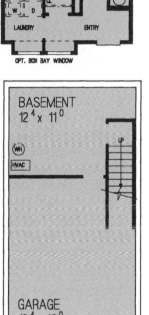

DECK
16⁰ x 5⁰

GREAT ROOM
12⁴ x 16⁴

OPT. FIREPLACE

UP

KITCHEN
9⁶ x 7¹⁰

DN

REF'S

POWDER

W D

LAUNDRY   ENTRY

CL

OPT. BOX BAY WINDOW

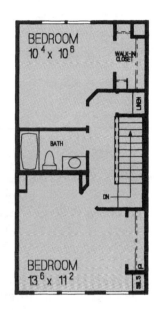

BEDROOM
10⁴ x 10⁶

WALK-IN CLOSET

LINEN

BATH

DN

BEDROOM
13⁶ x 11²

Width: 17'-0"
Depth: 34'-0"

BASEMENT
12⁴ x 11⁰

WH

HVAC

UP

GARAGE
12⁴ x 19⁰

Front View Enhanced Version

Rear View Enhanced Version

Front View Basic Version

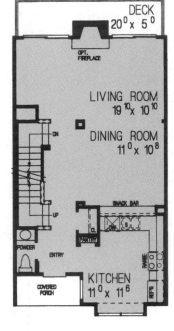

DECK
20⁰ x 5⁰

OPT.
FIREPLACE

LIVING ROOM
19¹⁰ x 10¹⁰

DINING ROOM
11⁰ x 10⁸

SNACK BAR

POWDER

ENTRY

COVERED
PORCH

KITCHEN
11⁰ x 11⁶

BEDROOM
10⁰ x 10⁶

BEDROOM
9⁶ x 13²

BATH

BATH

**MASTER
BEDROOM**
11⁶ x 13⁶

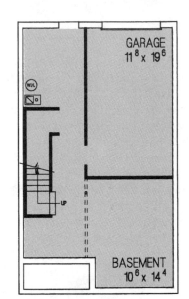

GARAGE
11⁸ x 19⁶

W.H.

BASEMENT
10⁶ x 14⁴

Width: 21'-0"
Depth: 36'-0"

Design 3736

First Floor: 685 square feet
Second Floor: 760 square feet
Total: 1,445 square feet

DESIGN BY
©Home Planners

◆ On this plan, the garage is under the rear of the house. This is designed for a narrow lot or to be joined with other townhouses to form a set. The basic version is complete by itself, while the enhanced version has exterior details such as gables and a box-bay window. The first floor features an efficient kitchen with a snack bar, a powder room and a combined living room/dining room with an optional fireplace. Upstairs are a private master suite, two bedrooms sharing a bath and a convenient laundry room.

Front View Enhanced Version

Rear View Enhanced Version

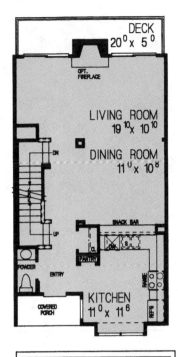

DECK
20⁰ x 5⁰

OPT. FIREPLACE

LIVING ROOM
19¹⁰ x 10¹⁰

DINING ROOM
11⁰ x 10⁸

DN

UP

POWDER

ENTRY

SNACK BAR

PANTRY

RANGE

REF.

KITCHEN
11⁰ x 11⁶

COVERED PORCH

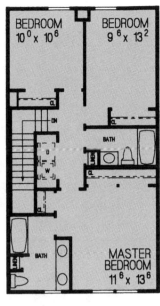

BEDROOM
10⁰ x 10⁶

BEDROOM
9⁶ x 13²

DN

BATH

BATH

W

MASTER BEDROOM
11⁶ x 13⁶

BATH

Width: 21'-0"
Depth: 36'-0"

BASEMENT
20² x 10⁴

W/L

UP

GARAGE
10⁸ x 21²

Front View Basic Version

DESIGN BY
© Home Planners

Design 3737

First Floor: 685 square feet
Second Floor: 760 square feet
Total: 1,445 square feet

◆ Built as a single home on a narrow lot or joined to two or more similar homes to form a row of townhouses, this is an efficient and affordable plan. The garage is tucked under the front of the house with the remainder of the basement being used for storage or expansion. The practical floor plan offers a living room and dining room on the first floor, with a front-facing kitchen. Upstairs, the master bedroom, at the front of the plan, sports a private bath, while two family bedrooms share a bath. For convenience, the laundry room is on the second floor.

Front View Enhanced Version

Rear View Enhanced Version

Design M188

Square Footage: 1,722

DESIGN BY
©Fillmore
Design Group

◆ Three bedrooms or two bedrooms with a study enhance this one-story plan. The study (or third bedroom) is to the left of the covered side entrance. The entry also includes a closet, garage and kitchen access and, through a wide doorway, the living room. A fireplace, TV nook, wide box-bay window and cathedral ceiling make this a showpiece living room. The kitchen opens to the rear patio through the breakfast area. Two bedrooms at the back of the plan are off a hallway. The master suite has a private bath, and a second full bath is beside Bedroom 2, which features a walk-in closet. This plan carries a choice of window styles.

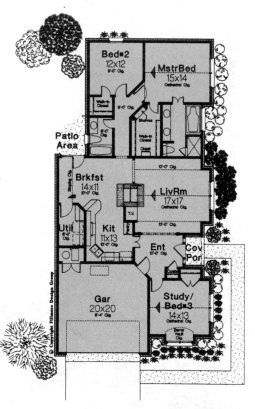

Width: 35'-0"
Depth: 70'-0"

Alternate View

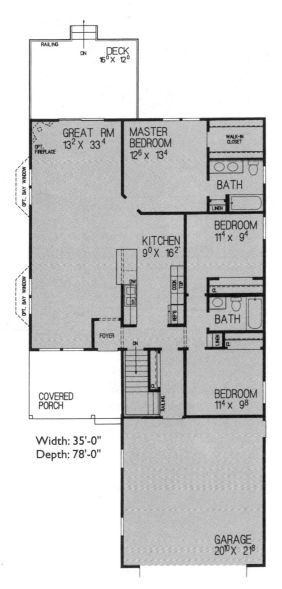

RAILING DN DECK 16⁰ X 12⁰

GREAT RM 13² X 33⁴

OPT. FIREPLACE

MASTER BEDROOM 12⁶ X 13⁴

WALK-IN CLOSET

BATH

OPT. BAY WINDOW

BEDROOM 11⁴ X 9⁴

KITCHEN 9⁰ X 16²

OPT. BAY WINDOW

FOYER

BATH

DN

COVERED PORCH

BEDROOM 11⁴ X 9⁸

GARAGE 20¹⁰ X 21⁸

Width: 35'-0"
Depth: 78'-0"

Design By
©Home Planners

◆ This eye-catching three-bedroom ranch home is designed specifically for narrow lots. All the many features you've been looking for in a family home can be found here. The master suite includes a bath and a walk-in closet. A second bath and a linen closet are located between the two family bedrooms. The huge great room offers an option for two bay windows. The blueprints for this house show how to build both a basic, low-cost version and an enhanced, upgraded version.

Basic Plan

Enhanced Plan

Design Q339

Square Footage: 1,007
Unfinished Lower Level:
1,007 square feet

DESIGN BY
©Select Home Designs

◆ To accommodate a very narrow lot, this plan can be built without the deck and the garage, but options are included for both. The lower floor can be finished later into a family room and additional bedrooms and a bath, if you choose. The cathedral entry offers steps up to the main living areas. The living room has a fireplace and leads to the L-shaped kitchen. Here you'll find abundant counter and cupboard space and room for a breakfast table. Sliding glass doors open to the optional deck. Bedrooms include a master bedroom and two family bedrooms.

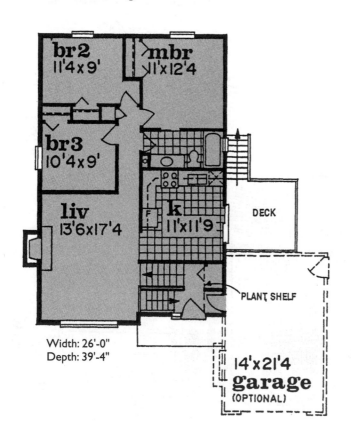

br2
11'4 x 9'

mbr
11' x 12'4

br3
10'4 x 9'

liv
13'6 x 17'4

k
11' x 11'9

DECK

PLANT SHELF

Width: 26'-0"
Depth: 39'-4"

14' x 21'4
garage
(OPTIONAL)

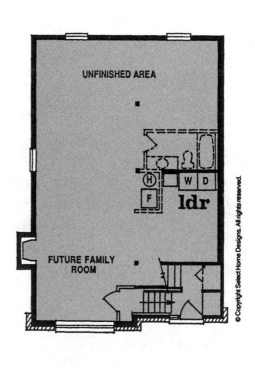

UNFINISHED AREA

W D

ldr

FUTURE FAMILY
ROOM

DESIGNS FOR FAMILY LIVING

Design 7469

First Floor: 1,106 square feet
Second Floor: 872 square feet
Total: 1,978 square feet

DESIGN BY
©Alan Mascord
Design Associates, Inc.

◆ Gables, shingles, various window shapes, a front deck and stone planters create an appealing blend of textures that call attention to this home. As befits a narrow lot, the garage is under the first floor. A U-shaped staircase rises from the garage to the foyer, or enter through the stylish front door. The dining and living rooms are open and optional French doors open from the dining room to the outside. A powder room and laundry room are tucked in a corner. The U-shaped kitchen offers a window sink and a cooktop island. The family room shares a through fireplace with the living room. A master suite, and two secondary bedrooms that share a bath are on the second floor. Please specify slab or basement foundation when ordering.

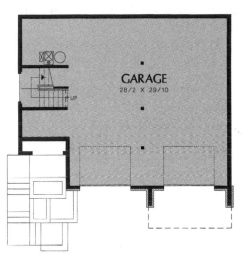

Width: 38'-0"
Depth: 35'-0"

69

Design 8119

First Floor: 1,158 square feet
Second Floor: 1,773 square feet
Third Floor: 173 square feet
Total: 3,104 square feet

DESIGN BY
© Larry E. Belk
Designs

◆ The facade of this home is a super prelude to an equally impressive interior. The front porch provides entry to a sleeping level, with the master suite on the right and a secondary bedroom on the left. Upstairs, living areas include a family room with a sitting alcove and a living room with special ceiling treatment. The kitchen serves a breakfast room as well as a barrel-vaulted dining room. A third bedroom and two balconies further the custom nature of this home. On the third floor, an observation room with outdoor access is an extra-special touch. Please specify crawlspace or slab foundation when ordering.

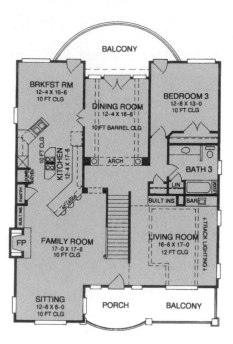

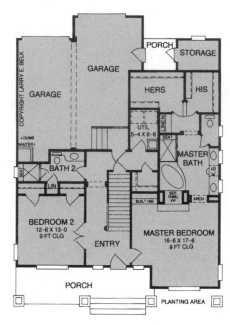

Width: 39'-10"
Depth: 58'-11"

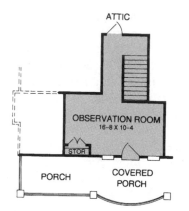

◆ The timeless influence of the French Quarter is exemplified in this home designed for river-front living. The double French-door entry opens into a living room/dining room area separated by a double archway. The living-room ceiling opens up through two stories to the cupola above. A railed balcony on the second floor overlooks the living room. A pass-through between the kitchen and dining room provides seating at a bar for informal dining. The spacious master bedroom includes a sitting area and a master bath with a walk-in closet. Two additional bedrooms, a bath and a bonus area for an office or game room are located upstairs. With ten-foot ceilings downstairs and nine-foot ceilings upstairs, there is a feeling of spaciousness. Fabulous decks on the front and back of the second story make this home perfect for entertaining. Please specify basement or slab foundation when ordering.

Design 8002

First Floor: 1,530 square feet
Second Floor: 968 square feet
Total: 2,498 square feet
Bonus Room: 326 square feet

DESIGN BY
©Larry E. Belk
Designs

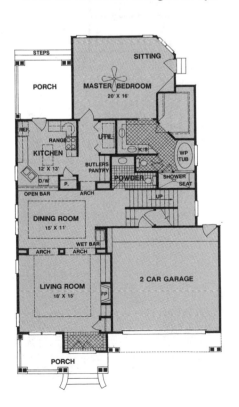

Interior View

Width: 40'-0"
Depth: 66'-0"

71

Design 2711

First Floor: 975 square feet
Second Floor: 1,024 square feet
Total: 1,999 square feet

L D

DESIGN BY
©Home Planners

◆ Sleek, modern lines define this two-story contemporary home. Open planning in the living areas creates a spaciousness found in much larger plans. The formal dining area and informal eating counter, both easily served by the U-shaped kitchen, share the cozy warmth of the centered fireplace and generous views to the rear grounds offered by the gathering room. Amenities abound in the second-floor master suite with a private balcony, walk-in closet, separate dressing area and knee-space vanity. Two secondary bedrooms and a full bath complete this floor.

QUOTE ONE®

Cost to build? See page 246 to order complete cost estimate to build this house in your area!

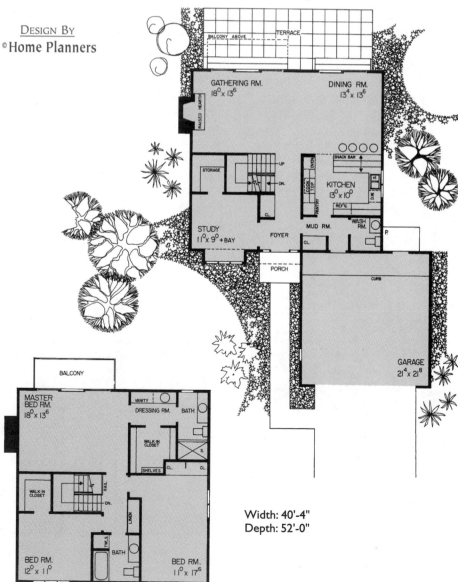

Width: 40'-4"
Depth: 52'-0"

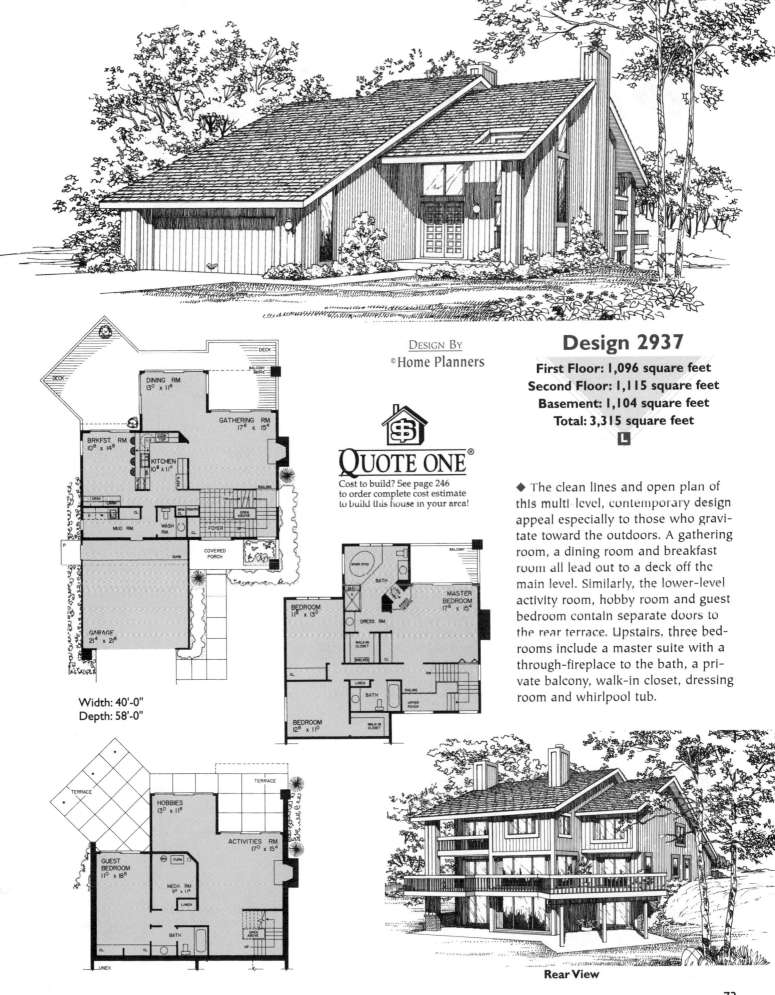

DESIGN BY
© Home Planners

Design 2937

First Floor: 1,096 square feet
Second Floor: 1,115 square feet
Basement: 1,104 square feet
Total: 3,315 square feet

L

QUOTE ONE®
Cost to build? See page 246
to order complete cost estimate
to build this house in your area!

Width: 40'-0"
Depth: 58'-0"

◆ The clean lines and open plan of this multi-level, contemporary design appeal especially to those who gravitate toward the outdoors. A gathering room, a dining room and breakfast room all lead out to a deck off the main level. Similarly, the lower-level activity room, hobby room and guest bedroom contain separate doors to the rear terrace. Upstairs, three bedrooms include a master suite with a through-fireplace to the bath, a private balcony, walk-in closet, dressing room and whirlpool tub.

Rear View

Design Q234

First Floor: 879
Second Floor: 869 square feet
Total: 1,748 square feet

◆ Special exterior details—a railed veranda, multi-paned windows and a dormer—lend country flavor to this three-bedroom home. A central hall at the entry holds a half-bath and a stairway to the second floor and allows passage to the formal living and dining rooms. The living room contains a fireplace; the dining room features a private veranda. The country kitchen is warmed by a fireplace and offers sliding glass doors to the rear patio, which boasts a built-in barbecue. An L-shaped work counter in the kitchen is complemented by a large pantry. The two-car garage is reached through the laundry area. On the second floor, the master suite offers a grand bath with a separate shower and tub. Two family bedrooms share a hall bath.

DESIGN BY
©Select Home Designs

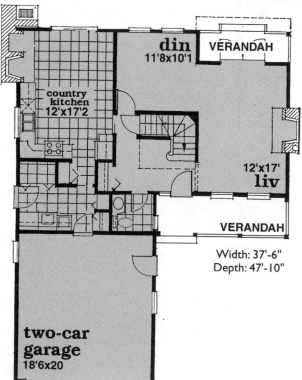

Width: 37'-6"
Depth: 47'-10"

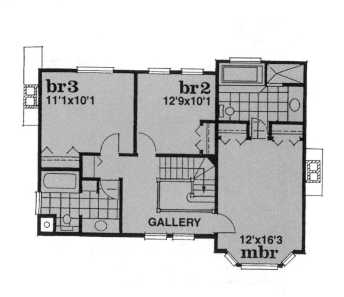

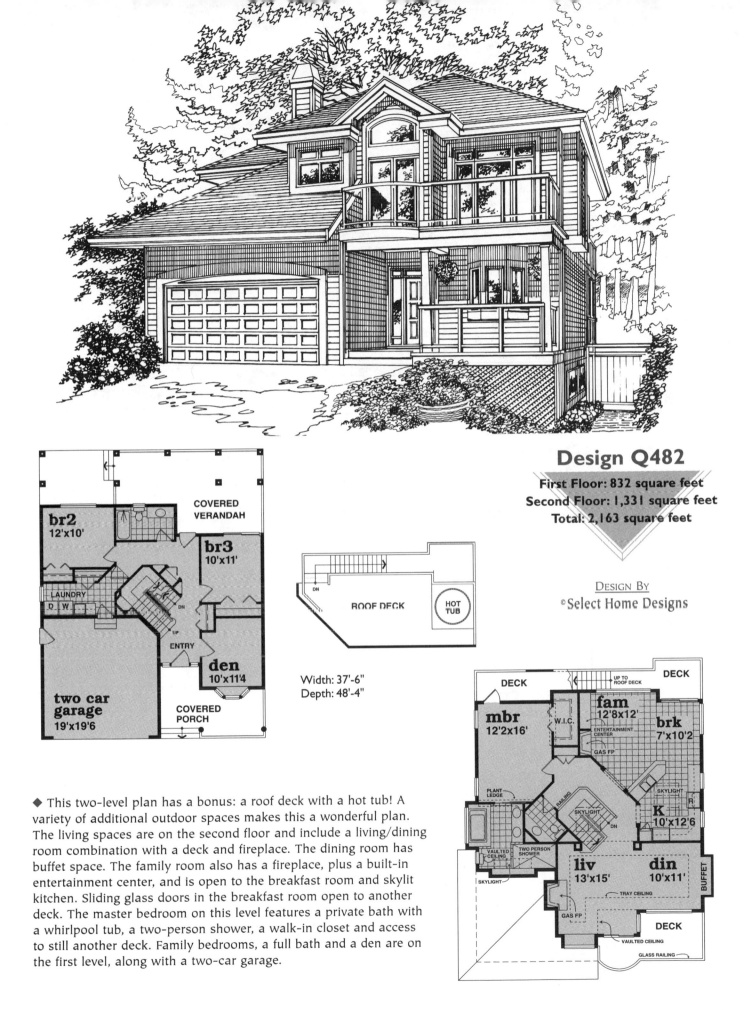

Design Q482

First Floor: 832 square feet
Second Floor: 1,331 square feet
Total: 2,163 square feet

DESIGN BY
©Select Home Designs

COVERED VERANDAH

br2
12'x10'

br3
10'x11'

LAUNDRY
D W

DN

UP

ENTRY

den
10'x11'4

two car garage
19'x19'6

COVERED PORCH

DN

ROOF DECK

HOT TUB

Width: 37'-6"
Depth: 48'-4"

DECK

DECK

UP TO ROOF DECK

mbr
12'2x16'

W.I.C.

fam
12'8'x12'

ENTERTAINMENT CENTER

GAS FP

brk
7'x10'2

PLANT LEDGE

RAILING

SKYLIGHT

DN

SKYLIGHT

K
10'x12'6

R

VAULTED CEILING

TWO PERSON SHOWER

SKYLIGHT

liv
13'x15'

din
10'x11'

BUFFET

TRAY CEILING

GAS FP

VAULTED CEILING

DECK

GLASS RAILING

◆ This two-level plan has a bonus: a roof deck with a hot tub! A variety of additional outdoor spaces makes this a wonderful plan. The living spaces are on the second floor and include a living/dining room combination with a deck and fireplace. The dining room has buffet space. The family room also has a fireplace, plus a built-in entertainment center, and is open to the breakfast room and skylit kitchen. Sliding glass doors in the breakfast room open to another deck. The master bedroom on this level features a private bath with a whirlpool tub, a two-person shower, a walk-in closet and access to still another deck. Family bedrooms, a full bath and a den are on the first level, along with a two-car garage.

Design V033

First Floor: 769 square feet
Second Floor: 872 square feet
Total: 1,641 square feet

DESIGN BY
©United Design
Associates, Inc.

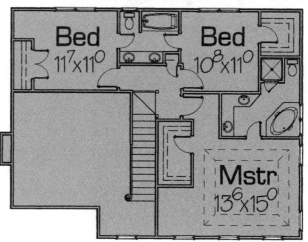

Width: 40'-4"
Depth: 37'-7"

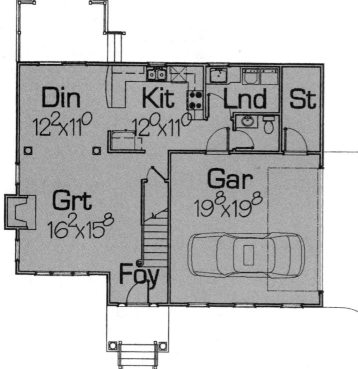

◆ Reminiscent of Classic American style, this elegant home features a beautiful vaulted foyer with an open staircase. Stunning transom windows in the great room let in natural light. The upstairs master suite includes a tray ceiling, large walk-in closet and master bath with a separate shower and garden or whirlpool tub. The kitchen and open dining area offer extensive views of the rear deck. A side-entry, two-car garage helps maintain the elegance of this design. The garage also contains a large storage area perfect for the lawnmower, weedeater and kids' bicycles.

◆ A graceful home with Old Southern charm, this design offers a sleek option for a narrow lot. Enter to an impressive two-story great room, with a fireplace, followed by a spacious dining room. The U-shaped kitchen is designed for efficiency and serves both dining room and breakfast bay equally well. The first-floor master suite is located at the rear of the plan and has an elegant tray ceiling, walk-in closet and private bath. Two more bedrooms (each with a walk-in closet), a roomy full bath, storage and linen space complete the second floor. A side porch serves both the great room and the breakfast room and offers a private area for the master bedroom.

Design 7647

First Floor: 1,545 square feet
Second Floor: 560 square feet
Total: 2,105 square feet

DESIGN BY
Donald A. Gardner
Architects, Inc.

MASTER BED RM.
16-4 x 17-0

master bath

walk-in closet

UTILITY
9-8 x 6-0

w | d

BRKFST.
8-7 x 11-8

KIT.
9-10 x 11-8

cl

pd. rm.

PORCH

PORCH

DINING
15-4 x 12-0

fireplace

up

GREAT RM.
23-2 x 16-10

(two story ceiling)

PORCH

© 1997 Donald A. Gardner Architects, Inc.

Width: 38'-0"
Depth: 64'-4"

GARAGE
22-4 x 25-4

BED RM.
12-4 x 11-8

walk-in closet

bath

BED RM.
12-4 x 12-0

lin. sto.

down

walk-in closet

great room below

© 1997 Donald A. Gardner Architects, Inc.

Design 7375

Square Footage: 1,212

DESIGN BY
©Design Basics, Inc.

◆ Attractive and uncomplicated, this two-bedroom home is perfect for first-time or empty-nest builders. Living, eating and cooking areas are designated as the center of activity in an open and unrestricted space. The master suite offers plenty of closet space and a private bath. Other features include a front coat closet for guests, a linen closet for hanging clothes in the laundry room and a warming fireplace in the great room, which is flanked by transom windows. A two-car garage provides a service entrance to the kitchen through the laundry room.

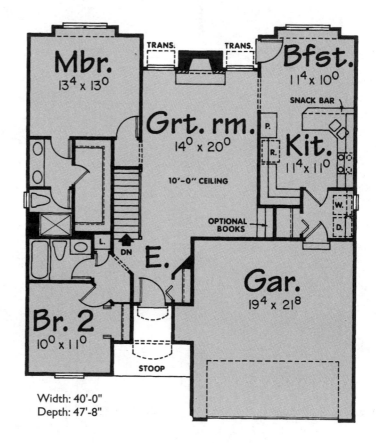

Mbr.
13^4 x 13^0

TRANS.   TRANS.

Bfst.
11^4 x 10^0

SNACK BAR

Grt. rm.
14^0 x 20^0

10'-0" CEILING

Kit.
11^4 x 11^0

P.
R.

W.
D.

OPTIONAL
BOOKS

E.

Gar.
19^4 x 21^8

DN

Br. 2
10^0 x 11^0

STOOP

Width: 40'-0"
Depth: 47'-8"

Design 9529/9530/9531

Square Footage: 1,420

DESIGN BY
©Alan Mascord
Design Associates, Inc.

◆ Your choice of three exteriors and roof styles is offered with a floor plan that's identical for all three styles. Enter the home through the garage service entrance or through the front entry. The den to the right of the foyer offers optional built-in shelves or a closet. The kitchen, great room and dining room provide an open living area, with sliding glass doors opening from the dining room to the rear terrace. Bedrooms to the left of the plan include a master suite—with a double-bowl vanity in the bath—and a secondary bedroom served by a hall bath.

Design 9529

Design 9530

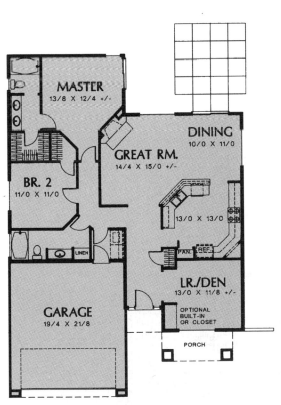

MASTER
13/8 X 12/4 +/-

DINING
10/0 X 11/0

GREAT RM.
14/4 X 15/0 +/-

BR. 2
11/0 X 11/0

13/0 X 13/0

PAN. REF.

LINEN

LR./DEN
13/0 X 11/8 +/-

GARAGE
19/4 X 21/8

OPTIONAL
BUILT-IN
OR CLOSET

PORCH

Width: 40'-0"
Depth: 58'-0"/59'-0"/58'-0"

Design 9531

Design 7654

First Floor: 1,055 square feet
Second Floor: 572 square feet
Total: 1,627 square feet

◆ What could be more charming than this country cottage? The covered front porch with special wood detailing invites you to put your feet up and take it easy. The interior is equally charming. The great room boasts a cathedral ceiling and fireplace while the adjacent kitchen and dining area has access to a rear covered porch to extend indoor/outdoor living. Two family bedrooms sharing a hall bath complete the main level. The master suite shares the second floor with attic storage and a roomy loft/study.

Width: 37'-4"
Depth: 43'-0"

DESIGN BY
Donald A. Gardner
Architects, Inc.

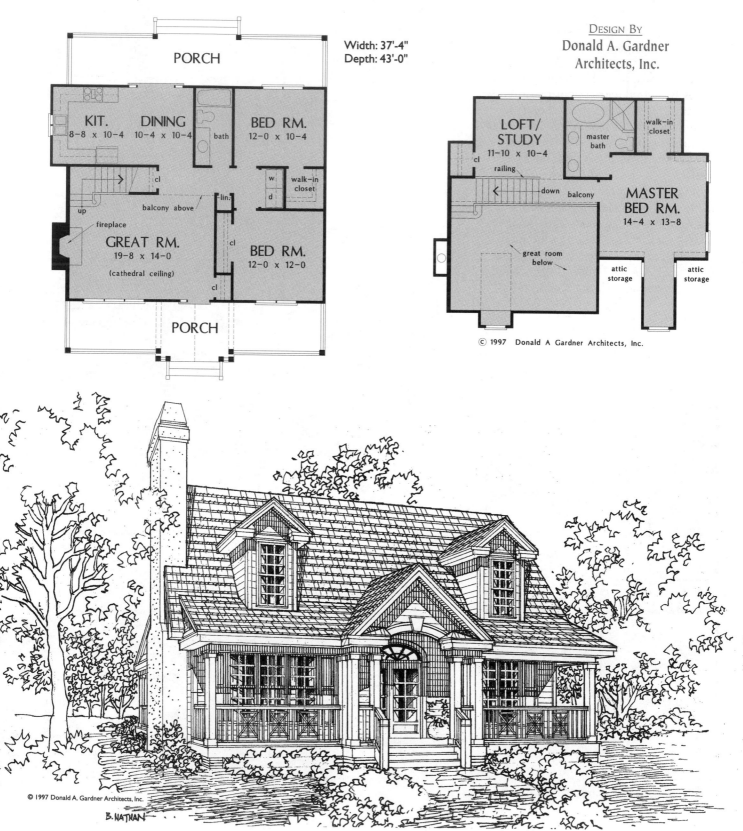

PORCH

KIT.
8-8 x 10-4

DINING
10-4 x 10-4

bath

BED RM.
12-0 x 10-4

cl

up

balcony above

lin.

w
d

walk-in closet

fireplace

GREAT RM.
19-8 x 14-0

(cathedral ceiling)

cl

cl

BED RM.
12-0 x 12-0

PORCH

LOFT/
STUDY
11-10 x 10-4

master bath

walk-in closet

cl

railing

down

balcony

great room below

MASTER
BED RM.
14-4 x 13-8

attic storage

attic storage

© 1997 Donald A Gardner Architects, Inc.

© 1997 Donald A. Gardner Architects, Inc.

B. NATHAN

80

◆ Craftsman styling and a welcoming porch create marvelous curb appeal for this design. A compact footprint allows economy in construction. A volume ceiling in the living and dining rooms and the kitchen makes this home seem larger than its modest square footage. The kitchen features generous cabinet space and flows directly into the dining room (note the optional buffet) to create a casual country feeling. The master bedroom offers a walk-in closet, full bath and a bumped-out window overlooking the rear yard. Two additional bedrooms also boast bumped-out windows and share a full bath. The lower level provides room for an additional bedroom, a den, a family room and a full bath.

Design Q527

Square Footage: 1,108 square feet
Unfinished Lower Level: 620 square feet
Unfinished Basement: 468 square feet

DESIGN BY
©Select Home Designs

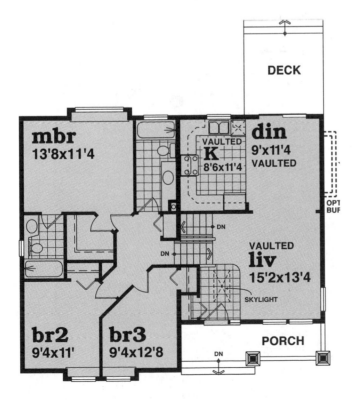

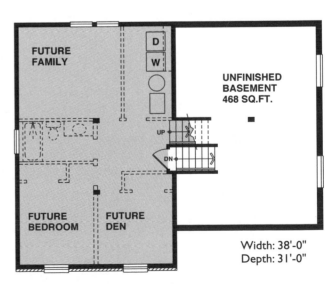

mbr 13'8x11'4

din 9'x11'4 VAULTED

VAULTED K 8'6x11'4

DECK

OPT BUF

VAULTED liv 15'2x13'4

SKYLIGHT

br2 9'4x11'

br3 9'4x12'8

PORCH

FUTURE FAMILY

FUTURE BEDROOM

FUTURE DEN

D W

UP

DN

UNFINISHED BASEMENT 468 SQ.FT.

Width: 38'-0"
Depth: 31'-0"

Design 7670

Square Footage: 1,444

DESIGN BY
Donald A. Gardner
Architects, Inc.

◆ Designed for longer lots, this home offers the ultimate in quiet living. Directly off the foyer, the front, U-shaped kitchen serves an elegant dining room that features a tray ceiling and pillars that separate it from the large great room. A fireplace, cathedral ceiling and access to the rear porch highlight the great room. The master suite features a coffered ceiling, a walk-in closet and a spacious bath. Two secondary bedrooms share a hall bath. The laundry area is conveniently located in the hall near the bedrooms.

master bath

lin.

cl

MASTER BED RM.
12-4 x 14-0

PORCH

BED RM.
11-0 x 11-0

w
d

walk-in closet

BED RM.
11-0 x 11-0

cl

bath

GREAT RM.
16-0 x 14-10

fireplace

(cathedral ceiling)

GARAGE
21-4 x 21-6

sto.

DINING
11-2 x 12-0

cl

FOYER
6-2 x
5-5

KITCHEN
11-6 x 10-0

Width: 40'-4"
Depth: 70'-0"

PORCH

© 1998 Donald A. Gardner, Inc.

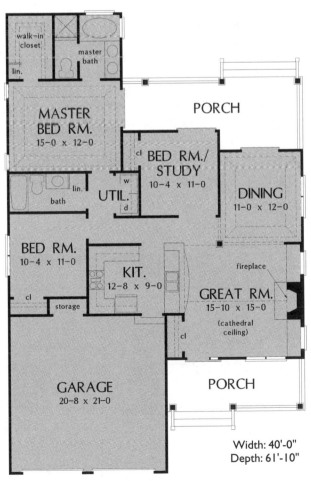

walk-in closet

lin.

master bath

MASTER BED RM.
15-0 x 12-0

PORCH

cl BED RM./
STUDY
10-4 x 11-0

bath lin.

UTIL.

w
d

DINING
11-0 x 12-0

BED RM.
10-4 x 11-0

cl

KIT.
12-8 x 9-0

storage

fireplace

GREAT RM.
15-10 x 15-0

(cathedral ceiling)

cl

GARAGE
20-8 x 21-0

PORCH

Width: 40'-0"
Depth: 61'-10"

© 1998   Donald A Gardner, Inc.

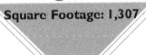

Design 7683
Square Footage: 1,307

DESIGN BY
**Donald A. Gardner
Architects, Inc.**

◆ Graceful stick-work lends Craftsman-type style to this fine three-bedroom home. The covered front porch ushers you into the spacious great room, where a cathedral ceiling, warming fireplace and built-ins enhance an already attractive room. Adjacent to the great room is the formal dining room, highlighted by a detailed ceiling and access to the rear porch. The U-shaped kitchen is also convenient to the great room, with a serving/snack bar providing a casual eating area. Three bedrooms—or make one a study—include a master suite with a detailed ceiling, walk-in closet and a private bath. Note the storage space in the two-car garage.

Design W019

First Floor: 778 square feet
Second Floor: 871 square feet
Total: 1,649 square feet

◆ Twin chimneys, symetrical gables and multi-pane windows reflect the charm that flows throughout this floor plan. The wide foyer opens at the left to the living room that houses one of the fireplaces, or it leads directly ahead to the country kitchen. Amenities in the kitchen include a cooktop island, a walk-in pantry and access to the rear porch, which is big enough for alfresco dining. The master suite takes up the right side of the plan. It features the second fireplace, a walk-in closet and a bath that offers a double-bowl vanity. Two family bedrooms on the second floor share a compartmented bath and a balcony overlooking the foyer. Please specify basement or crawlspace foundation when ordering.

DESIGN BY
©TAG Architects

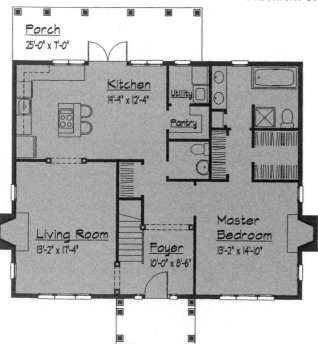

Porch
25'-0" x 7'-0"

Kitchen
19'-4" x 12'-4"

Utility

Pantry

Living Room
13'-2" x 17'-4"

Foyer
10'-0" x 8'-6"

Master Bedroom
13'-2" x 14'-10"

Width: 38'-0"
Depth: 45'-6"

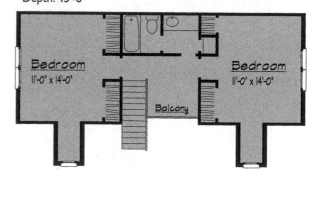

Bedroom
11'-0" x 14'-0"

Bedroom
11'-0" x 14'-0"

Balcony

◆ Porches front and back enhance this light-filled, country-style home. A dormer window over the foyer lets in natural light and provides a sense of space that makes this home seem larger than its modest square footage. Dormer windows add character to the upstairs bedrooms, which receive plenty of natural light from wide windows. The master suite on the first floor receives light from two front windows and two windows flanking the fireplace. Another fireplace warms the living room, which has the same window arrangement as the master bedroom. Please specify basement or crawlspace foundation when ordering.

Design W016

First Floor: 1,178 square feet
Second Floor: 571 square feet
Total: 1,749 square feet

DESIGN BY
©TAG Architects

Width: 38'-0"
Depth: 45'-0"

Porch
25'-0" x 7'-0"

Kitchen
19'-9" x 12'-4"

Utility

Pantry

Living Room
13'-2" x 17'-4"

Foyer
10'-0" x 8'-6"

Master Bedroom
13'-2" x 14'-10"

Porch
38'-0" x 7'-0"

Bedroom
11'-0" x 14'-0"

Bedroom
11'-0" x 14'-0"

Balcony

Design 7248

First Floor: 845 square feet
Second Floor: 760 square feet
Total: 1,605 square feet

◆ With its gabled roof, brick accents and covered front porch, this design has a lot going for it! Inside, a large, two-story great room with a fireplace is open to a formal dining room, which has space for a built-in hutch. The kitchen offers a snack bar, a separate breakfast area for family meals and a built-in desk. The nearby laundry area provides a window, a broom closet and a hanging rod. Upstairs, three bedrooms dominate, including a stunning master suite with French doors both at the entry and the sumptuous bath. Two secondary bedrooms share a bath and a linen closet.

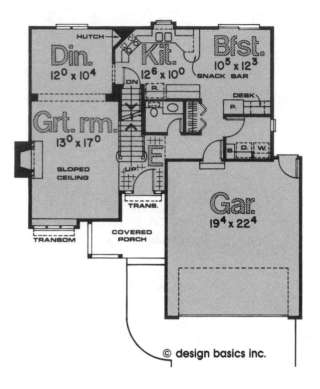

DESIGN BY
©Design Basics, Inc.

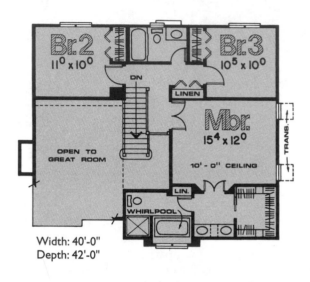

Width: 40'-0"
Depth: 42'-0"

◆ An impressive exterior distinguished by handsome wood columns leads to an equally grand interior. Inside, a spacious entry opens to an inviting great room. The dining room is steps away from the kitchen, complete with a snack bar and a breakfast area that combine to make meal preparation a breeze. The master suite invites relaxation in the luxurious master bath with its whirlpool tub. The second floor contains Bedrooms 2, 3 and 4, which share a full bath.

Design 9380

First Floor: 1,327 square feet
Second Floor: 518 square feet
Total: 1,845 square feet

DESIGN BY
©Design Basics, Inc.

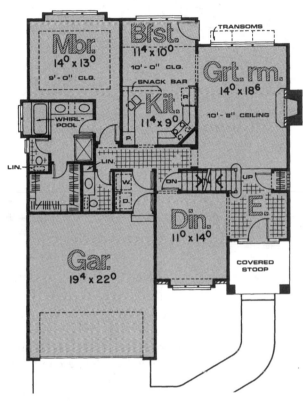

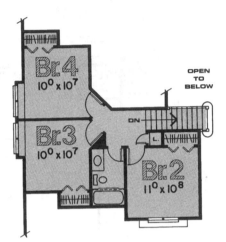

Width: 40'-8"
Depth: 53'-0"

Design 7026

First Floor: 866 square feet
Second Floor: 788 square feet
Total: 1,654 square feet

◆ An L-shaped front porch provides an ideal place to unwind and leads into the dining room or to a staircase to the second floor. The family room and breakfast area include a snack bar, a fireplace and sliding glass doors that open to the outside. The kitchen provides a window sink, a pantry and quick access to the dining room. Upstairs, the master suite features a separate tub and shower, and two secondary bedrooms share a hall bath. The garage includes additional storage space or the perfect spot for a work bench.

DESIGN BY
©Design Basics, Inc.

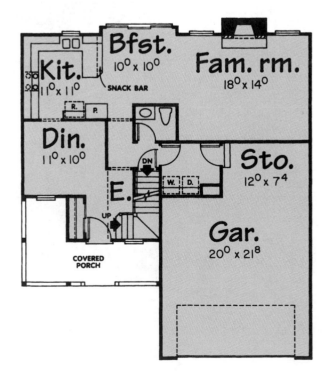

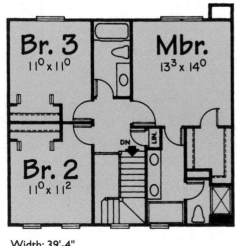

Width: 39'-4"
Depth: 45'-0"

◆ A fireplace and transom windows highlight the great room, while the kitchen provides a breakfast bay and access to outside. The master suite, located on the first floor for privacy, enjoys a walk-in closet and a compartmented bath that offers a double-bowl vanity. Near the service entrance from the garage, you'll find the laundry room and powder room. The unfinished bonus room on the second floor could be a recreation room or a fourth bedroom, joining Bedrooms 2 and 3, which share the hall bath.

Design 7376

First Floor: 1,324 square feet
Second Floor: 391 square feet
Total: 1,715 square feet
Bonus Room: 212 square feet

DESIGN BY
©Design Basics, Inc.

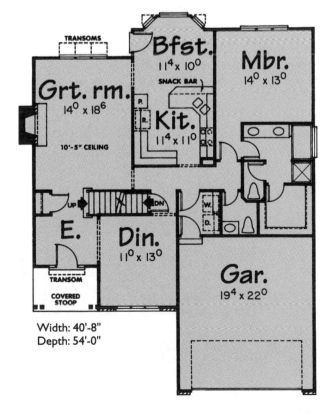

TRANSOMS

Bfst.
11⁴ x 10⁰

Mbr.
14⁰ x 13⁰

SNACK BAR

Grt. rm.
14⁰ x 18⁶

Kit.
11⁴ x 11⁰

10'-5" CEILING

UP   DN

E.

Din.
11⁰ x 13⁰

W.
D.

Gar.
19⁴ x 22⁰

TRANSOM

COVERED
STOOP

Width: 40'-8"
Depth: 54'-0"

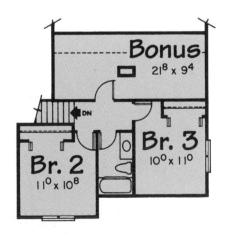

Bonus
21⁸ x 9⁴

DN

Br. 2
11⁰ x 10⁸

Br. 3
10⁰ x 11⁰

Design E143

First Floor: 1,505 square feet
Second Floor: 555 square feet
Total: 2,060 square feet

DESIGN BY
©Chatham Home
Planning, Inc.

◆ Covered porches in front and back soften the natural light flooding in through the many windows in this design, while a dramatic dining bay with pretty, arch-topped windows lets the sun shine in full force. Adjacent to the dining room, the kitchen and breakfast room provide access to the laundry room and the rear porch. A handsome fireplace and built-in shelves dress up the living room. The bedroom to the right of the foyer might be converted to an office. To the rear is the master suite, featuring a walk-in closet, a double-bowl vanity and oval tub. Each of the two bedrooms upstairs has its own vanity and walk-in closet.

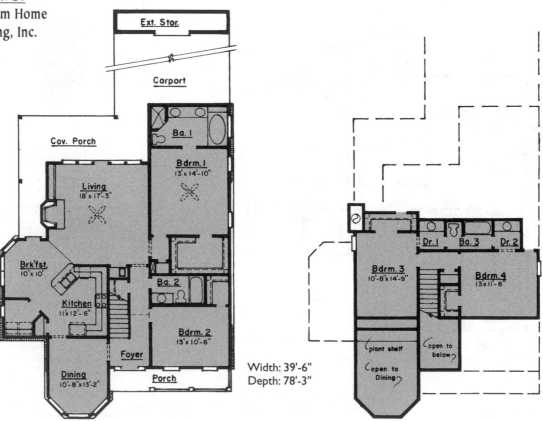

Width: 39'-6"
Depth: 78'-3"

◆ Charming and compact, this delightful two-story cabin is perfect for the small family or empty-nesters. Designed with casual living in mind, the two-story great room is completely open to the dining area and the spacious island kitchen. The master suite—on the first floor for privacy and convenience—features a roomy bath and a walk-in closet. Upstairs, two comfortable bedrooms—one has a dormer window, the other offers a balcony overlook to the great room—share a full hall bath.

Design 9697

First Floor: 1,039 square feet
Second Floor: 583 square feet
Total: 1,622 square feet

DESIGN BY
Donald A. Gardner
Architects, Inc.

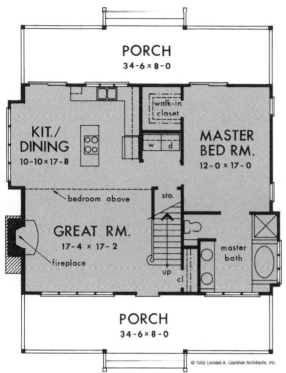

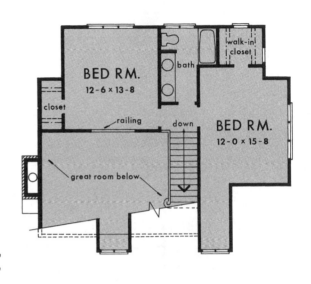

Width: 37'-9"
Depth: 44'-8"

© 1992 Donald A. Gardner Architects, Inc.

Design P266

First Floor: 834 square feet
Second Floor: 872 square feet
Total: 1,706 square feet

DESIGN BY
© Frank Betz
Associates, Inc.

◆ Elegant height, arches and distinguishing shutters draw attention to this stately home. Inside, an interior balcony overlooks the two-story family room with its fireplace. The efficient L-shaped kitchen adjoins the formal dining room and opens to the breakfast room, which has a door to the covered rear porch. The service entrance is through the garage and leads past a powder room. All three bedrooms are upstairs, including the master suite with a huge compartmented bath and two walk-in closets. Please specify basement or crawlspace foundation when ordering.

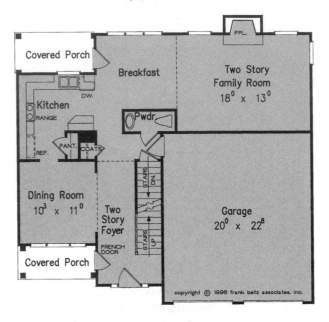

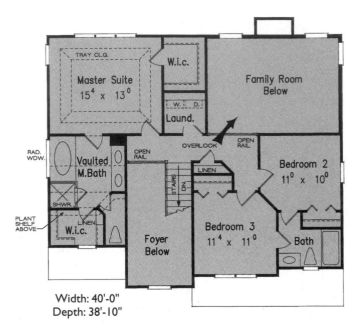

Width: 40'-0"
Depth: 38'-10"

◆ A covered-porch entry to this delightful two-story home gives way to an interesting foyer with an angled stairway. The formal living and dining rooms to the left provide a massive open space for relaxing and entertaining. The island kitchen is open to a bayed breakfast room and connects to the garage via a laundry and powder room. Upstairs, three bedrooms include two family bedrooms that share a hall bath and an indulgent master suite with a pampering master bath and a huge walk-in closet.

Design 7251

First Floor: 884 square feet
Second Floor: 848 square feet
Total: 1,732 square feet

DESIGN BY
©Design Basics, Inc.

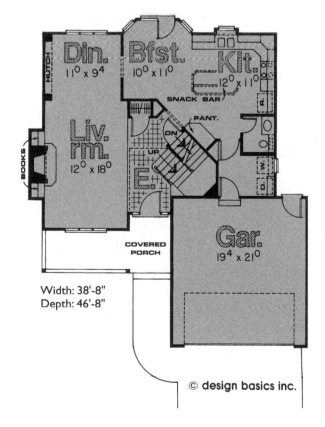

Din.
11⁰ x 9⁴

HUTCH

Bfst.
10⁰ x 11⁰

Kit.
12⁰ x 11⁰

SNACK BAR

Liv. rm.
12⁰ x 18⁰

BOOKS

PANT.

DN

UP

R.

D. W.

Gar.
19⁴ x 21⁰

COVERED PORCH

Width: 38'-8"
Depth: 46'-8"

© design basics inc.

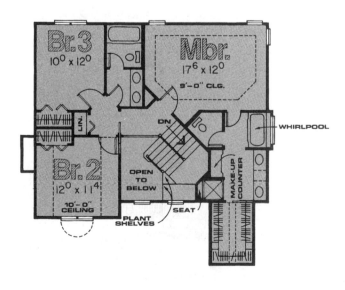

Br.3
10⁰ x 12⁰

Mbr.
17⁶ x 12⁰

9'-0" CLG.

LIN.

DN

WHIRLPOOL

Br.2
12⁰ x 11⁴

10'-0" CEILING

OPEN TO BELOW

MAKE-UP COUNTER

SEAT

PLANT SHELVES

Design 7328

First Floor: 845 square feet
Second Floor: 883 square feet
Total: 1,728 square feet

◆ A quaint covered porch suggests comfortable living in this tidy two-story design. The great room features a raised-hearth fireplace and a sloped ceiling. Transom windows provide lots of natural light. The wrap-around kitchen with peninsula snack bar is located between the formal dining room and the breakfast room. On the second floor, the master suite opens with double doors and soars to a ten-foot ceiling. Amenities here include a compartmented bath with a double-bowl vanity, a whirlpool tub and a walk-in closet. Three other bedrooms share a hall bath.

DESIGN BY
©Design Basics, Inc.

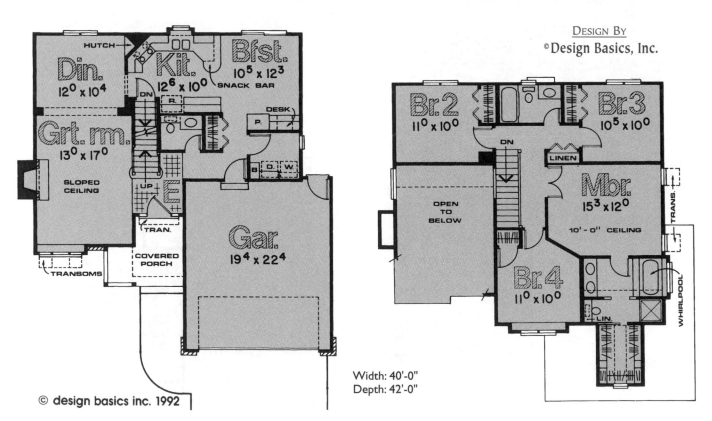

Width: 40'-0"
Depth: 42'-0"

© design basics inc. 1992

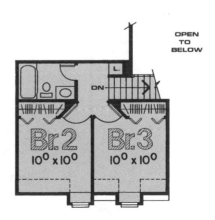

Design 7216

First Floor: 1,327 square feet
Second Floor: 348 square feet
Total: 1,675 square feet

DESIGN BY
©Design Basics, Inc.

◆ The Palladian arch sheltering the entry demonstrates exceptional style. Inside, a wide cased opening leads to the bright formal dining room on the right. The great room, with its wall of windows and brick fireplace, creates an inviting atmosphere. The open breakfast area enjoys large windows, a snack bar shared with the kitchen and access to outside. The master bedroom, with a boxed ceiling and an expansive window area, affords maximum privacy. Two secondary bedrooms and a full bath are upstairs.

Mbr.
$14^0 \times 13^0$
8'-0" CEILING

Bfst.
$11^4 \times 10^0$
10'-0" CEILING

SNACK BAR

Grt. rm.
$14^0 \times 18^8$
10'-8" CEILING

TRANSOMS

WHIRL-POOL

Kit.
$11^4 \times 9^0$

LIN.

LIN.

DN

UP

W.

D.

Din.
$11^0 \times 14^0$

Gar.
$19^4 \times 22^0$

COVERED STOOP

© design basics inc. 1992

Width: 40'-8"
Depth: 53'-0"

OPEN TO BELOW

DN

Br. 2
$10^0 \times 10^0$

Br. 3
$10^0 \times 10^0$

Design P456

First Floor: 1,412 square feet
Second Floor: 425 square feet
Total: 1,837 square feet
Bonus Room: 368 square feet

DESIGN BY
©Frank Betz
Associates, Inc.

◆ Stone and siding create a textured facade relieved by gables and arched windows. Inside, the two-story foyer leads past the formal dining and living rooms and staircase to the vaulted, two-story family room. A fireplace accents the family room, which is open to the breakfast nook and kitchen. The master bedroom on this floor offers a tray ceiling and a French door to a private compartmented bath that ends in a walk-in closet. Two bedrooms on the second floor share a bath and an overlook to the family room and foyer. Options include a loft and a bonus room. Please specify basement or crawlspace foundation when ordering.

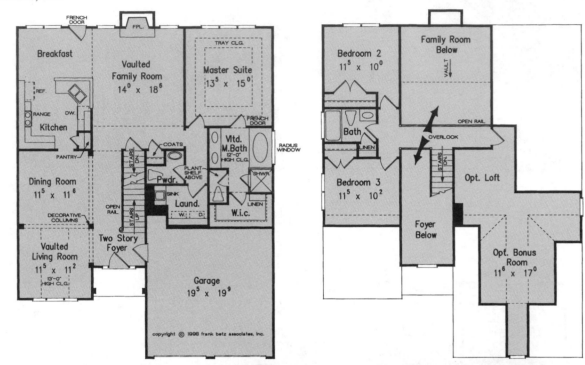

Width: 40'-0"
Depth: 53'-4"

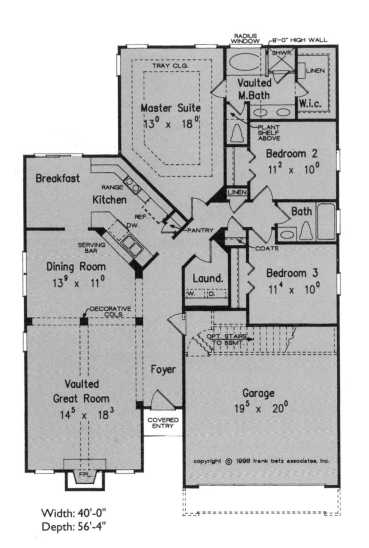

RADIUS WINDOW · 8'-0" HIGH WALL

TRAY CLG.

Master Suite
13⁰ x 18⁰

Vaulted
M.Bath

SHWR

LINEN

W.i.c.

Breakfast

RANGE

Kitchen

REF. DW.

PLANT SHELF ABOVE

Bedroom 2
11² x 10⁰

LINEN

Bath

PANTRY

SERVING BAR

Dining Room
13⁹ x 11⁰

DECORATIVE COLS.

COATS

Laund.
W. D.

Bedroom 3
11⁴ x 10⁰

OPT. STAIRS TO BSMT.

Foyer

Vaulted
Great Room
14⁵ x 18³

Garage
19⁵ x 20⁰

COVERED ENTRY

FPL

copyright © 1998 frank betz associates, inc.

Width: 40'-0"
Depth: 56'-4"

Design P455
Square Footage: 1,573

DESIGN BY
©Frank Betz
Associates, Inc.

◆ A herring-bone brick design on the fireplace exterior is the attention-getter of this comfortable one-story home. Through the covered entry, the foyer leads into an angled hallway. Off the hall, decorative columns separate the vaulted great room, which houses the handsome fireplace, from the dining room. The efficient kitchen leads to a breakfast room with the dining room just a step away. The master suite at the back of the plan includes a vaulted bath and a walk-in closet. Two bedrooms share a hall bath. The laundry room, across from the kitchen, is convenient to the three bedrooms. Please specify basement or crawlspace foundation when ordering.

DESIGN BY
©Alan Mascord
Design Associates, Inc.

◆ With split-bedroom sleeping arrangements and a wonderfully open living space, this plan seems much larger than it really is. The master suite and the great room feature vaulted ceilings, which give them a lofty feeling. A breakfast nook complements the kitchen, which provides a preparation island, a pass-through to the great room and access to the rear patio. Upstairs, two secondary bedrooms share a bath and a balcony that overlooks the great room. There's also a bonus room that can be developed in any way you choose. The garage easily holds two cars.

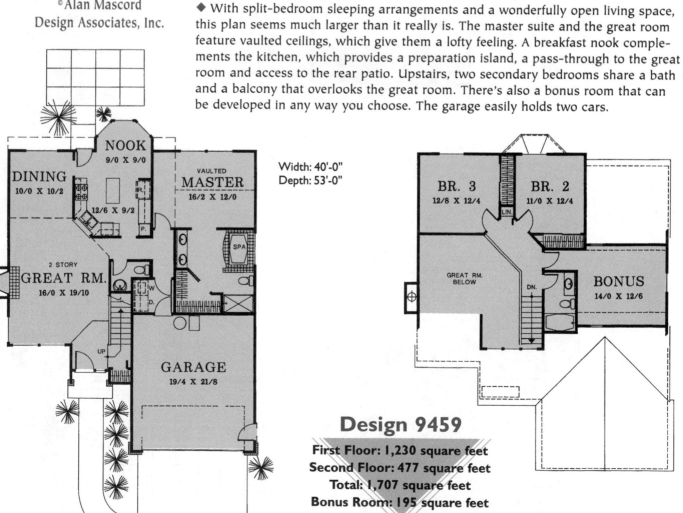

Width: 40'-0"
Depth: 53'-0"

NOOK
9/0 X 9/0

DINING
10/0 X 10/2

VAULTED
MASTER
16/2 X 12/0

12/6 X 9/2

2 STORY
GREAT RM.
16/0 X 19/10

SPA

GARAGE
19/4 X 21/8

UP

W
D.

P.

BR. 3
12/8 X 12/4

BR. 2
11/0 X 12/4

LIN.

GREAT RM.
BELOW

DN.

BONUS
14/0 X 12/6

Design 9459

First Floor: 1,230 square feet
Second Floor: 477 square feet
Total: 1,707 square feet
Bonus Room: 195 square feet

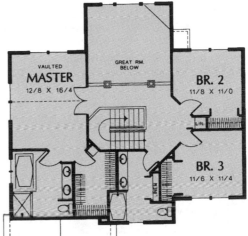

Design 9591

First Floor: 1,176 square feet
Second Floor: 994 square feet
Total: 2,170 square feet

DESIGN BY
©Alan Mascord
Design Associates, Inc.

◆ An angled door to the rear covered porch elegantly echoes the angled door at the front, thus setting the style for this amenity-filled design. Flanking the foyer to the left is the formal dining room and to the right, through double French doors, is a den or parlor. The great room opens out into the comfortable breakfast nook, sharing the warmth of its corner fireplace and giving this plan a spacious feeling. Gourmets will enjoy the large kitchen that offers a work island and access to the laundry room and powder room. Upstairs, the master suite is separated from two secondary bedrooms for privacy and offers a luxurious bath and a walk-in closet.

TWO STORY
GREAT RM.
14/0 X 17/4

MEDIA CENTER

DEN/PARLOR
11/8 X 10/8
(9' CLG)

NOOK
12/8 X 11/0
(9' CLG)

14/8 X 11/0

REF.

PAN

DINING
12/0 X 11/0
(9' CLG.)

GARAGE
20/4 X 20/2

Width: 40'-0"
Depth: 64'-0"

VAULTED
MASTER
12/8 X 16/4

GREAT RM. BELOW

BR. 2
11/8 X 11/0

BR. 3
11/6 X 11/4

99

Design Z036

Square Footage: 1,059

DESIGN BY
©Drummond Designs, Inc.

◆ A trianglular stoop leads to a three-part front door and adds to the appeal of this pristine, light-filled, one-story home. The focal point in the family room is the fire-place framed by soaring arched windows. The eat-in kitchen includes a walk-in pantry, a corner window sink and sliding doors to the outside. Two bedrooms share a bath that includes a shower, a garden tub and a double-bowl vanity. This home is designed with a basement foundation.

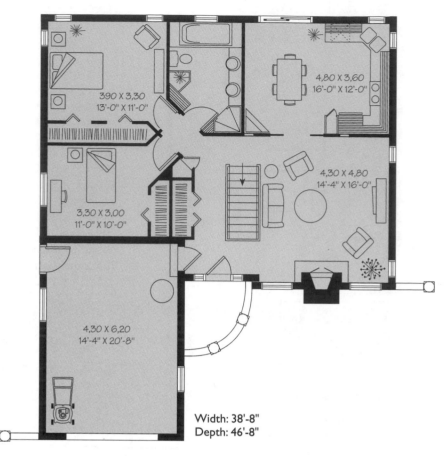

390 X 3,30
13'-0" X 11'-0"

4,80 X 3,60
16'-0" X 12'-0"

3,30 X 3,00
11'-0" X 10'-0"

4,30 X 4,80
14'-4" X 16'-0"

4,30 X 6,20
14'-4" X 20'-8"

Width: 38'-8"
Depth: 46'-8"

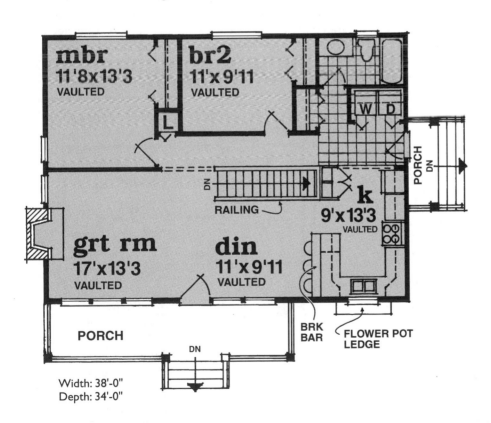

mbr
11'8x13'3
VAULTED

br2
11'x9'11
VAULTED

L

W | D

PORCH
DN

DN

DN
RAILING

k
9'x13'3
VAULTED

grt rm
17'x13'3
VAULTED

din
11'x9'11
VAULTED

PORCH

DN

BRK
BAR

FLOWER POT
LEDGE

Width: 38'-0"
Depth: 34'-0"

Design Q515
Square Footage: 1,064

◆ This farmhouse fits space-efficient features into its compact design. The front porch opens into a vaulted great room and its adjoining dining room. Twin dormer windows flood this area with natural light and accentuate the high ceilings. A hearth in the great room also warms the dining room. The U-shaped kitchen provides a breakfast bar open to the dining room and a sink overlooking a flower box. A side-door in the laundry room furnishes access to the outside. Vaulted bedrooms positioned along the back of the plan contain wall closets and share a full bath that has a soaking tub. An open-rail staircase leads to the optional basement, which can be developed into living or sleeping space at a later time, if needed.

Design Q276

First Floor: 957 square feet
Second Floor: 930 square feet
Total: 1,887 square feet
Bonus Room: 221 square feet

DESIGN BY
©Select Home Designs

◆ Decorated with two circle-head windows, this traditional design is both comfortable and appealing. The covered veranda leads to an entry foyer that is located in the center of the plan. To the left are the formal living areas—a living room with fireplace and a dining room with buffet space. The stairway to the second floor is at the entry; behind it is the U-shaped kitchen and octagonal breakfast bay. The sunken family room features a fireplace. Three bedrooms upstairs are separated by a railed gallery—master suite on one side and family bedrooms on the other. A large bonus room can be finished in the future for additional sleeping space or for a home office.

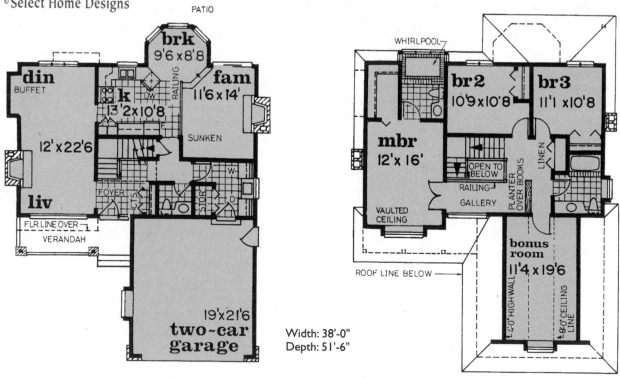

Width: 38'-0"
Depth: 51'-6"

102

Design Q342

Square Footage: 1,184
Bonus Space: 902 square feet

DESIGN BY

©Select Home Designs

Width: 38'-6"
Depth: 60'-4"

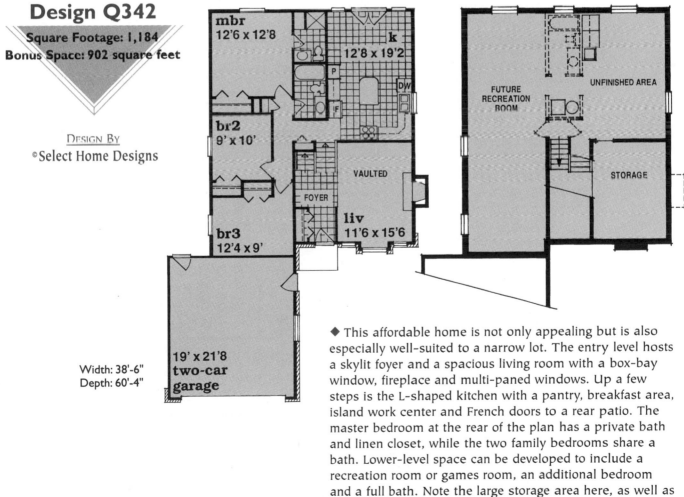

mbr
12'6 x 12'8

k
12'8 x 19'2

br2
9' x 10'

br3
12'4 x 9'

P

DW

F

VAULTED

FOYER

liv
11'6 x 15'6

19' x 21'8
two-car
garage

FUTURE
RECREATION
ROOM

UNFINISHED AREA

STORAGE

◆ This affordable home is not only appealing but is also especially well-suited to a narrow lot. The entry level hosts a skylit foyer and a spacious living room with a box-bay window, fireplace and multi-paned windows. Up a few steps is the L-shaped kitchen with a pantry, breakfast area, island work center and French doors to a rear patio. The master bedroom at the rear of the plan has a private bath and linen closet, while the two family bedrooms share a bath. Lower-level space can be developed to include a recreation room or games room, an additional bedroom and a full bath. Note the large storage area here, as well as laundry space. A two-car garage sits in front of the bedrooms to protect them from street noise.

© HOME DESIGN SERVICES, INC.

J.N. HANSEN P.T.L

Design 8789

Square Footage: 1,834

DESIGN BY
© Home Design
Services, Inc.

◆ Loaded with four bedrooms and expansive views from every room of the house, this creative design is perfect for the growing family. Inside the foyer, double doors open to a bedroom or den. While two other bedrooms are off a hall to the right, the left side of the plan contains the open living area that includes the dining room, family room, living room and kitchen. Sliding glass doors open from the living room to the rear covered patio. The master bedroom boasts a curved window, a walk-in closet and a bath with a double-bowl vanity.

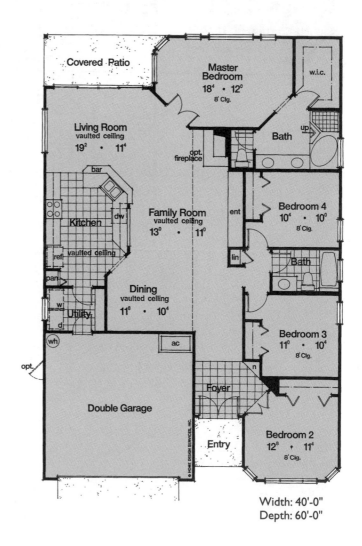

Width: 40'-0"
Depth: 60'-0"

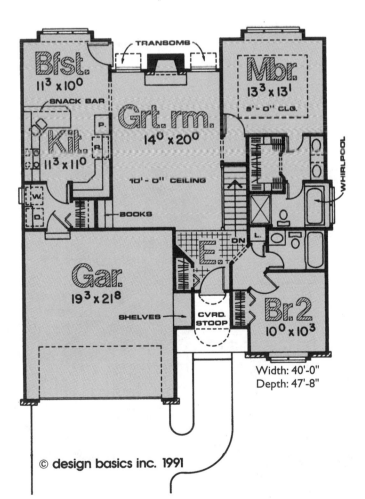

TRANSOMS

Bfst.
11³ x 10⁰

SNACK BAR

Kit.
11³ x 11⁰

Grt. rm.
14⁰ x 20⁰

10' - 0" CEILING

BOOKS

P.

R.

W.
D.

Gar.
19³ x 21⁸

SHELVES

CVRD.
STOOP

Mbr.
13³ x 13¹

8' - 0" CLG.

WHIRLPOOL

DN

L.

Br. 2
10⁰ x 10³

Width: 40'-0"
Depth: 47'-8"

© design basics inc. 1991

Design 9371

Square Footage: 1,205

DESIGN BY
©Design Basics, Inc.

◆ Although only 1,205 square feet, this home feels considerably larger. The angled entry features two plant shelves and a roomy closet. Straight ahead, the vaulted great room provides a window-flanked fireplace, a built-in bookcase and easy access to the kitchen and breakfast room. This area offers a snack bar, a wrapping counter, a pantry and access to the garage through the laundry room. The secondary bedroom extends privacy for guests or it could easily serve as a den. The master bedroom is highlighted by a box ceiling and a bath with a whirlpool tub and dual sinks.

Design C530

Square Footage: 1,598

DESIGN BY
©Piercy & Barclay
Designers, Inc.

◆ A skylight brightens the vaulted entry of this volume design. To the right of the entry, the kitchen extends to a vaulted breakfast nook. An eating bar in the kitchen is for snacks and casual meals while the dining room and patio for alfresco meals are at the rear of the plan. The dining room opens to the living room to make a large gathering space. Three bedrooms include a master suite. There's an option of a daylight basement with a stairway. Please specify basement or crawlspace foundation when ordering.

**Optional Basement
Staircase**

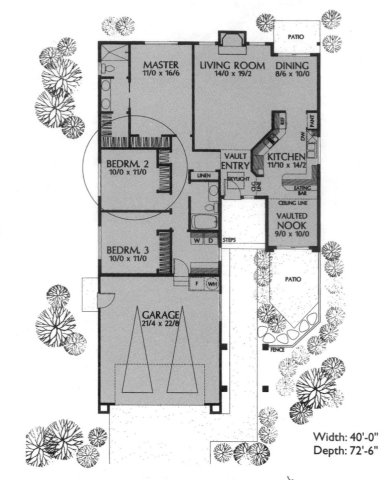

Width: 40'-0"
Depth: 72'-6"

◆ Large arch-top windows fill this home with natural light. The striking floor-to-ceiling window at the front of the design brightens the master bedroom and its dressing area. Two more bedrooms and a bath are off the upstairs hall, which overlooks the first floor. On the first floor, the vaulted living room combines with the dining room to create a large gathering space. Through the breakfast nook is the deck and patio, which are also accessed from the family room. A two-car garage is tucked under the master bedroom.

Design C531

First Floor: 1,075 square feet
Second Floor: 830 square feet
Total: 1,905 square feet

DESIGN BY
©Piercy & Barclay
Designers, Inc.

PATIO

RAILING

DECK

DW

FAMILY RM.
17/0 x 12/0

NOOK
9/0 x 12/0

KITCHEN
13/0 x 10/0

REF

BATH

DN

DINING
11/0 x 9/0

UTIL.

UP

ENTRY

W D

WH F

VAULTED
LIVING RM.
12/0 x 14/6

GARAGE
20/0 x 20/8

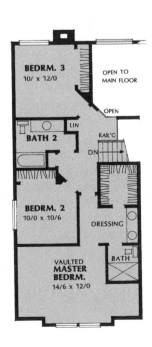

BEDRM. 3
10/ x 12/0

OPEN TO
MAIN FLOOR

OPEN

BATH 2

LIN

RAIL'G

DN

BEDRM. 2
10/0 x 10/6

DRESSING

BATH

VAULTED
MASTER
BEDRM.
14/6 x 12/0

Width: 40'-0"
Depth: 46'-6"

Design F150

Square Footage: 2,001

DESIGN BY
©R.L. Pfotenhauer

◆ Petite yet sweet, this home is perfect for a narrow lot. Full of amenities, this is also a great starter or empty-nester home. Inside, the foyer is flanked by a cozy study (or a third bedroom) to the left and the kitchen/nook area to the right. Here, the gourmet of the family is sure to be pleased with plenty of counter and cabinet space to work with. The spacious great room includes a warming fireplace and combines with the dining area to make entertaining a breeze. The master bedroom suite provides a corner sitting bay, a walk-in closet and a lavish bath.

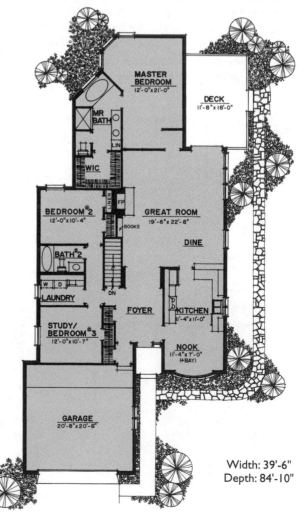

Width: 39'-6"
Depth: 84'-10"

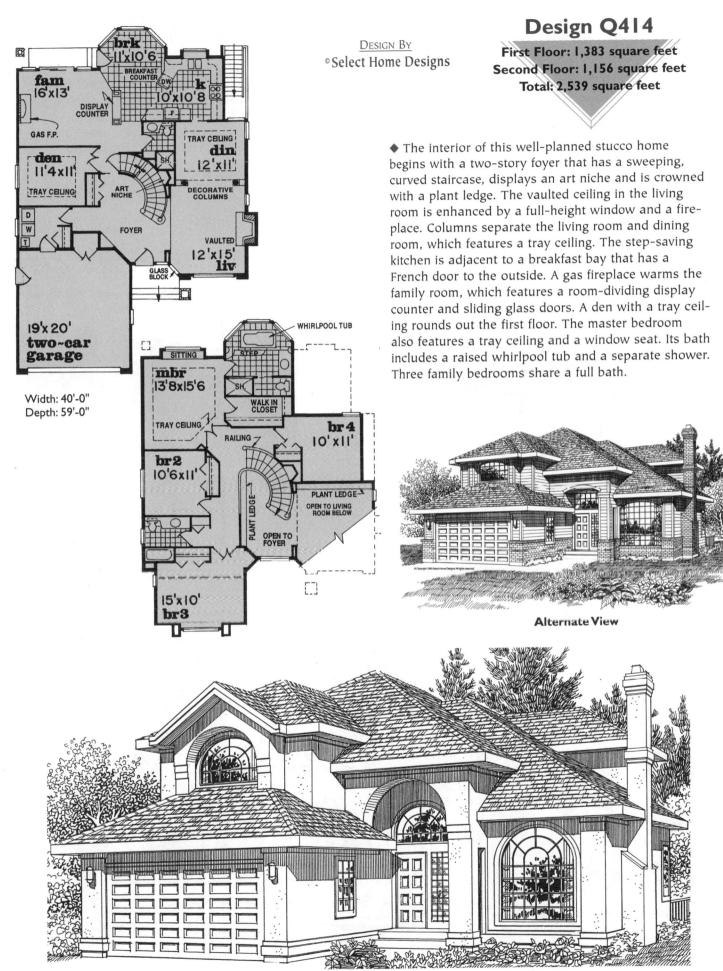

DESIGN BY
©Select Home Designs

Design Q414

First Floor: 1,383 square feet
Second Floor: 1,156 square feet
Total: 2,539 square feet

brk
11'x10'6
BREAKFAST COUNTER

fam
16'x13'

DISPLAY COUNTER

DW

k
10'x10'8

F

GAS F.P.

TRAY CEILING
din
12'x11'

den
11'4x11

SH.

TRAY CEILING

ART NICHE

DECORATIVE COLUMNS

D
W
T

FOYER

VAULTED
12'x15'
liv

GLASS BLOCK

19'x20'
two-car garage

Width: 40'-0"
Depth: 59'-0"

WHIRLPOOL TUB

SITTING

STEP

mbr
13'8x15'6

SH.

WALK IN CLOSET

TRAY CEILING

RAILING

br4
10'x11'

br2
10'6x11'

PLANT LEDGE
OPEN TO LIVING ROOM BELOW

PLANT LEDGE

OPEN TO FOYER

15'x10'
br3

◆ The interior of this well-planned stucco home begins with a two-story foyer that has a sweeping, curved staircase, displays an art niche and is crowned with a plant ledge. The vaulted ceiling in the living room is enhanced by a full-height window and a fireplace. Columns separate the living room and dining room, which features a tray ceiling. The step-saving kitchen is adjacent to a breakfast bay that has a French door to the outside. A gas fireplace warms the family room, which features a room-dividing display counter and sliding glass doors. A den with a tray ceiling rounds out the first floor. The master bedroom also features a tray ceiling and a window seat. Its bath includes a raised whirlpool tub and a separate shower. Three family bedrooms share a full bath.

Alternate View

109

Design 8659

First Floor: 1,230 square feet
Second Floor: 649 square feet
Total: 1,879 square feet

◆ The tiled foyer of this two-story home opens to a living and dining space with soaring ceilings. A covered patio invites outdoor livability in a design that's reminiscent of Bermuda architecture. The family-oriented kitchen has an oversized breakfast area with a volume ceiling and a view of the front yard. The master bedroom occupies the rear of the first floor and offers privacy with its compartmented bath. A corner soaking tub, a separate shower and two vanities provide a luxurious setting. Upstairs, a loft overlooking the living spaces below could become a third bedroom. One of the family bedrooms features a walk-in closet. Both bedrooms utilize a generous hall bath.

DESIGN BY
©Home Design
Services, Inc.

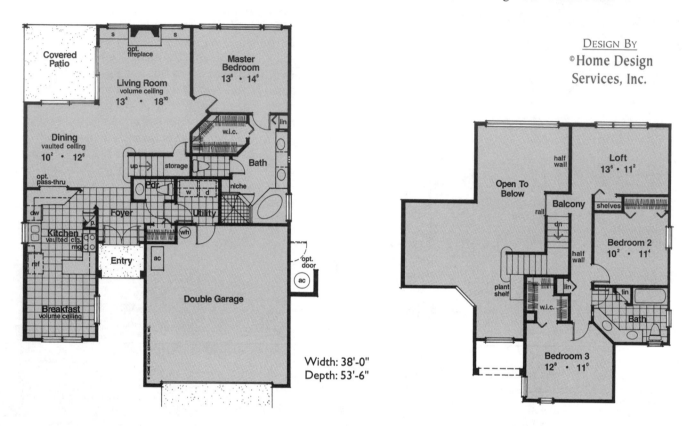

Width: 38'-0"
Depth: 53'-6"

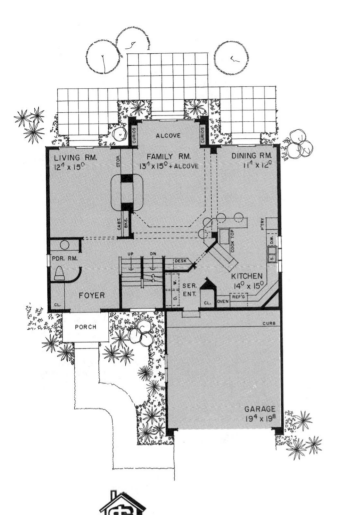

LIVING RM.
12⁹ x 15⁰

FAMILY RM.
13⁷ x 15⁰ + ALCOVE

DINING RM.
11⁴ x 12⁰

ALCOVE

CURIOS

CURIOS

STOR.

CABT.

BKC.

PTRY.

PDR. RM.

UP   DN

DESK

COOK TOP

S. D.W.

FOYER

W. D.

SER. ENT.

CL.

OVEN   REF'G

KITCHEN
14⁰ x 15⁰

CL.

PORCH

CURB

GARAGE
19⁴ x 19⁸

Design 3562

DESIGN BY
©Home Planners

First Floor: 1,182 square feet
Second Floor: 927 square feet
Total: 2,109 square feet
L D

◆ Interesting detailing marks the exterior of this home as a beauty. Double doors on the left open to a large foyer with a handy coat closet and a powder room with a curved wall. Living areas of the home are open and well planned. The formal living room shares a through-fireplace with the large family room, which is enhanced by a cabinet-lined alcove. The adjoining dining room has a pass-through counter to the L-shaped kitchen. Each of the three main rooms on this floor features sliding glass doors to the rear terrace. Upstairs, the master bath offers a whirlpool tub, two walk-in closets and a good-sized dressing area. Two family bedrooms share a full bath.

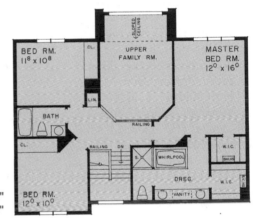

BED RM.
11⁸ x 10⁸

CL.

UPPER
FAMILY RM.

SLOPED CEILING

MASTER
BED RM.
12⁰ x 16⁰

LIN.

BATH

RAILING

CL.

RAILING   DN

S.

WHIRLPOOL

W.I.C.

SHLVS.

BED RM.
12⁰ x 10⁰

DRESS.

VANITY

W.I.C.

Width: 40'-0"
Depth: 54'-0"

Design K501

First Floor: 1,514 square feet
Second Floor: 632 square feet
Total: 2,146 square feet

DESIGN BY
©Lucia Custom
Home Designers

◆ Three designs give options for the exterior of this home—all three come with the same floor plan. The entry opens into a small foyer and the open area of living room and two-story dining room. A powder room and a U-shaped stairway are on the way to the kitchen, which offers a large work island, a walk-in pantry, a breakfast nook and a laundry room. The family room, at the rear of the plan, accesses the rear patio (through sliding glass doors) and the master suite. The master bath features a double-bowl vanity, a corner window tub and a walk-in closet. Three second-floor bedrooms share a bath that has a double-bowl vanity. A fifth bedroom may be added over the dining room.

View A

View B

View C

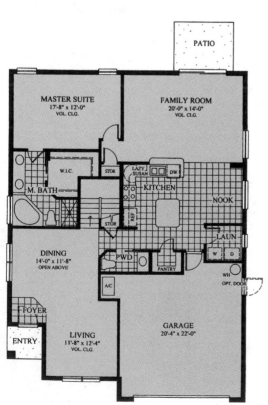

Width: 39'-4"
Depth: 53'-4"

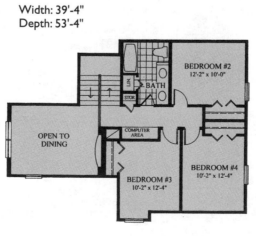

Fireplace Option

Optional 5th Bedroom

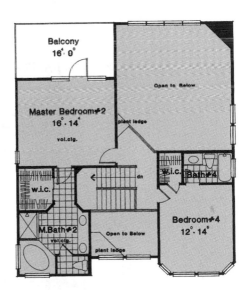

Design K502

First Floor: 1,619 square feet
Second Floor: 846 square feet
Total: 2,465 square feet

DESIGN BY
©Lucia Custom
Home Designers

Width: 37'-4"
Depth: 69'-0"

First Floor labels: Master Bedroom #1 16⁰·18⁴; Living / Dining 19⁰·21⁰; opt. fireplace; vol.clg.; shelves; M.Bath #1; w.i.c.; Bath #3; knee space; Foyer; up; ref; pan; Kitchen 12⁰·12⁰; sink; dw; Nook 12⁰·9¹⁰; Bedroom #3 /Den 11⁰·12⁰; Entry; Util.; wh; a/c; cu; Garage

Second Floor labels: Balcony 16⁴·0⁰; Open to Below; Master Bedroom #2 16⁰·14⁴; plant ledge; vol.clg.; w.i.c.; dn; w.i.c.; Bath #4; M.Bath #2; vol.clg.; Open to Below; plant ledge; Bedroom #4 12⁰·14⁰

◆ Generous bay windows and an arched window above the entry give this home an opulent look. From the foyer, you can enter the kitchen and breakfast nook, which is housed in one of the wide bay windows. Or you can enter the den through French doors on the left—this could be a third bedroom. Or continue past the den to the laundry room and a hall bath. If you walk straight ahead from the foyer, you will end up in the combination living/dining room, which offers an optional corner fireplace and French doors to the outside. The master suite off this area includes a compartmented bath and a walk-in closet. The second floor houses another master suite—this one with a private balcony. There's also a secondary bedroom with a smaller walk-in closet and private bath.

Enhanced Plan

Design 3723

First Floor: 1,004 square feet
Second Floor: 1,004 square feet
Total: 2,008 square feet

DESIGN BY
©Home Planners

◆ This spacious two-story home offers many deluxe features and lots of living space. The entrance foyer includes a powder room to the left. Adjacent to the kitchen is a large family room. An open living and dining room creates a feeling of spaciousness. The second floor features a magnificent master suite with a full-sized bath and a walk-in closet. A full bath services the remaining three bedrooms. Options include a fireplace, a box-bay window, decorative louvers, a rear deck and a two-car garage. The blueprints for this house show how to build both the basic, low-cost version and the enhanced, upgraded version.

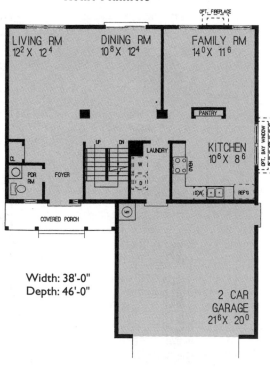

Width: 38'-0"
Depth: 46'-0"

LIVING RM 12² X 12⁴
DINING RM 10⁸ X 12⁴
FAMILY RM 14⁰ X 11⁶
OPT. FIREPLACE
PANTRY
OPT. BAY WINDOW
FOYER
UP DN
LAUNDRY
KITCHEN 10⁶ X 8⁶
PDR RM
COVERED PORCH
2 CAR GARAGE 21⁶ X 20⁰

BEDROOM 11⁴ X 9²
BEDROOM 10⁶ X 11⁴
MASTER BEDROOM 12⁴ X 16⁸
BATH
LIN.
BEDROOM 11⁴ X 10⁰
DN
WALK-IN CLOSET 9² X 10⁰
SHELVES
MASTER BATH
LIN.

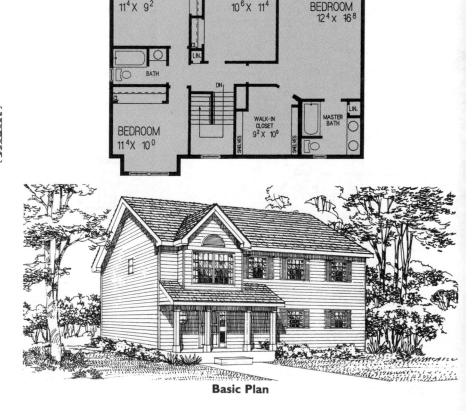

Basic Plan

AT HOME IN THE CITY OR COUNTRY

Design 8156

First Floor: 954 square feet
Second Floor: 682 square feet
Total: 1,636 square feet

◆ Traditional in design, this starter home bundles features demanded by today's homeowners into a small package. Two-story living and dining rooms give the home a spacious feel, with the living-room fireplace offering warmth on cool evenings. The efficiently designed kitchen features a small breakfast nook and a sunny window over the kitchen sink. The first-floor master suite offers a seated vanity and an oval whirlpool tub/shower combination. The laundry room is across the hall. Upstairs, three bedrooms, a bath and a loft area complete the plan. Please specify crawlspace or slab foundation when ordering.

DESIGN BY
© Larry E. Belk
Designs

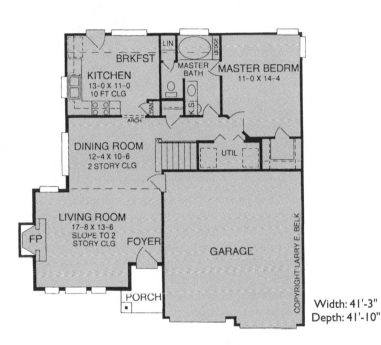

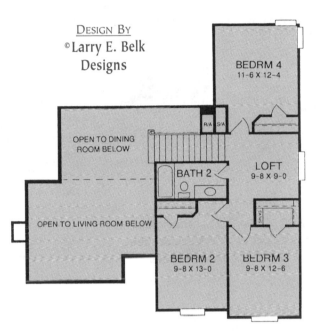

Width: 41'-3"
Depth: 41'-10"

Design T092

First Floor: 1,225 square feet
Second Floor: 563 square feet
Total: 1,788 square feet

DESIGN BY
Stephen Fuller

◆ A two-story home with mixed exterior materials is hard to beat. Both casual and formal occasions are accommodated in the great room, which boasts a fireplace, and the formal dining room, which opens through columns from the foyer. An informal breakfast room complements the gourmet kitchen; its bay window makes family dining a treat. The master suite, on the first floor, features a compartmented bath with a walk-in closet, corner tub and separate shower. Two family bedrooms on the second floor share a bath that is accessed through private vanity areas. Unfinished bonus space on the second floor can function as storage or be developed into a recreation room or fourth bedroom. This home is designed with a basement foundation.

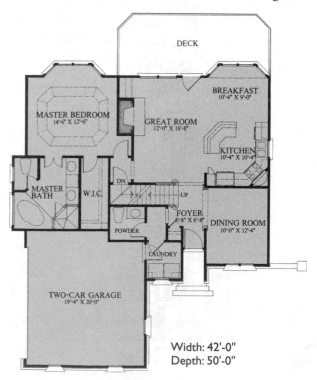

Width: 42'-0"
Depth: 50'-0"

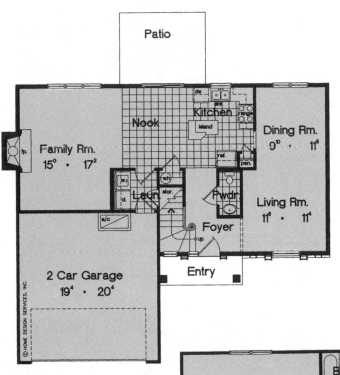

Patio

Nook

Kitchen

Dining Rm.
9¹⁰ · 11⁸

Family Rm.
15⁰ · 17²

island

fp

Laun.

stor.

Pwdr.

Living Rm.
11⁸ · 11⁴

Foyer

a/c

up

2 Car Garage
19⁴ · 20⁴

Entry

Width: 44'-0"
Depth: 38'-8"

Design 8762

First Floor: 1,051 square feet
Second Floor: 949 square feet
Total: 2,000 square feet

◆ A traditionally styled home with a story-book entrance offers today's family space to change and grow. The foyer features a powder room and a stairway to the second floor. The open living/dining room area is large enough for entertaining. A work island/snack counter, window sink and breakfast nook highlight the kitchen. A fireplace warms the family room. Upstairs four bedrooms include a master suite with a walk-in closet and private bath. The three family bedrooms share a compartmented bath that provides a double-bowl vanity. One of these bedrooms has a walk-in closet.

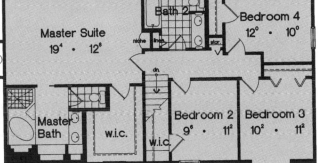

Bath 2

Master Suite
19⁴ · 12⁸

Bedroom 4
12⁰ · 10⁰

niche

lnen

stor.

dn

Master
Bath

w.i.c.

w.i.c.

Bedroom 2
9⁰ · 11²

Bedroom 3
10² · 11²

© American Home Gallery, Ltd.

Design T079

First Floor: 1,140 square feet
Second Floor: 1,360 square feet
Total: 2,500 square feet

DESIGN BY
Stephen Fuller

◆ Whether you're building within city limits or out in the country, this traditional design works well and exhibits many of the finest features of modern livability. The foyer opens up into two stories—18-feet high—and offers a powder room, a coat closet and a U-shaped staircase to the second floor. The living and dining rooms are open to each other, providing a divine space for entertaining. The family will enjoy the breakfast bay and the great room with its fireplace. This design comes complete with four bedrooms, three full baths and a study off Bedroom 2, which also features a private bath. Bedrooms 3 and 4 share a bath. This home is designed with a basement foundation.

BREAKFAST
11'-6" X 6'-0"

GREAT ROOM
23'-0" X 13'-6"

KITCHEN
14'-0" X 12'-0"

TWO CAR GARAGE
20'-0" X 22'-0"

DINING ROOM
11'-0" X 12'-0"

FOYER
8'-0" X 7'-0"

LIVING ROOM
11'-0" X 12'-0"

Width: 43'-6"
Depth: 45'-0"

MASTER BEDROOM
16'-6" X 13'-6"

MASTER BATH
9'-0" X 13'-6"

BEDROOM NO.4
11'-0" X 12'-0"

BEDROOM NO.2
14'-0" X 12'-6"

STUDY
9'-0" X 7'-0"

BEDROOM NO.3
11'-6" X 12'-0"

Design A139

First Floor: 1,527 square feet
Second Floor: 1,532 square feet
Total: 3,059 square feet

DESIGN BY
©Living Concepts
Home Planning

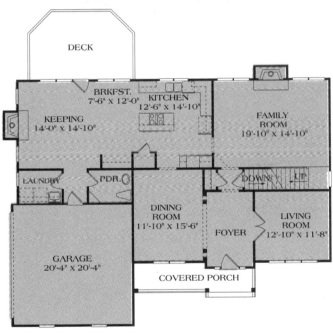

DECK

BRKFST.
7'-6" X 12'-0"

KITCHEN
12'-6" X 14'-10"

KEEPING
14'-0" X 14'-10"

FAMILY
ROOM
19'-10" X 14'-10"

LAUNDRY

PDR.

DOWN

UP

DINING
ROOM
11'-10" X 15'-6"

FOYER

LIVING
ROOM
12'-10" X 11'-8"

GARAGE
20'-4" X 20'-4"

COVERED PORCH

Width: 44'-4"
Depth: 55'-0"

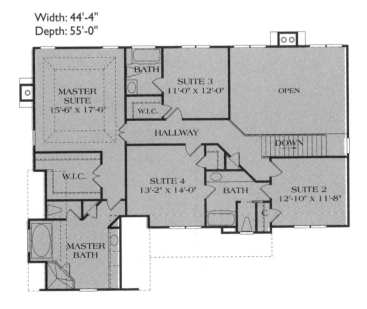

MASTER
SUITE
15'-6" X 17'-6"

BATH

SUITE 3
11'-0" X 12'-0"

OPEN

W.I.C.

HALLWAY

DOWN

W.I.C.

SUITE 4
13'-2" X 14'-0"

BATH

SUITE 2
12'-10" X 11'-8"

MASTER
BATH

◆ A charming covered porch shelters the entrance to this happy French garden design. With the formal living room and dining room at the front, the foyer leads through double doors to a family room with a fireplace flanked by tall windows. The kitchen, which provides an island cooktop, blends seamlessly with the breakfast area and the keeping room, which features a fireplace and access to the rear deck. An angled hallway on the second level overlooks the family room below. A vaulted ceiling, an oversized walk-in closet and a garden tub highlight the master suite. Two of the three family bedrooms share a compartmented bath, while another bedroom boasts a private bath and a walk-in closet.

119

Design P452

First Floor: 916 square feet
Second Floor: 895 square feet
Total: 1,811 square feet
Bonus Room: 262 square feet

DESIGN BY
©Frank Betz
Associates, Inc.

◆ Gables at varying heights, a traditional front porch and shuttered windows give a small-town look to this family home. The two-story foyer leads to the dining room on the left or to the family room, which is straight ahead past the powder room, coat closet and entrance to the garage. The family room is open to the kitchen, which boasts a work island, a corner-window sink and access to the laundry room. The second floor provides a master suite that has two walk-in closets, two family bedrooms that share a bath but have walk-in closets, an overlook to the foyer below and an optional bonus room. Please specify basement or crawlspace foundation when ordering.

Width: 44'-0"
Depth: 38'-0"

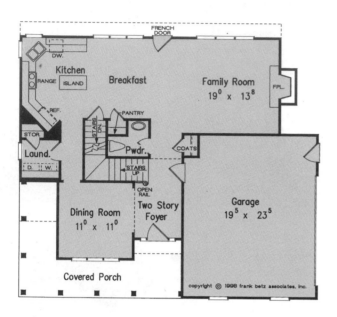

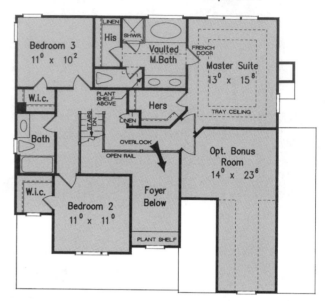

This home, as shown in the photograph, may differ from the actual blueprints. For more detailed information, please check the floor plans carefully.

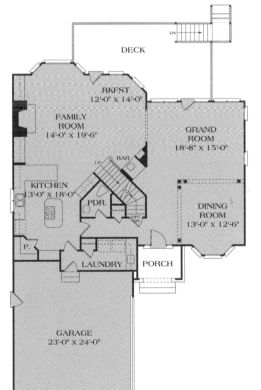

Width: 45'-8"
Depth: 66'-0"

Design A305

First Floor: 1,558 square feet
Second Floor: 1,511 square feet
Total: 3,069 square feet

DESIGN BY
©Living Concepts
Home Planning

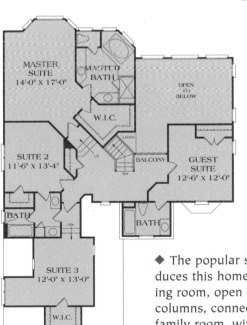

◆ The popular stucco-and-stone blend introduces this home as something special. The dining room, open on two sides but defined by columns, connects with the grand room. The family room, with a fireplace and built-in shelves, features not only a bay window but an open breakfast bay and a wet bar. A cooktop island, a walk-in pantry and nearby laundry and powder rooms accent the kitchen. The second floor includes four bedroom suites and three baths. The master suite provides a walk-in closet and a bath that offers separate vanities.

Design P357

First Floor: 1,179 square feet
Second Floor: 460 square feet
Total: 1,639 square feet
Bonus Room: 350 square feet

◆ With vaulted ceilings in the dining room and great room, as well as a tray ceiling in the master suite, and a two-story foyer filled with natural light, this inviting design offers a wealth of sunlight and space. An optional bonus room adds 350 square feet. The counter-filled kitchen opens to a large breakfast area with rear-yard access. Each bedroom is separated enough to offer privacy to every occupant. Please specify basement or crawlspace foundation when ordering.

DESIGN BY
© **Frank Betz**
Associates, Inc.

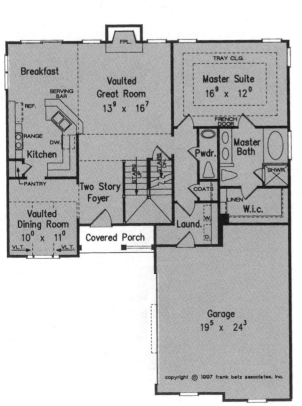

Width: 41'-6"
Depth: 52'-0"

MASTER BEDRM
15-0 X 15-6
10 FT CLG

DETACHED GARAGE

PORCH

CLERESTORY WINDOW

CLERESTORY WINDOW

MASTER BATH

HERS

HIS

PAN

LIVING ROOM
19-8 X 15-6
2 STORY CLG

FP

BUILT-INS

BUILT-INS

KITCHEN
14-0 X 12-6
10 FT CLG

SERVE LEDGE

ARCH

BRKFST RM
8-4 X 9-0
10 FT CLG

PWDR

PORCH

ARCH

FOYER
2 STORY CLG

DINING ROOM
12-4 X 13-0
10 FT CLG

PORCH

Width: 41'-10"
Depth: 56'-5"

COPYRIGHT LARRY E. BELK

Design 8144

First Floor: 1,482 square feet
Second Floor: 631 square feet
Total: 2,113 square feet

DESIGN BY
©Larry E. Belk
Designs

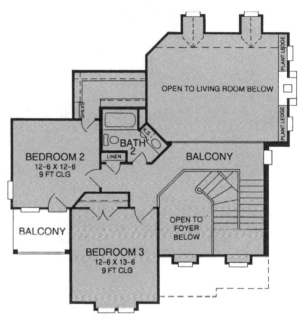

PLANT LEDGE

PLANT LEDGE

OPEN TO LIVING ROOM BELOW

SHLVS

BATH 2

LINEN

BEDROOM 2
12-6 X 12-6
9 FT CLG

BALCONY

BALCONY

OPEN TO FOYER BELOW

BEDROOM 3
12-6 X 13-6
9 FT CLG

◆ A charming elevation gives this home its curbside appeal. Inside, the two-story foyer opens through archways to the living room and dining room. Clerestory windows flood the living room with natural light. The kitchen and breakfast room are nearby. An angled sink, with a serving ledge and pass-through, opens the kitchen to the living room beyond. An old-time side porch off the kitchen enhances the look of the home and provides convenient access to the outside. The master bath has all the frills and includes two walk-in closets. Two bedrooms and a bath are located upstairs. A lovely balcony is located off Bedroom 2. Please specify slab or crawlspace foundation when ordering.

Design X004

First Floor: 905 square feet
Second Floor: 1,120 square feet
Total: 2,025 square feet

DESIGN BY
©Jannis Vann &
Associates, Inc.

◆ The metal-roofed porch and gables of varying heights and angles create an appealing exterior for this traditional brick and siding home. Inside, a spacious living area opens to a deck and flows into the breakfast room. This area leads to the efficient kitchen that offers plenty of cabinets and counter space. Upstairs, three bedrooms include a deluxe master suite, with a loft at the top of the stairs available for a fourth bedroom, home office or play area. Please specify basement, crawlspace or slab foundation when ordering.

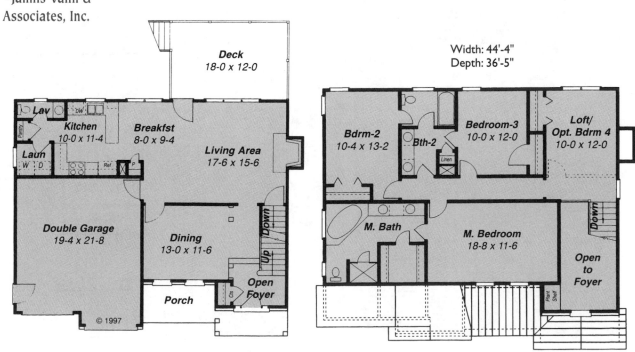

Deck
18-0 x 12-0

Lav

Kitchen
10-0 x 11-4

Breakfst
8-0 x 9-4

Living Area
17-6 x 15-6

Laun

Double Garage
19-4 x 21-8

Dining
13-0 x 11-6

Up / Down

Open Foyer

Porch

© 1997

Width: 44'-4"
Depth: 36'-5"

Bdrm-2
10-4 x 13-2

Bth-2

Bedroom-3
10-0 x 12-0

Loft/
Opt. Bdrm 4
10-0 x 12-0

M. Bath

M. Bedroom
18-8 x 11-6

Down

Open
to
Foyer

◆ The pleasing character of this house does not stop behind its distinguished facade. The foyer opens up into the eat-in kitchen and an encompassing great room with a fireplace. Stairs lead from the great room to the second floor—and here's where you'll find the laundry! The master suite spares none of the amenities: full bath with a double-bowl vanity, a separate shower and tub and a walk-in closet. Bedrooms 2 and 3 share a full bath. This home is designed with a basement foundation.

Design T097

First Floor: 830 square feet
Second Floor: 1,060 square feet
Total: 1,890 square feet

DESIGN BY
Stephen Fuller

© American Home Gallery, Ltd.

Width: 41'-0"
Depth: 40'-6"

DECK

BREAKFAST
10'-0" x 7'-0"

GREAT ROOM
18'-6" x 15'-6"

KITCHEN
12'-0" x 10'-10"

UP

DN

FOYER

DINING
9'-6" x 12'-10"

POWDER

TWO-CAR GARAGE
20'-0" x 21'-0"

PORCH

MASTER SUITE
14'-10" x 15'-8"

M. BATH

LAUN
6'-0" x 5'-8"

W.I.C.

BEDROOM No. 2
12'-0" X 14'-0"

BATH

BEDROOM No.3
10'-0" x 12'-10"

125

Design 7338

First Floor: 927 square feet
Second Floor: 865 square feet
Total: 1,792 square feet

DESIGN BY
©Design Basics, Inc.

◆ Reminiscent of a New England cottage, this home opens with a two-story entry that leads directly to the formal dining room. The generous great room beyond the entry features captivating windows and a fireplace. The kitchen includes a box window, a planning desk and access to the laundry room, which leads to the service entrance from the garage. The breakfast room, between the great room and the kitchen, has sliding glass doors to the rear property. For convenience, there is a centrally located powder room on the first floor. The master suite on the second floor offers a walk-in closet, a whirlpool tub and separate vanities. Note the built-in seat opposite the walk-in closet and the unfinished bonus room that could be a study or exercise room. Two family bedrooms share a full bath.

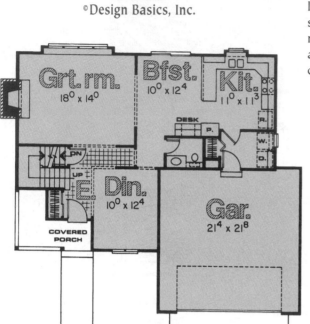

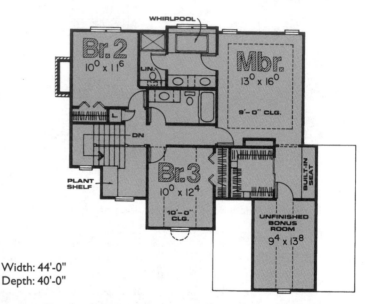

Width: 44'-0"
Depth: 40'-0"

E. NATHAN

© 1996 Donald A. Gardner Architects, Inc.

MASTER BED RM.
13-8 x 12-0

BED RM.
11-0 x 10-0

walk-in closet

DECK

walk-in closet

lin.

bath

ci

master bath

d w

UTIL.

BED RM.
11-0 x 10-0

KITCHEN
12-0 x 10-0

cl

cl

storage

DINING
10-0 x 11-4

GREAT RM.
15-0 x 18-4
(cathedral ceiling)

GARAGE
13-4 x 20-0

fireplace

PORCH

© 1996 Donald A. Gardner Architects, Inc.

Width: 41'-8"
Depth: 51'-4"

Design 7615

Square Footage: 1,362

DESIGN BY
Donald A. Gardner
Architects, Inc.

◆ This one-story home invites cool summer evenings spent lounging on the front porch or enjoying family gatherings around the fireplace. The central great room, with its cathedral ceiling, opens to the dining room. The efficient kitchen has a door to the rear deck. Three bedrooms include two family bedrooms with a shared bath and a master suite with a walk-in closet and a large master bath. The utility and laundry area is conveniently located by the bedrooms.

© 1995 Donald A. Gardner Architects, Inc.

B. NATHAN

Design 9793

Square Footage: 1,109
**Optional Bedroom:
169 square feet**

DESIGN BY
Donald A. Gardner
Architects, Inc.

◆ A spacious cathedral ceiling expands the feel of this compact plan that is filled with popular features. Open to each other for increased spaciousness, the living areas feature a fireplace in the great room and an island to increase work space in the kitchen. A deck off the kitchen amplifies living and entertaining space. The master bedroom is accentuated by a double window with a circle top for extra volume and light. The private bath opens up with a skylight and includes a relaxing garden tub and double-bowl vanity. The second bedroom is located near a skylit full bath, linen closet and utility room. An optional bedroom through the utility room is available.

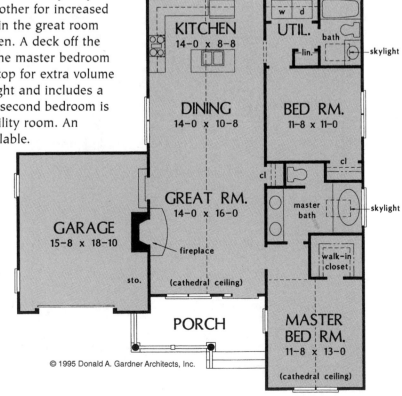

DECK

(optional bedroom)

KITCHEN
14-0 x 8-8

UTIL.

w d

bath

lin.

skylight

DINING
14-0 x 10-8

BED RM.
11-8 x 11-0

cl

cl

GREAT RM.
14-0 x 16-0

master
bath

skylight

GARAGE
15-8 x 18-10

fireplace

walk-in
closet

sto.

(cathedral ceiling)

PORCH

MASTER
BED RM.
11-8 x 13-0

(cathedral ceiling)

© 1995 Donald A. Gardner Architects, Inc.

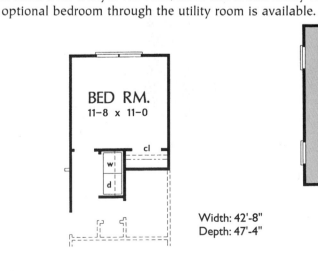

BED RM.
11-8 x 11-0

cl

w

d

Width: 42'-8"
Depth: 47'-4"

◆ Either a starter home or a retreat for empty-nesters, this home is compact and stylish. From the Palladian window in front to the rear sliding glass door that leads outside, the living/dining area extends in an open area under the cathedral ceiling. A large bay window provides natural light in the dining area and the L-shaped kitchen, which enjoys a window sink and a snack counter. Three bedrooms share a roomy bath that features a garden tub and a separate shower. This home is designed with a basement foundation.

Design Z027

Square Footage: 1,104

DESIGN BY
©Drummond Designs, Inc.

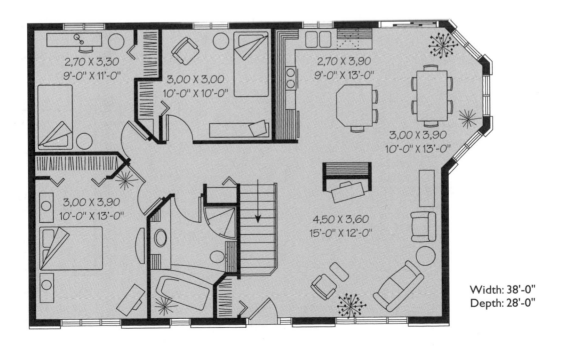

2,70 X 3,30
9'-0" X 11'-0"

3,00 X 3,00
10'-0" X 10'-0"

2,70 X 3,90
9'-0" X 13'-0"

3,00 X 3,90
10'-0" X 13'-0"

3,00 X 3,90
10'-0" X 13'-0"

4,50 X 3,60
15'-0" X 12'-0"

Width: 38'-0"
Depth: 28'-0"

B. NATHAN

© 1996 Donald A. Gardner Architects, Inc.

Design 7614

Square Footage: 1,306

DESIGN BY
Donald A. Gardner
Architects, Inc.

◆ A central kitchen is the focal point for this country ranch home. It includes a snack bar and is conveniently close to both the living area and the sleeping quarters. The great room and dining area are combined, offering a fireplace, a cathedral ceiling and access to the front porch. Notice that the washer and dryer are handy to the kitchen as well as to the family bedrooms and the shared full bath. The master bedroom and bath include a cathedral ceiling, a walk-in closet and a skylit whirlpool tub.

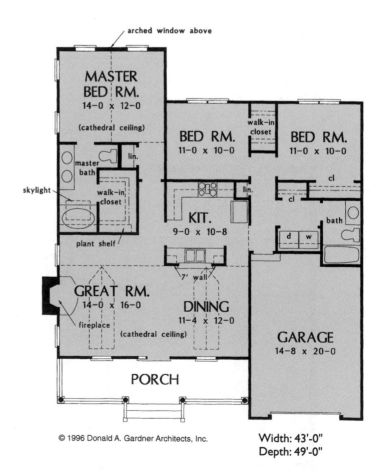

arched window above

MASTER BED RM.
14-0 x 12-0
(cathedral ceiling)

master bath

skylight

lin.

walk-in closet

plant shelf

BED RM.
11-0 x 10-0

walk-in closet

BED RM.
11-0 x 10-0

lin.

cl

cl

bath

KIT.
9-0 x 10-8

d   w

GREAT RM.
14-0 x 16-0

fireplace

7' wall

DINING
11-4 x 12-0
(cathedral ceiling)

GARAGE
14-8 x 20-0

PORCH

© 1996 Donald A. Gardner Architects, Inc.

Width: 43'-0"
Depth: 49'-0"

DESIGN BY
©Greg Marquis
& Associates

Design B162

First Floor: 1,269 square feet
Second Floor: 741 square feet
Total: 2,010 square feet
Optional Bonus Room:
313 square feet

Garage
22 x 24/7

Dining
13 x 11
9' Clg.

Utility

W D

Desk

Kitchen
Bar
12/11 x 11/9

P

Up

Down

Stoop

Master
13/4 x 16
9' Clg.

Family Room
14/3 x 18
9' Clg.

Foyer

Porch
21 x 8

Width: 43'-0"
Depth: 69'-4"

Optional Bonus
24/7 x 11/4

Kid's Living
10/8 x 11/3
8' Clg.

Attic Storage

Rail

Down

Bedroom #3
13/4 x 11
8' Clg.

Slopod Clg.

Linen

Bedroom #2
14/4 x 15/7
8' Clg.

◆ As cozy inside as it looks from the outside, this comfortable three-bedroom plan provides amenities galore. The family room, with a fireplace, is directly off the porch and leads to the master suite on the left and to the kitchen and dining room straight ahead. The master suite includes a walk-in closet and a bath that contains a double-bowl vanity. The kitchen offers a sink island and sliding glass doors to the outside. The service entrance from the garage is in the dining room, and the utility room and a powder room are nearby. There's a side entrance that leads to the dining room. Two bedrooms upstairs share a bath, a living room, and an optional bonus room.

Design W002

First Floor: 832 square feet
Second Floor: 789 square feet
Total: 1,621 square feet

Design By
©TAG Architects

◆ A wraparound porch introduces this practical design that's full of amenities. Windows open up the living room on three sides to let in natural light and let you keep an eye on kids playing on the porch. The U-shaped kitchen is open to a bright breakfast room and only a few steps from the laundry room. A spacious dining room and a powder room complete the first floor. The second floor contains a master bedroom—with a walk-in closet and private bath—and two secondary bedrooms that share a hall bath. Please specify basement, crawlspace or slab foundation when ordering.

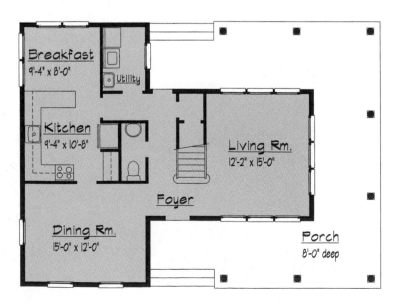

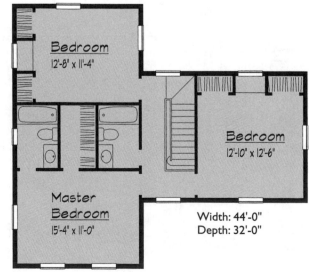

132

◆ What a combination—a charming turn-of-the-century exterior with a contemporary interior! A wraparound railed porch and rear deck expand the living space to outdoor entertaining. Vaulted ceilings throughout the great room and dining room add spaciousness while a fireplace warms the area. An open kitchen plan includes a preparation island, breakfast bar and window over the sink. The master suite is on the first floor for privacy and convenience. It boasts a roomy walk-in closet and private bath with a garden whirlpool tub, a separate shower and a double-bowl vanity. Two vaulted family bedrooms on the second floor share a full bath. Note the loft area and extra storage space. Please specify basement or crawlspace foundation when ordering.

Design Q520

First Floor: 1,050 square feet
Second Floor: 533 square feet
Total: 1,583 square feet

DESIGN BY
©Select Home Designs

Width: 42'-0"
Depth: 38'-0"

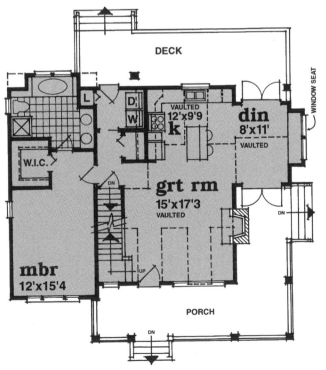

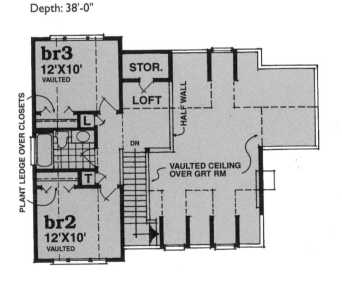

Design U190

First Floor: 1,168 square feet
Second Floor: 494 square feet
Total: 1,662 square feet

DESIGN BY
©Ahmann Design, Inc.

◆ The entry of this transitional home, which is designed for a hillside lot, takes you downstairs to a two-story living room. The dining room/kitchen combination shares a three-way gas fireplace with the living room. The master bedroom on this floor includes a private bath, a walk-in closet and the laundry room nearby. Here, too, is a powder room and a service entrance from the two-car garage. Two bedrooms on the upper level share a full bath.

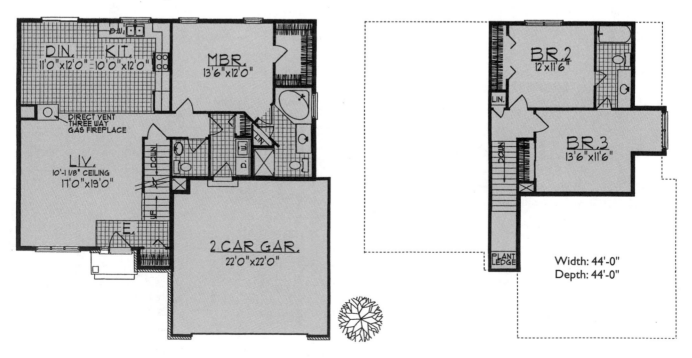

DIN.
11'0"x12'0"

KIT.
10'0"x12'0"

MBR.
13'6"x12'0"

DIRECT VENT
THREE WAY
GAS FIREPLACE

LIV.
10'-11/8" CEILING
17'0"x19'0"

2 CAR GAR.
22'0"x22'0"

BR.2
12'x11'6"

LIN.

DOWN

BR.3
13'6"x11'6"

PLANT
LEDGE

Width: 44'-0"
Depth: 44'-0"

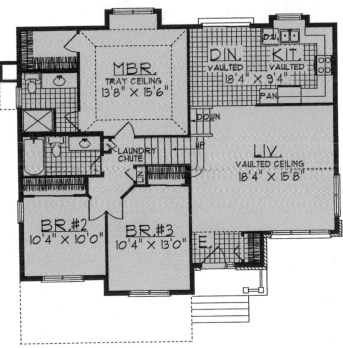

Design U109

Main Floor: 1,289 square feet
Lower Floor: 443 square feet
Total: 1,732 square feet

DESIGN BY
©Ahmann Design, Inc.

Width: 43'-0"
Depth: 40'-0"

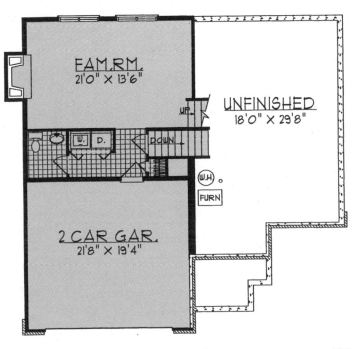

◆ Enter this multi-level home through the front door or through the garage on the lower floor. The family room, laundry room, powder room and unfinished space are also on the lower floor. Stairs from this level lead up to the living room, which features a vaulted ceiling and wide corner windows. Step down a few steps to the master suite with its private bath, walk-in closet and box-bay window. Two family bedrooms share a bath and a laundry chute. Please specify basement or slab foundation when ordering.

Design Q265

Square Footage: 1,197
**Unfinished Lower Level:
522 square feet**

DESIGN BY
©Select Home Designs

◆ Perfect for a hillside lot, this design combines brick and horizontal siding for a lovely effect. Double doors with a transom create a fine entry. A few steps up is the main living area, with a living/dining room combination. The living room features a fireplace, while the dining room offers sliding glass doors to the rear deck. The kitchen and attached breakfast room are nearby and also open to the deck. Three bedrooms are found on the left side of the plan. The master suite provides a private bath with a garden sink and corner shower. Family bedrooms share a full bath. If you choose to develop the lower level, you'll gain 522 square feet and a family room with a fireplace, plus a full bath. The laundry room and garage, with storage space, sit on the lower level.

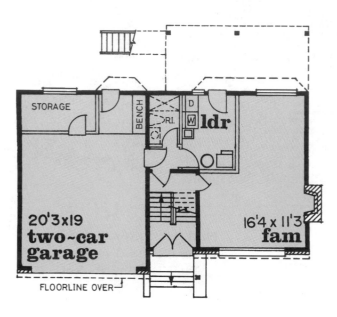

STORAGE

BENCH

DRI.

D W

ldr

20'3x19
**two~car
garage**

16'4 x 11'3
fam

FLOORLINE OVER

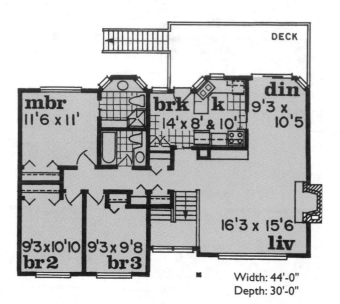

DECK

mbr
11'6 x 11'

brk
14' x 8' & 10'

k

din
9'3 x
10'5

9'3x10'10
br2

9'3 x 9'8
br3

16'3 x 15'6
liv

Width: 44'-0"
Depth: 30'-0"

◆ This traditional design offers not only an interestingly textured exterior, but also plenty of room for future expansion. The main level contains an open living room and dining room, warmed by a fireplace and open to the rear deck through sliding glass doors. The kitchen and breakfast room are reached easily from either the living room or dining room and have access to the deck. The master bedroom and two family bedrooms are on the left side of the plan. The master bedroom has its own bath, while family bedrooms share a full bath. The lower level offers 1,052 square feet of unfinished space for two additional bedrooms, a den, a full bath and a family room with a fireplace. The laundry room is also on this level.

Design Q264

Square Footage: 1,194
Unfinished Lower Level: 1,052 square feet

DESIGN BY
©Select Home Designs

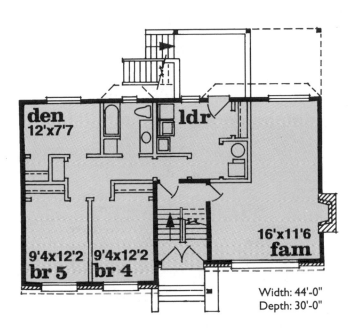

Width: 44'-0"
Depth: 30'-0"

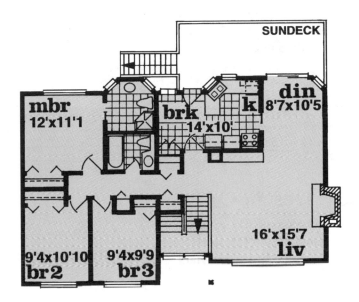

Design Q472

First Floor: 1,099 square feet
Second Floor: 535 square feet
Total: 1,634 square feet

DESIGN BY
© Select Home Designs

◆ Several different options enhance this floor plan. The exterior is graced by a wrapping veranda, round columns, stone facing with cedar shingled accents and a trio of dormers. Inside, the open plan includes a vaulted great room with a fireplace, a vaulted dining room, a vaulted kitchen and three bedrooms. The kitchen offers a pass-through to the dining room. The master suite contains a walk-in closet with a dressing room, sitting area and full skylit bath. Family bedrooms are on the second floor and share a full bath. An optional loft is also available on the second floor. If you choose, you can reconfigure the master bath to allow for a half-bath in the laundry. Please specify basement or crawlspace foundation when ordering.

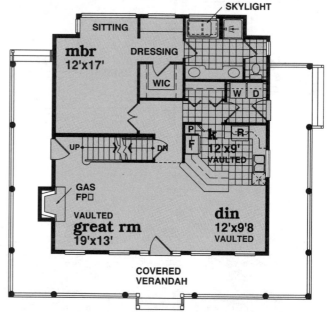

SKYLIGHT
SITTING
mbr 12'x17'
DRESSING
WIC
W D
UP DN
P R
k 12'x9' VAULTED
F
GAS FP
VAULTED
great rm 19'x13'
din 12'x9'8 VAULTED
COVERED VERANDAH

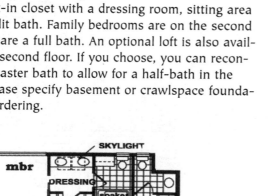

mbr
DRESSING
WIC
soaker tub
SKYLIGHT
W D

Optional Master Bath

Width: 44'-8"
Depth: 41'-4"

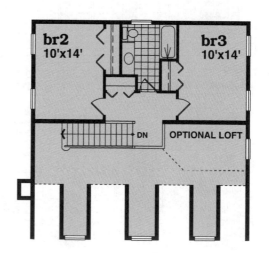

br2 10'x14'
br3 10'x14'
DN
OPTIONAL LOFT

◆ Dormer windows, columns, a balustrade on the front porch and a window flower box create an inviting facade. Inside, the vaulted foyer provides a coat closet and a powder room. The family living area includes a vaulted great room with a fireplace and a kitchen open to a vaulted breakfast room. The dining room on the other side of the kitchen is also vaulted. On the opposite side of the plan, the master suite provides a compartmented bath and a walk-in closet. Access to the garage is through the laundry room. Upstairs, two bedrooms share a bath, a balcony and a loft. The loft can be made into a fourth bedroom. Please specify basement or crawlspace foundation when ordering.

Design P447

First Floor: 1,189 square feet
Second Floor: 551 square feet
Total: 1,740 square feet
Optional Loft: 131 square feet

DESIGN BY
©Frank Betz
Associates, Inc.

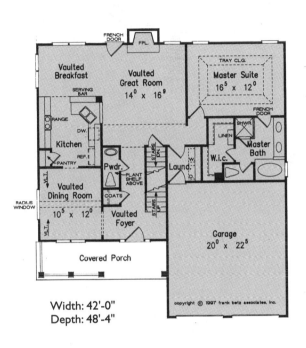

Width: 42'-0"
Depth: 48'-4"

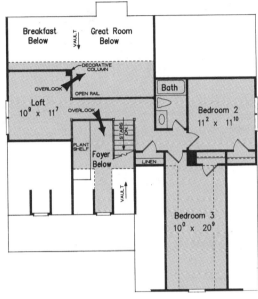

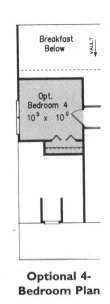

Optional 4-Bedroom Plan

Design E142

First Floor: 1,499 square feet
Second Floor: 1,012 square feet
Total: 2,511 square feet

◆ You can't beat the charm of this country home with its shady covered front porch and bright bay windows in the dining room and breakfast nook. The kitchen, with a cooktop island, is convenient to both formal and casual dining areas. The spacious living room offers a fireplace, built-in bookshelves and access to the rear patio. The rest of the main floor is granted to the master suite, which includes a double-vanity bath with an oval tub and separate shower. Upstairs, two of the three family bedrooms have dormer windows. All three of these bedrooms provide walk-in closets.

DESIGN BY
©Chatham Home
Planning, Inc.

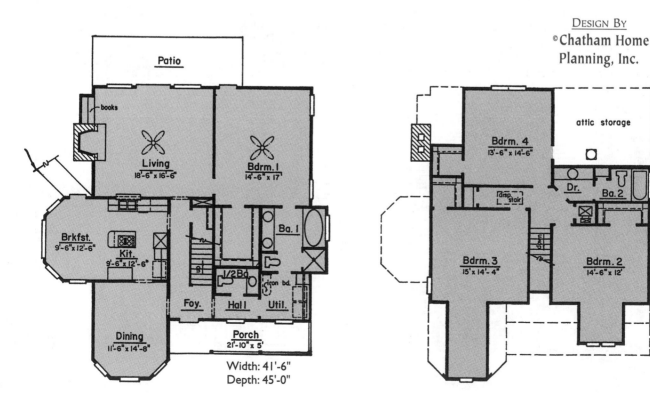

Width: 41'-6"
Depth: 45'-0"

◆ Compact, but so livable, this traditional two-story design boasts details usually found only in much larger designs. Begin with the covered front porch which opens to a light filled two-story foyer and open-railed staircase to the second floor. Beyond is the large great room with vaulted ceiling and fireplace. The attached dining area is also vaulted and features sliding glass doors to the rear yard. The U-shaped kitchen has a pass-through to the great room. The master suite, on the first floor, is replete with a tray ceiling, walk-in closet and bath with double-bowl sink and separate tub and shower. A powder room is located in the service entrance that leads to the two-car garage. The second floor holds two family bedrooms and a full bath. Note the convenient linen closet located in the second-floor hall. Please specify basement or crawl-space foundation when ordering.

Design P385

First Floor: 976 square feet
Second Floor: 368 square feet
Total: 1,344 square feet

DESIGN BY
©Frank Betz
Associates, Inc.

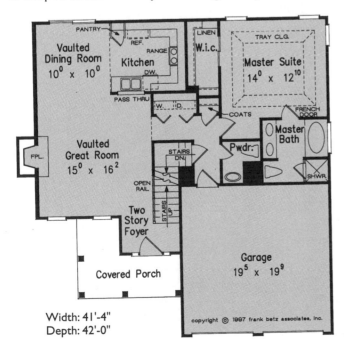

Width: 41'-4"
Depth: 42'-0"

copyright © 1997 frank betz associates, inc.

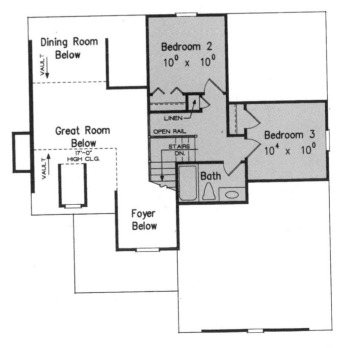

Design U164

First Floor: 1,014 square feet
Second Floor: 910 square feet
Total: 1,924 square feet

DESIGN BY
© Ahmann Design, Inc.

◆ A plant ledge and a coat closet in the two-story foyer set the scene for a plan that serves a family's aesthetic and practical needs. The dining room, with a box-bay window, is adjacent to the kitchen, which offers a window sink and an eating bar. Access to the rear of the property is provided by French doors in the adjoining breakfast nook. Windows along one wall of the great room share the spotlight with a fireplace. Around the corner are the powder room and laundry room. Upstairs, the master bedroom, with a cathedral ceiling, enjoys a private bath and a walk-in closet. Two family bedrooms share a bath that has a double-bowl vanity.

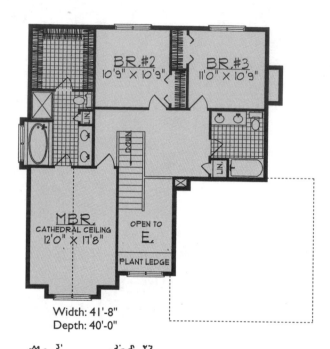

BR.#2
10'9" X 10'9"

BR.#3
11'0" X 10'9"

DOWN

LIN.

MBR.
CATHEDRAL CEILING
12'0" X 17'8"

OPEN TO
E.

PLANT LEDGE

Width: 41'-8"
Depth: 40'-0"

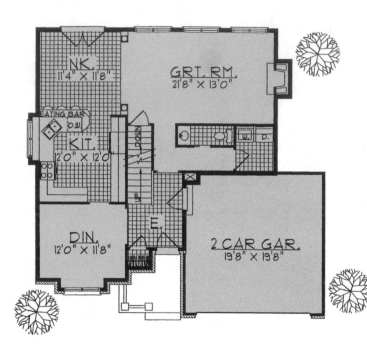

NK.
11'4" X 11'8"

GRT. RM.
21'8" X 13'0"

EATING BAR

KIT.
12'0" X 12'0"

DIN.
12'0" X 11'8"

E.

2 CAR GAR.
19'8" X 19'8"

© design basics inc.

◆ Unique window treatments, brick accents and classic siding dress up this impressive two-story home. The entry, topped by a plant shelf, opens on the left to a cozy great room with a warming fireplace. A breakfast room with a wall of windows and a built-in bookcase provides a place for casual meals and conversations with the resident gourmet. Upstairs, two family bedrooms share a full bath. A terrific master suite offers a compartmented whirlpool bath.

Design 7310

First Floor: 831 square feet
Second Floor: 790 square feet
Total: 1,621 square feet

DESIGN BY
©Design Basics, Inc.

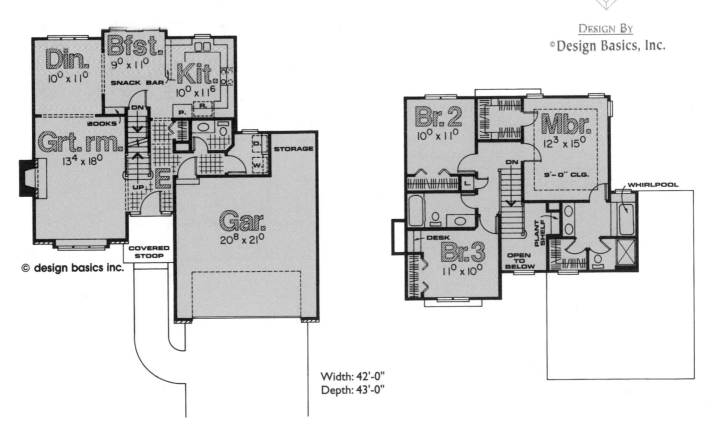

Din.
10⁰ x 11⁰

Bfst.
9⁰ x 11⁰

SNACK BAR

Kit.
10⁰ x 11⁶

DN

P.

R.

BOOKS

Grt. rm.
13⁴ x 18⁰

UP

D.

W.

STORAGE

Gar.
20⁸ x 21⁰

COVERED STOOP

© design basics inc.

Br. 2
10⁰ x 11⁰

Mbr.
12³ x 15⁰

DN

9'-0" CLG.

WHIRLPOOL

L.

DESK

Br. 3
11⁰ x 10⁰

OPEN TO BELOW

PLANT SHELF

Width: 42'-0"
Depth: 43'-0"

143

Design Q252

Square Footage: 1,475

DESIGN BY
©Select Home Designs

◆ A railed veranda, turned posts and filigrees complement a lovely Palladian window on the exterior of this home. The foyer is brightly lit by a skylight, and leads to the living room, which has a vaulted ceiling, a fireplace and built-in bookshelves. The dining room overlooks a covered veranda that opens from the breakfast room. A well organized kitchen features an L-shaped work area and a butcher-block island. Clustered sleeping quarters include a master suite and two family bedrooms sharing a full bath that offers a double vanity. Please specify basement or crawlspace foundation when ordering.

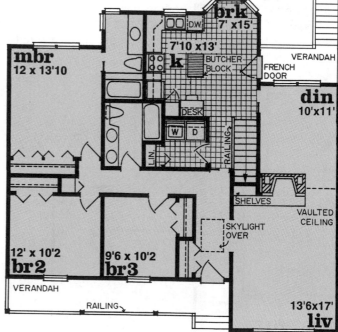

Width: 44'-0"
Depth: 43'-0"

Rear View

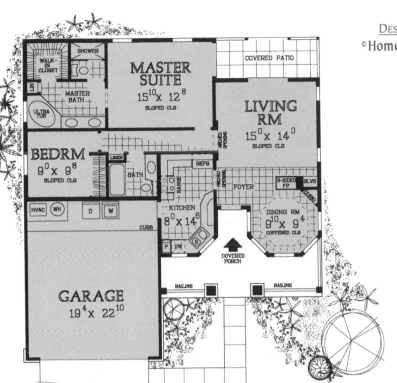

Width: 44'-4"
Depth: 47'-4"

QUOTE ONE®

Cost to build? See page 246
to order complete cost estimate
to build this house in your area!

Design 3659

Square Footage: 1,118

L

DESIGN BY
©Home Planners

◆ Compact yet comfortable, this home has many appealing amenities. From the covered front porch, the entrance foyer opens to the sunlit, octagonal dining room and the large living room. To the left of the foyer is the efficient kitchen that has the added bonus of no cross-room traffic. The luxurious master suite includes a lavish bath complete with a corner tub, a separate shower, a walk-in closet and a double-bowl vanity. A secondary bedroom has access to a full hall bath.

Covered Front Porch

145

Design 3460

Square Footage: 1,389

L

DESIGN BY
©Home Planners

◆ A double dose of charm, this special farmhouse plan offers two elevations in its blueprint package. Though rooflines and porch options are different, the floor plan is basically the same and very livable. A formal living room has a warming fireplace and a delightful bay window. The kitchen separates this area from the more casual family room. Three bedrooms include two family bedrooms served by a shared bath and a lovely master suite with its own private bath. Each room has a vaulted ceiling and large windows to let the outdoors in beautifully.

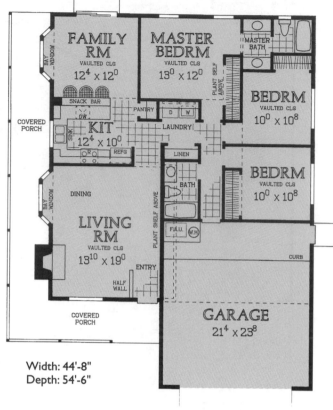

Width: 44'-8"
Depth: 54'-6"

Alternate View

Design 5531

Width: 42'-0"
Depth: 65'-6"

◆ Whether you choose Design 5531 or Design 5533, every inch of space in this one-story home is designed to provide the ultimate in comfort and enjoyment. The front facing great room offers a sloped ceiling, a box-bay window, an inviting fireplace and access to a formal dining area with a bay window. The U-shaped kitchen maximizes counter space and provides entry to both the dining area and the family room with its bayed breakfast area and rear-patio access. Located at the rear of the home for privacy, the master bedroom features a bay window, backyard entry and a master bath with a linen closet, a separate shower and a whirlpool tub. Two family bedrooms, or one bedroom and a den, share a full bath. A two-car garage and a convenient laundry room complete this amenity-filled plan.

Design 5531/5533

Square Footage: 1,952/1,971

DESIGN BY
©**Home Planners**

Width: 42'-8"
Depth: 65'-10"

Design 5533

Design B571

First Floor: 964 square feet
Second Floor: 925 square feet
Total: 1,889 square feet

DESIGN BY
©Studer Residential
Designs, Inc.

◆ A cozy front porch and an open floor plan are only two of the details that add up to a thoughtful design. You'll enjoy entertaining in the great room with its sloped ceiling and warming fireplace. The spacious dining area can be as formal or informal as your lifestyle demands and provides access to the screened porch for alfresco din-ing. The kitchen, with a sink island and walk-in pantry, functions as an efficient work area. Tucked behind the stairway to the second floor are a hobby area, a laundry room and a service entrance from the garage. The master suite, with a deluxe bath and walk-in closet, is located on the second floor with two family bedrooms that share a bath.

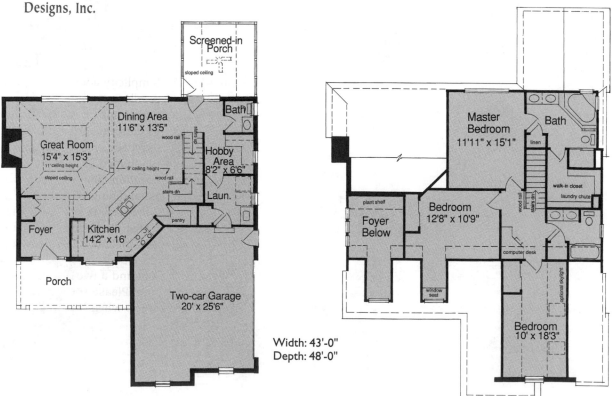

Width: 43'-0"
Depth: 48'-0"

Design 8250

Square Footage: 1,322

DESIGN BY
©Larry E. Belk
Designs

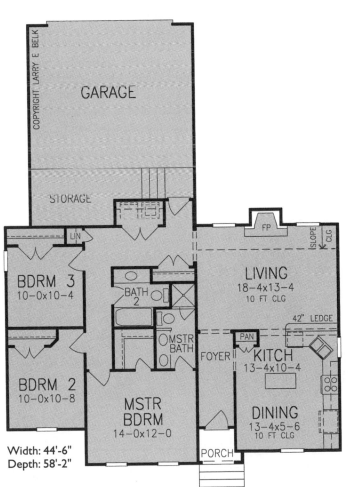

GARAGE

COPYRIGHT LARRY E BELK

STORAGE

LIN

BDRM 3
10-0x10-4

BATH
2

BDRM 2
10-0x10-8

MSTR
BDRM
14-0x12-0

OMSTR
BATH

FOYER

FP

SLOPE

CLG

LIVING
18-4x13-4
10 FT CLG

42" LEDGE

PAN

KITCH
13-4x10-4

DINING
13-4x5-6
10 FT CLG

PORCH

Width: 44'-6"
Depth: 58'-2"

◆ Classic simplicity adorns this traditional design and calls up memories of gentler times. Though compact in design, its ten-foot ceilings contribute the sense of spaciousness typically enjoyed in much larger plans. The L-shaped kitchen features an island preparation counter and a roomy area for casual dining. The glow of the focal-point fireplace is shared by the kitchen and dining area. Bedrooms—clustered for convenience—include a private master suite, two secondary bedrooms and a full bath. A laundry room and a two-car garage complete the plan. Please specify crawlspace or slab foundation when ordering.

149

Design U236

First Floor: 992 square feet
Second Floor: 950 square feet
Total: 1,942 square feet

DESIGN BY
©Ahmann Design, Inc.

Width: 44'-4"
Depth: 40'-0"

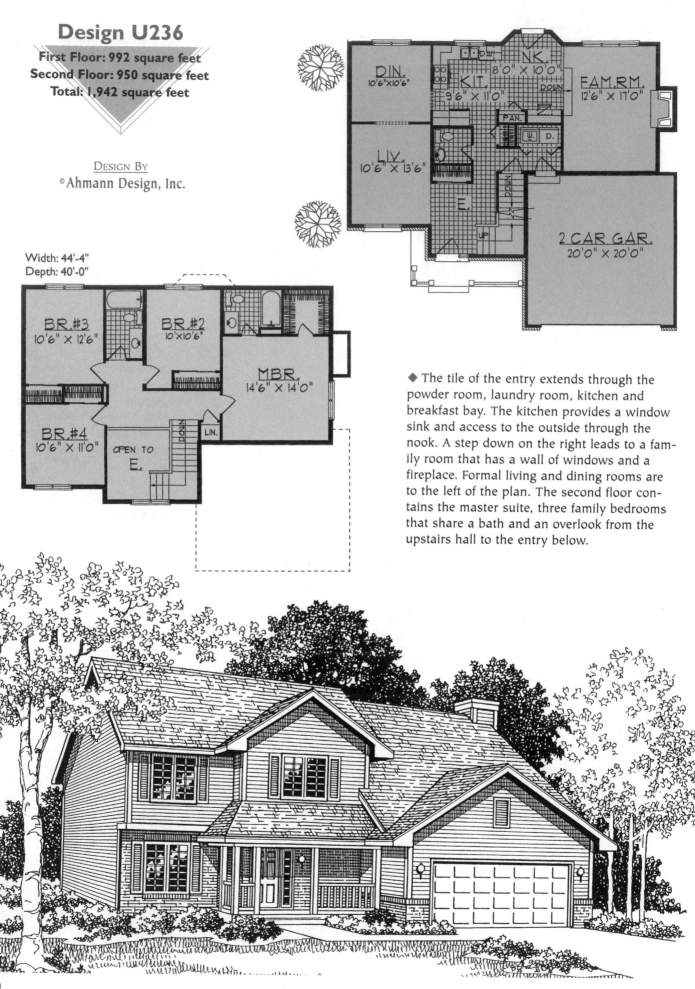

DIN.
10'6"x10'6"

NK.
8'0" X 10'0"

KIT.
9'6" X 11'0"

FAM. RM.
12'6" X 17'0"

PAN.

LIV.
10'6" X 13'6"

W. D.

E.

2 CAR GAR.
20'0" X 20'0"

UP

DOWN

BR. #3
10'6" X 12'6"

BR. #2
10'x10'6"

MBR.
14'6" X 14'0"

LIN.

BR. #4
10'6" X 11'0"

OPEN TO E.

◆ The tile of the entry extends through the powder room, laundry room, kitchen and breakfast bay. The kitchen provides a window sink and access to the outside through the nook. A step down on the right leads to a family room that has a wall of windows and a fireplace. Formal living and dining rooms are to the left of the plan. The second floor contains the master suite, three family bedrooms that share a bath and an overlook from the upstairs hall to the entry below.

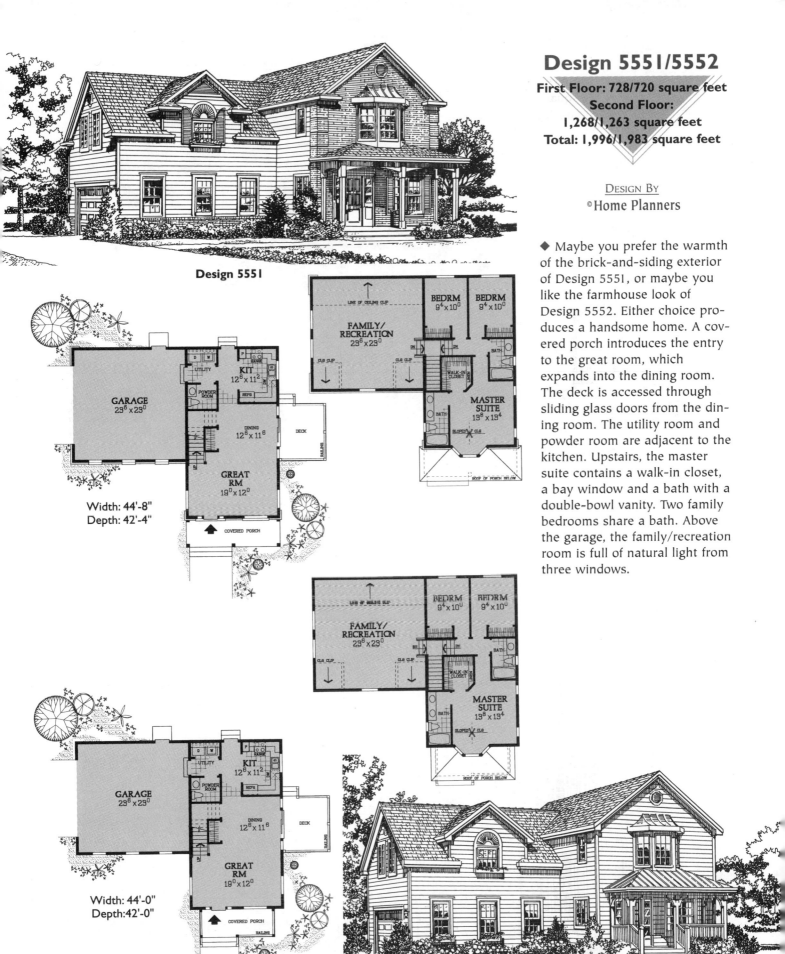

Design 5551

Width: 44'-8"
Depth: 42'-4"

GARAGE 23⁸ x 23⁰

UTILITY

KIT 12⁸ x 11²

POWDER ROOM

REFG

DINING 12⁸ x 11⁶

DECK

GREAT RM 19⁰ x 12⁰

COVERED PORCH

FAMILY/ RECREATION 23⁸ x 23⁰

BEDRM 9⁴ x 10⁰

BEDRM 9⁴ x 10⁰

BATH

WALK-IN CLOSET

MASTER SUITE 13⁸ x 13⁴

BATH

SLOPED CLG

ROOF OF PORCH BELOW

Width: 44'-0"
Depth: 42'-0"

GARAGE 23⁸ x 23⁰

UTILITY

KIT 12⁸ x 11²

POWDER ROOM

REFG

DINING 12⁸ x 11⁶

DECK

GREAT RM 19⁰ x 12⁰

COVERED PORCH

FAMILY/ RECREATION 23⁸ x 23⁰

BEDRM 9⁴ x 10⁰

BEDRM 9⁴ x 10⁰

BATH

WALK-IN CLOSET

MASTER SUITE 13⁸ x 13⁴

BATH

SLOPED CLG

ROOF OF PORCH BELOW

Design 5551/5552

First Floor: 728/720 square feet
Second Floor:
1,268/1,263 square feet
Total: 1,996/1,983 square feet

DESIGN BY
© Home Planners

◆ Maybe you prefer the warmth of the brick-and-siding exterior of Design 5551, or maybe you like the farmhouse look of Design 5552. Either choice produces a handsome home. A covered porch introduces the entry to the great room, which expands into the dining room. The deck is accessed through sliding glass doors from the dining room. The utility room and powder room are adjacent to the kitchen. Upstairs, the master suite contains a walk-in closet, a bay window and a bath with a double-bowl vanity. Two family bedrooms share a bath. Above the garage, the family/recreation room is full of natural light from three windows.

Design 5552

Design Z006

First Floor: 1,227 square feet
Second Floor: 590 square feet
Total: 1,817 square feet

DESIGN BY
©Drummond Designs, Inc.

◆ Graceful windows and entry columns enhance the contemporary lines of this design. A home office is on each level—use one as a library or a media room. The open dining/living room area flows into the kitchen, which opens to the family room. A powder room and laundry room complete the first floor. Upstairs, the master suite includes a sitting area and private access to a bath. Two family bedrooms round out the second floor. This home is designed with a basement foundation.

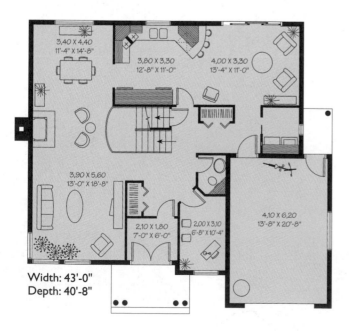

Width: 43'-0"
Depth: 40'-8"

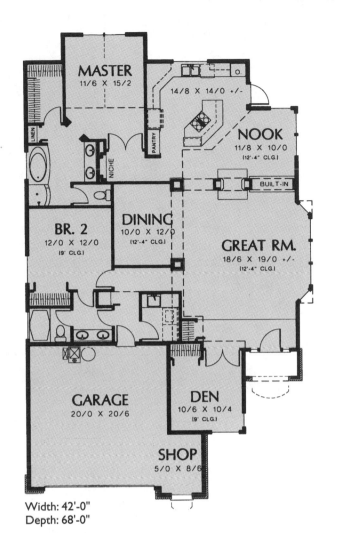

MASTER
11/6 X 15/2

14/8 X 14/0 +/-

LINEN

PANTRY

NICHE

NOOK
11/8 X 10/0
(12'-4" CLG.)

BUILT-IN

BR. 2
12/0 X 12/0
(9' CLG.)

DINING
10/0 X 12/0
(12'-4" CLG.)

GREAT RM.
18/6 X 19/0 +/-
(12'-4" CLG.)

GARAGE
20/0 X 20/6

DEN
10/6 X 10/4
(9' CLG.)

SHOP
5/0 X 8/6

Width: 42'-0"
Depth: 68'-0"

Design 7449

Square Footage: 1,864

DESIGN BY
© Alan Mascord
Design Associates, Inc.

◆ With an offset front entry and brick-and-siding detail, this home is the model of sheltered style. The entry opens directly into the large great room, but a secluded den is just to the left through double doors. A through-fireplace serves both the great room and nook, while columns separate the formal dining room from the great room. A lovely island kitchen features everything the gourmet cook might request: pantry, abundant counterspace, an over-the-sink window and outdoor access. Both bedrooms have private baths. The master bath is a study in indulgence with a whirlpool tub, separate shower, compartmented toilet, double sink and walk-in closet. The two-car garage has space enough for a workshop.

Design Z031

Square Footage: 1,208

DESIGN BY
©Drummond Designs, Inc.

◆ This lovely European design has a rustic nature with a very comfortable floor plan. A superb fan-light dresses the entry, which leads to a bright, open interior. The living room has a fireplace and a bay window in the turret, which allows natural light to extend to the dining area. An L-shaped kitchen provides a breakfast nook with doors to a charming patio. Blueprints include both a one-bedroom and a two-bedroom option. This home is designed with a basement foundation.

3,70 X 4,10
12'-4" X 13'-8"

4,20 X 3,90
14'-0" X 13'-0"

3,30 X 3,60
11'-0" X 12'-0"

4,10 X 4,80
13'-8" X 16'-0"

3,70 X 6,70
12'-4" X 22'-4"

Width: 41'-0"
Depth: 45'-0"

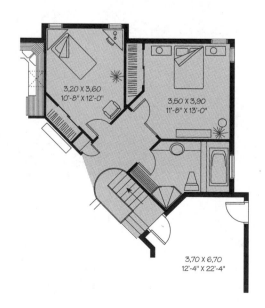

3,20 X 3,60
10'-8" X 12'-0"

3,50 X 3,90
11'-8" X 13'-0"

3,70 X 6,70
12'-4" X 22'-4"

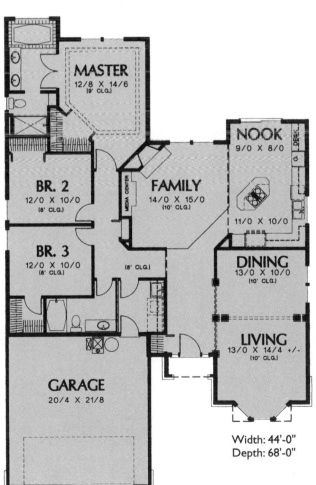

Width: 44'-0"
Depth: 68'-0"

MASTER
12/8 X 14/6
(9' CLG.)

BR. 2
12/0 X 10/0
(8' CLG.)

BR. 3
12/0 X 10/0
(8' CLG.)

GARAGE
20/4 X 21/8

MEDIA CENTER

FAMILY
14/0 X 15/0
(10' CLG.)

(8' CLG.)

NOOK
9/0 X 8/0

11/0 X 10/0

DINING
13/0 X 10/0
(10' CLG.)

LIVING
13/0 X 14/4 +/-
(10' CLG.)

DECK

Design 7447

Square Footage: 1,790

DESIGN BY
© Alan Mascord
Design Associates, Inc.

◆ Horizontal wood siding and brick accents gives this clever design exterior charm. The floor plan is practical but contains many amenities to boost livability. A central hall unites the living areas and defines formal from informal spaces. The living and dining rooms are graced with columns and ten-foot ceilings. The family room also features a ten-foot ceiling plus a warming fireplace and media center. An island kitchen and breakfast nook are close by. The nook has sliding glass doors to the rear yard. One of the two family bedrooms sports a walk-in closet. The master suite offers a tray ceiling and walk-in closet. Its bath includes a large spa tub, a separate shower and a double bowl vanity.

Design Q379

First Floor: 1,077 square feet
Second Floor: 933 square feet
Total: 2,010 square feet

DESIGN BY
©Select Home Designs

◆ The bold entry of this home is complemented by a curved-top window to its right. Dramatic rooflines and a solid chimney mass add their touches to the overall effect. A vaulted foyer continues the drama inside. Accents in the living room include a tray ceiling and a fireplace. An archway with columns separates the living and dining rooms (note the box-bay window in the dining room). An island kitchen with a breakfast bar and breakfast nook opens to a large family room with a fireplace. Sliding glass doors in the nook allow access to a rear patio. A service entrance leads past the laundry alcove and into a two-car garage with shop space. Bedrooms on the second floor include a master suite and two family bedrooms. Desk space at the railed gallery is perfect for a computer station.

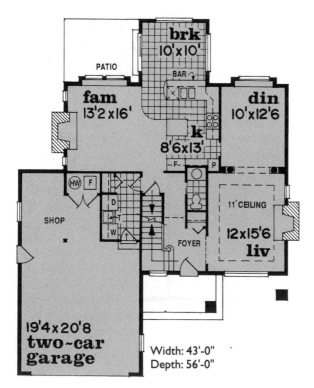

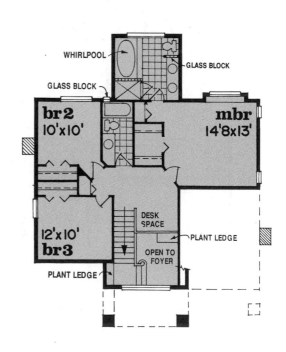

Width: 43'-0"
Depth: 56'-0"

High-rise windows and window boxes filled with flowers give this home an airy, romantic appearance. The entry hallway includes a coat closet and a powder room. The open living/dining area is highlighted by a fireplace and corner windows. The V-shaped kitchen shares a snack bar with the family room. That same V-shape is echoed upstairs in the bath that is shared by the master bedroom and one secondary bedroom. The remaining two bedrooms share an adjoining bath. This home is designed with a basement foundation.

Design Z014

First Floor: 926 square feet
Second Floor: 988 square feet
Total: 1,914 square feet

DESIGN BY
©Drummond Designs, Inc.

Width: 42'-0"
Depth: 34'-0"

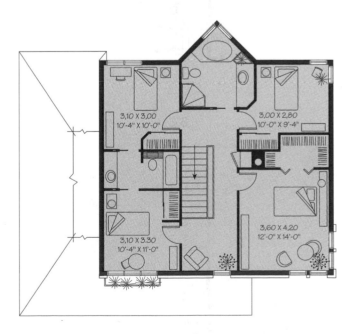

Design 9339

First Floor: 1,517 square feet
Second Floor: 234 square feet
Total: 1,751 square feet

DESIGN BY
©Design Basics, Inc.

◆ Brick and wood siding, window detailing and a covered front entrance produce a beautiful design. The entry gives way to a dining room and a great room, which is open to a breakfast bay. Amenities in the kitchen include a planning desk, a snack bar and access to the garage through the laundry room. The first floor holds a secondary bedroom and the master suite, which provides a walk-in closet, a corner whirlpool tub and two vanities. The secondary bedroom is served by an adjacent bath. The second floor bedroom has a private bath, a clothes closet and a linen closet.

Width: 42'-0"
Depth: 54'-0"

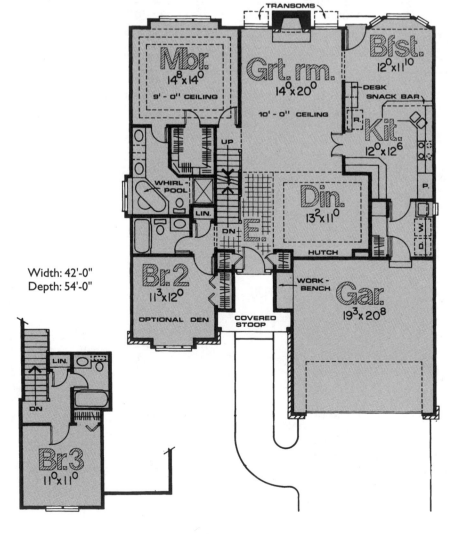

158

Alternate Elevation A

Design K500

First Floor: 1,553 square feet
Second Floor: 391 square feet
Total: 1,944 square feet

DESIGN BY
©Lucia Custom
Home Designers

◆ Your choice of three exteriors is only one option available with this flexible design. The floor plan and other options are identical for all three exteriors. The study to the left of the foyer could be a third bedroom as it adjoins a bath. The great room, dining room and kitchen make up an open area. An entertainment center and a fireplace are optional. From this area, access is through French doors to a covered porch and an optional deck. A bedroom and bath are housed on the second floor along with a loft area and an overlook to the great room below. There's also an optional closet and unfinished bonus space.

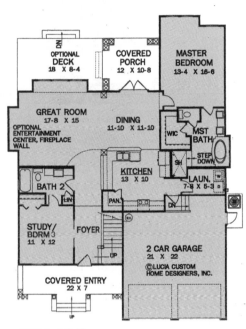

Width: 44'-0"
Depth: 62'-8"

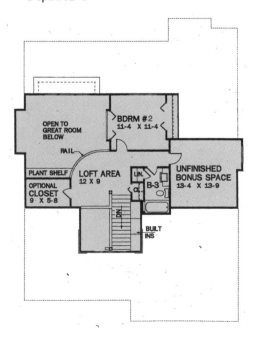

Alternate Elevation B

Alternate Elevation C

Design 6680

First Floor: 1,007 square feet
Second Floor: 869 square feet
Total: 1,876 square feet

DESIGN BY
©The Sater
Design Collection

Width: 43'-8"
Depth: 53'-6"

© The Sater Group, Inc.

br. 3
11'-0" x 10'-6"
8'-0" clg.

open to grand
room below

overlook

up

down

w.i.c.

master
11'-6" x 14'-6"
8'-0" clg.

covered balcony

© The Sater Group, Inc.

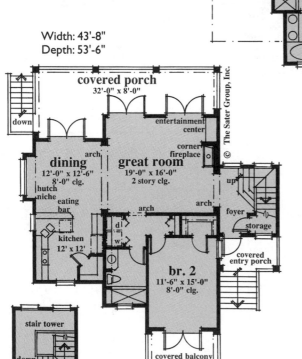

covered porch
32'-0" x 8'-0"

down

entertainment
center

corner
fireplace

dining
12'-0" x 12'-6"
8'-0" clg.

arch

great room
19'-0" x 16'-0"
2 story clg.

hutch
niche

eating
bar

kitchen
12' x 12'

d
w

arch

arch

up

foyer

storage

covered
entry porch

br. 2
11'-6" x 15'-0"
8'-0" clg.

stair tower

down

covered balcony
12'-6" x 9'-0"

◆ An enchanting center gable announces a graceful, honest architecture that's at home with the easygoing nature of this three-bedroom, coastal design. Gentle arches add pleasing definition to an open interior. The well-appointed kitchen features a corner walk-in pantry, an eating bar for easy meals and an angled double sink. A bedroom is located next to the bath and boasts a private balcony. The second floor contains the master suite and a gallery hall—with a balcony overlook to the great room—that leads to an additional suite. The plan includes pier and crawlspace foundation options.

Rear View

160

◆ A faux widow's walk creates a stunning complement to the observation balcony and two sun decks. Inside, the open living and dining area is defined by two pairs of French doors that frame a two-story wall of glass, and built-ins flank the living room fireplace. The efficient kitchen features a walk-in pantry, a work island and a door to the covered porch. Split sleeping quarters offer privacy to the first-floor master suite. Upstairs, two guest suites provide private baths. A gallery loft leads to a computer area with a built-in desk and a balcony overlook.

Design 6693

First Floor: 1,642 square feet
Second Floor: 1,165 square feet
Lower Floor Entry: 150
Total: 2,957 square feet

DESIGN BY
©The Sater
Design Collection

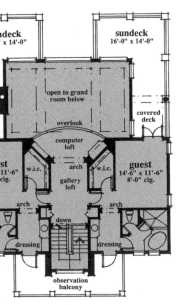

Width: 44'-6"
Depth: 58'-0"

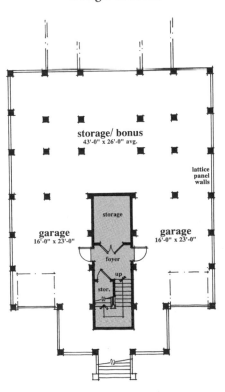

Design M557

First Floor: 2,155 square feet
Second Floor: 522 square feet
Total: 2,677 square feet

DESIGN BY
©Andy McDonald
Design Group

◆ More than twice as long as it is wide, this plan presents a charming and deceptive facade. From the front gallery, the open family room provides a spacious area for gathering together. To the side are a study and a master suite that includes a private bath. Behind the family room, you'll find a keeping room, with a fireplace and built-in shelves, and a breakfast area that opens to the courtyard. A second bedroom and bath are located at the rear of the plan, while a third and fourth bedroom (sharing a bath) are on the second floor.

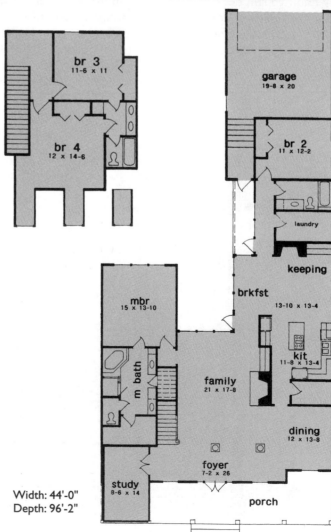

br 3
11-6 x 11

br 4
12 x 14-6

garage
19-8 x 20

br 2
11 x 12-2

laundry

keeping

brkfst

mbr
15 x 13-10

m bath

family
21 x 17-8

kit
11-8 x 13-4

dining
12 x 13-8

foyer
7-2 x 26

study
8-6 x 14

porch

Width: 44'-0"
Depth: 96'-2"

GRAND TRADITIONS IN SMALL SPACES

DESIGN BY
Stephen Fuller

Design T145

First Floor: 1,501 square feet
Second Floor: 1,252 square feet
Total: 2,753 square feet

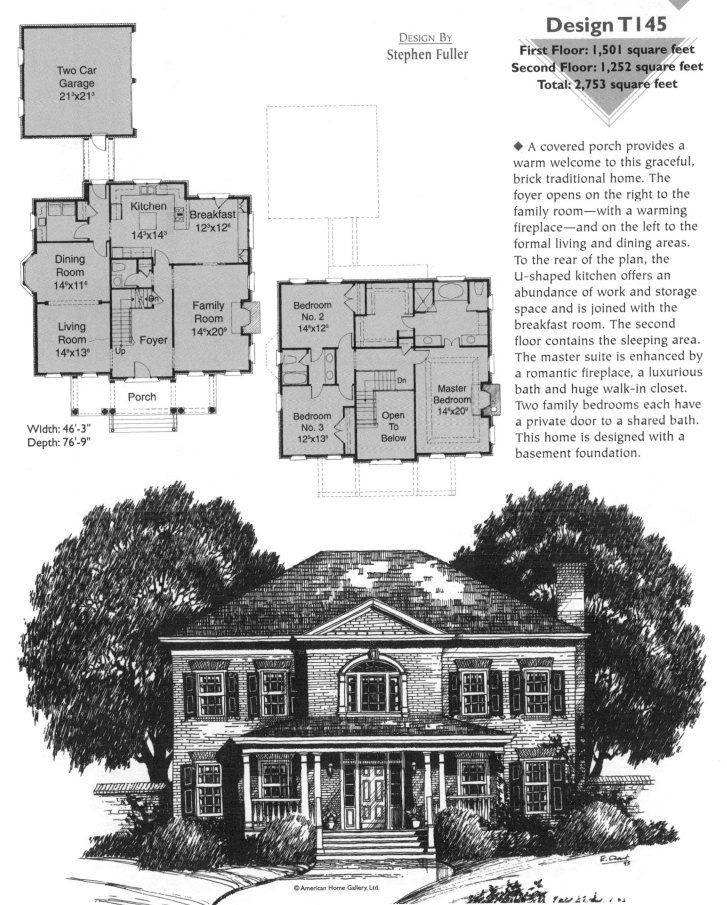

Two Car
Garage
21³x21³

Kitchen
14³x14³

Breakfast
12³x12⁶

Dining
Room
14⁶x11⁶

Living
Room
14⁶x13⁶

Foyer

Family
Room
14⁶x20⁹

Up
Dn

Porch

Width: 46'-3"
Depth: 76'-9"

Bedroom
No. 2
14⁶x12³

Bedroom
No. 3
12³x13⁶

Open
To
Below

Dn

Master
Bedroom
14⁶x20⁹

◆ A covered porch provides a warm welcome to this graceful, brick traditional home. The foyer opens on the right to the family room—with a warming fireplace—and on the left to the formal living and dining areas. To the rear of the plan, the U-shaped kitchen offers an abundance of work and storage space and is joined with the breakfast room. The second floor contains the sleeping area. The master suite is enhanced by a romantic fireplace, a luxurious bath and huge walk-in closet. Two family bedrooms each have a private door to a shared bath. This home is designed with a basement foundation.

Design 2622

First Floor: 700 square feet
Second Floor: 700 square feet
Total: 1,400 square feet

L D

DESIGN BY
©Home Planners

◆ Coping on a tight budget? This Colonial adaptation provides a functional design that allows for future expansion. Note the cozy fireplace in the living room and the roomy L-shaped kitchen with a window sink and breakfast-nook space. The upstairs holds two bedrooms, a full bath and master bedroom with an attached bath. A large storage area over the garage can become an office, recreation room or a bedroom.

QUOTE ONE®

Cost to build? See page 246
to order complete cost estimate
to build this house in your area!

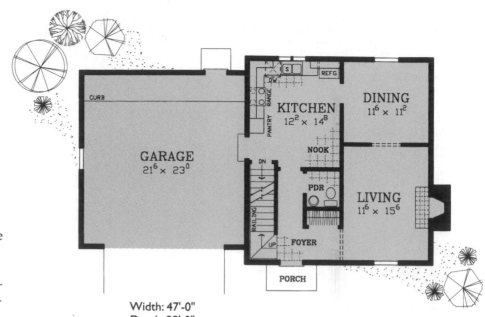

Width: 47'-0"
Depth: 28'-0"

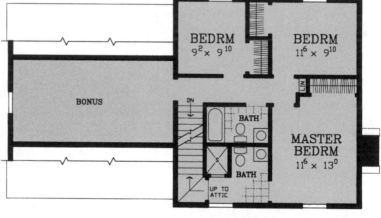

Design F132

First Floor: 1,890 square feet
Second Floor: 1,874 square feet
Total: 3,764 square feet

DESIGN BY
©R.L. Pfotenhauer

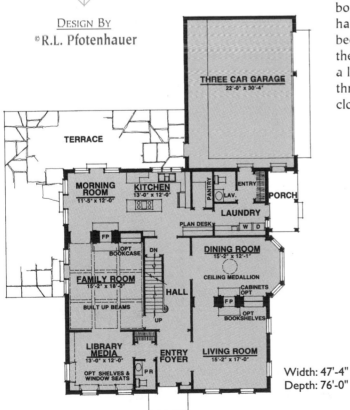

◆ Many built-in and optional amenities abound within this impressive Colonial design. The library, or media room, offers the option of adding shelves and window seats, while the living/dining room features a shared fireplace and the option of adding cabinets and bookshelves. The family room shares a fireplace with the morning room and and gives an option for built-in bookcases. A walk-in pantry, a laundry room and two half-baths complete the first floor. While three family bedrooms share a full hall bath with separate sinks, the master bedroom is a study in opulence. It features a large sitting room with a mini breakfast bar, a through-fireplace to the whirlpool tub, two walk-in closets and a skylit tray ceiling in the master bath.

Width: 47'-4"
Depth: 76'-0"

Design Y023

First Floor: 1,334 square feet
Second Floor: 437 square feet
Total: 1,771 square feet
Bonus Room: 224 square feet

DESIGN BY
©The Nelson
Group, Inc.

◆ The many charms of this design include the master suite at the rear of the plan, an L-shaped kitchen with a work island, a breakfast room that opens to both the rear porch and the garage and the double-bowl vanity in the compartmented bath shared by the upstairs bedrooms. The master suite is somewhat separated from the rest of the floor plan by a powder room and laundry room. It offers a lavish bath, entered through double French doors, and two walk-in closets. Separate vanities and a whirlpool tub add to the attractions. Please specify basement, crawl-space or slab foundation when ordering.

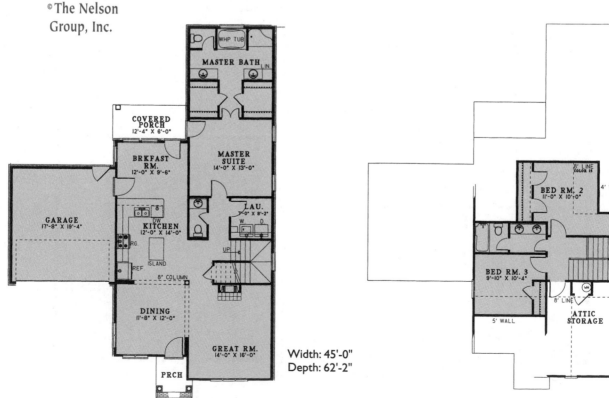

Width: 45'-0"
Depth: 62'-2"

Design 1361

First Floor: 965 square feet
Second Floor: 740 square feet
Total: 1,705 square feet

L D

DESIGN BY
©Home Planners

FAMILY RM.
17⁰x12⁶

DINING RM.
11⁰x12⁶

KIT.
10⁸x12⁶

EATING

LIVING RM.
17⁰x12⁶

GARAGE
19⁸x20⁶

ENTRY HALL

UP

CURB

PORCH

TERRACE

Width: 46'-5"
Depth: 34'-3"

MASTER
BED RM.
15⁰x11⁶

BED RM.
11⁰x10⁰

BED RM.
11⁰x13⁰

BATH

DN.

LIN.

◆ An abundance of livability is offered by this traditional adaptation, which is economical to build. The entry hall gives way to a central, L-shaped kitchen. The formal dining room opens to the right. The spacious living room allows a variety of furniture arrangements. In the family room, casual living takes off with direct access to the rear terrace. Note the first-floor laundry conveniently located between the kitchen and the family room. Upstairs, three bedrooms include a master bedroom with a private bath. Double closets guarantee ample space for wardrobes. One of the secondary bedrooms features a walk-in closet. Don't forget the handy broom closet and the pantry located just off the kitchen.

Design E124

First Floor: 1,651 square feet
Second Floor: 1,150 square feet
Total: 2,801 square feet

DESIGN BY
©Chatham Home
Planning, Inc.

◆ Two wraparound covered porches and beautiful bay windows enhance the living in this functional four-bedroom home. The foyer opens to the formal dining room, then leads straight ahead to the large living room with its fireplace and a wall of windows looking out to the rear porch. Between these rooms are the efficient U-shaped kitchen and bayed breakfast nook. The sleeping zone on the right of the plan includes a guest room, with convenient access from the foyer, and the master suite that offers a sumptuous bath with twin dressing areas, vanities and walk-in closets. Upstairs, two family bedrooms share a full bath and a game room. Please specify crawlspace or slab foundation when ordering.

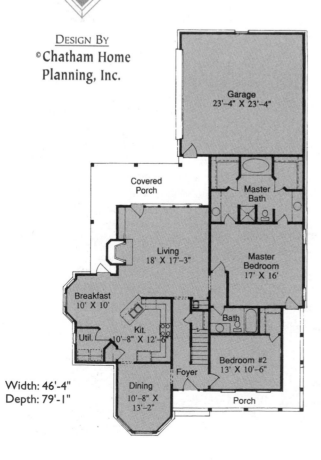

Width: 46'-4"
Depth: 79'-1"

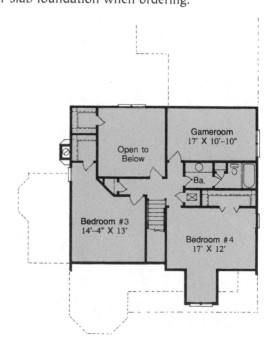

Design 9312

First Floor: 1,150 square feet
Second Floor: 1,120 square feet
Total: 2,270 square feet

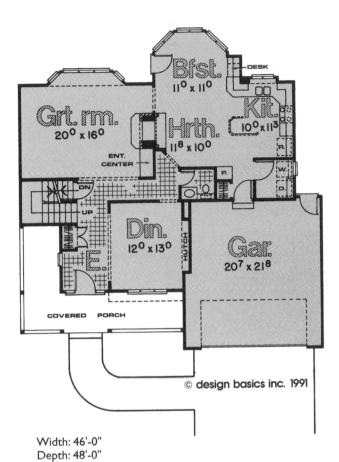

DESIGN BY
©Design Basics, Inc.

© design basics inc. 1991

Width: 46'-0"
Depth: 48'-0"

◆ The spacious two-story entry provides a fine introduction to the formal dining room. A fireplace and a bay window add appeal to the great room. Families will love the spacious kitchen, breakfast bay and hearth room. Enhancements to this casual living area include a through-fireplace, a work island and a planning desk. Upstairs, three secondary bedrooms and a sumptuous master suite feature privacy. Bedroom 3 is highlighted by a half-circle window while Bedroom 4 features a built-in desk and a box-bay window.

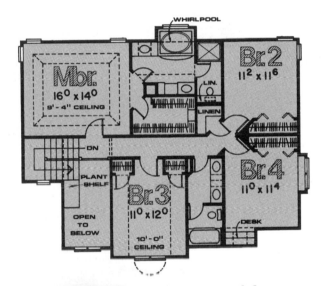

Design 7663

First Floor: 1,336 square feet
Second Floor: 523 square feet
Total: 1,859 square feet
Bonus Room: 225 square feet

DESIGN BY
**Donald A. Gardner
Architects, Inc.**

◆ From the shelter of the front porch, the foyer leads up the stairway to the second floor or directly ahead to the great room. A centered fireplace warms the great room, which opens to the rear covered porch through lovely French doors. The U-shaped kitchen serves a snack counter as well as the formal dining room, with its own porch access. A tray ceiling, a garden tub, a double-bowl vanity and a walk-in closet highlight the master suite. Two upper-level bedrooms are connected by a gallery hall with an overlook to the great-room.

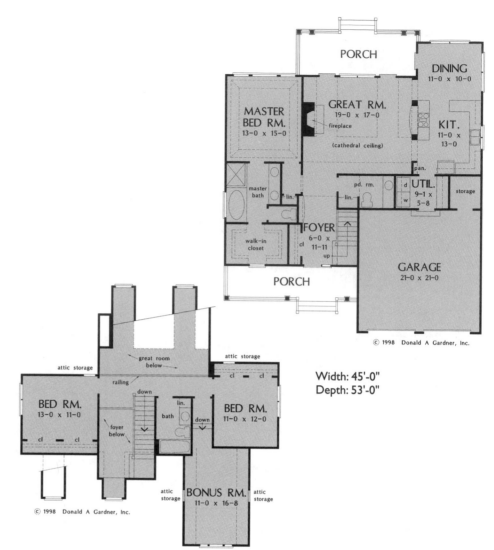

© 1998 Donald A Gardner, Inc.

Width: 45'-0"
Depth: 53'-0"

© 1998 Donald A Gardner, Inc.

© 1998 Donald A Gardner Architects, Inc.

170

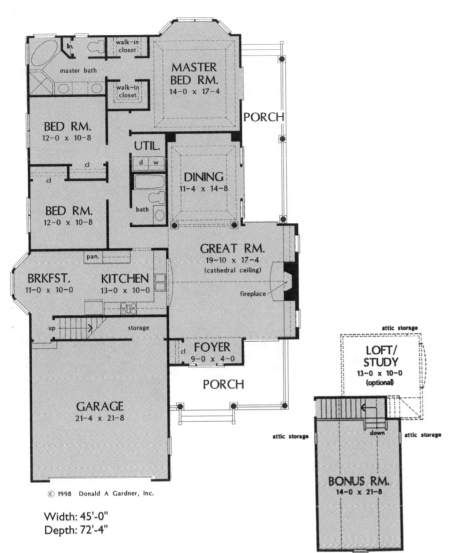

Design 7705

Square Footage: 1,795
Bonus Room: 368 square feet

DESIGN BY
Donald A. Gardner
Architects, Inc.

◆ This lovely home incorporates style and practicality in an economical and charming package. A cathedral ceiling enhances the great room that also displays a fireplace and built-ins. An optional loft/study above the kitchen overlooks the great room. The kitchen serves the breakfast bay, the dining room and the great room. Sleeping arrangements include a delightful master suite, with two walk-in closets, and two family bedrooms that share a hall bath. A bonus room over the garage offers room for future expansion.

Width: 45'-0"
Depth: 72'-4"

© 1998 Donald A Gardner, Inc.

© 1998 Donald A. Gardner, Inc.

171

Design V030

Square Footage: 1,504

©United Design
Associates, Inc.

◆ This Southern coastal cottage offers a vaulted great room, a dining area and a kitchen much larger than those typically found in homes of this size. The master suite is located at the rear of the plan with the opportunity of beautiful views. The suite includes a tray ceiling, a large walk-in closet and a master bath with a separate shower and garden or whirlpool tub. With an inviting front porch perfect for enjoying your favorite book, a romantic fireplace, interior architectural columns and numerous windows, this plan offers the simple charm of a country cottage.

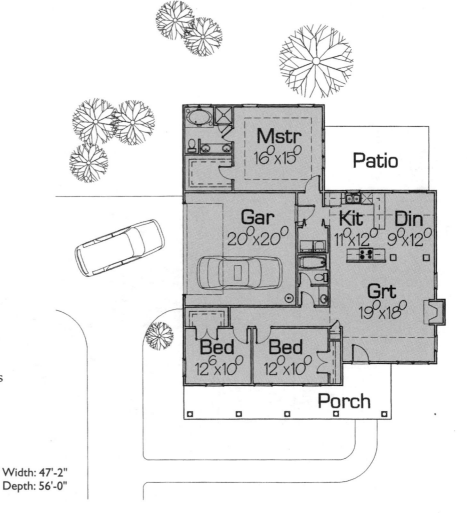

Width: 47'-2"
Depth: 56'-0"

Mstr 16⁰x15⁰
Patio
Gar 20⁰x20⁰
Kit 11⁰x12⁰
Din 9⁰x12⁰
Grt 19⁰x18⁰
Bed 12⁶x10⁰
Bed 12⁰x10⁰
Porch

© 1994 Donald A. Gardner Architects, Inc.

B. NATHAN

DESIGN BY
Donald A. Gardner
Architects, Inc.

Design 9758

First Floor: 1,313 square feet
Second Floor: 573 square feet
Total: 1,886 square feet

GARAGE
21-4 x 22-0

DECK

SCREEN PORCH
11-4 x 14-0

DINING
11-10 x 12-0

KIT.
9-0 x 13-10

BRKFST.
13-0 x 9-8

UTIL.
7-0 x 6-4

pd. rm.

cl

d. w.

walk-in closet

master bath

GREAT RM.
13-4 x 19-4

fireplace

MASTER BED RM.
13-4 x 13-0

FOYER
7-4 x 6-2

up

cl

PORCH

© 1994 Donald A. Gardner Architects, Inc.

◆ A covered porch on this three-bedroom home bids a warm country welcome. To the left of the two-story foyer is a great room featuring a fireplace and a pair of columns leading to the dining room. Conveniently located nearby is the U-shaped kitchen and breakfast area—opening to the screened porch and inviting casual outdoor living. The first-floor master suite contains a generous walk-in closet and a lavish bath featuring a double-bowl vanity, a whirlpool tub and a separate shower. Upstairs, two additional bedrooms highlighted by pairs of closets and dormers share a full bath.

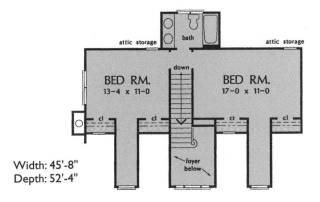

attic storage

bath

attic storage

BED RM.
13-4 x 11-0

down

BED RM.
17-0 x 11-0

cl

cl

cl

cl

foyer below

Width: 45'-8"
Depth: 52'-4"

173

Design A148

First Floor: 844 square feet
Second Floor: 875 square feet
Total: 1,719 square feet
Bonus Room: 242 square feet

DESIGN BY
©Living Concepts
Home Planning

◆ A Palladian window adds interest to the modified gable roofline of this livable three-bedroom design. Columns and tall glass panels flank the covered entryway. A hall closet and a powder room line the foyer. The great room with a fireplace, the kitchen and a breakfast area with patio access are across the back. The master suite and two family bedrooms are on the second floor. Please specify crawlspace or slab foundation when ordering.

DECK/PATIO

GREAT ROOM
18'-4" x 13'-8"

BREAKFAST

KITCHEN
11'-4" x 11'-0"

PANTRY

PDR.

FOYER

UP

DINING ROOM
11'-4" x 12'-0"

GARAGE
20'-0" x 22'-4"

LOGGIA

Width: 45'-0"
Depth: 37'-0"

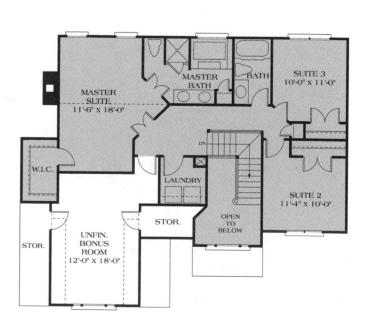

MASTER SUITE
11'-6" x 18'-0"

MASTER BATH

BATH

SUITE 3
10'-0" x 11'-0"

W.I.C.

DN

LAUNDRY

SUITE 2
11'-4" x 10'-0"

STOR.

UNFIN. BONUS ROOM
12'-0" x 18'-0"

STOR.

OPEN TO BELOW

◆ Decorative window trim enhances the exterior of this classic-country three-bedroom plan. Tall columns separate the formal living room and dining room. A large family room with a fireplace opens to the U-shaped kitchen and breakfast area. Two family bedrooms with a shared bath and the master suite with a private bath occupy the second floor, along with an unfinished bonus room. Please specify crawlspace or slab foundation when ordering.

Design A151

First Floor: 1,056 square feet
Second Floor: 967 square feet
Total: 2,023 square feet
Bonus Room: 291 square feet

DESIGN BY
© Living Concepts
Home Planning

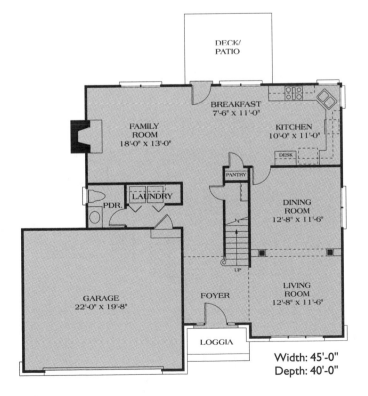

DECK/
PATIO

BREAKFAST
7'-6" X 11'-0"

FAMILY
ROOM
18'-0" X 13'-0"

KITCHEN
10'-0" X 11'-0"

DESK

PANTRY

LAUNDRY

PDR.

DINING
ROOM
12'-8" X 11'-6"

GARAGE
22'-0" X 19'-8"

FOYER

UP

LIVING
ROOM
12'-8" X 11'-6"

LOGGIA

Width: 45'-0"
Depth: 40'-0"

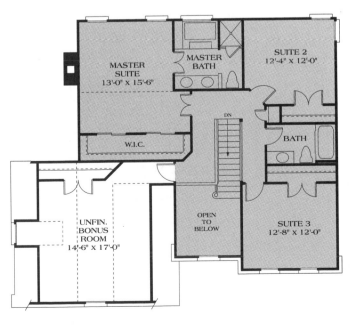

MASTER
SUITE
13'-0" X 15'-6"

MASTER
BATH

SUITE 2
12'-4" X 12'-0"

W.I.C.

DN

BATH

UNFIN.
BONUS
ROOM
14'-6" X 17'-0"

OPEN
TO
BELOW

SUITE 3
12'-8" X 12'-0"

Design A159

First Floor: 1,635 square feet
Second Floor: 917 square feet
Total: 2,552 square feet
Bonus Room: 271 square feet

◆ Graceful columns and multi-pane windows frame the entrance to this understated two-story traditional design. The view from the foyer extends through the gathering room and out onto the covered veranda. The dining room, with its lovely bay window, is to the left of the foyer and connects to the kitchen. Here the angled bar and corner breakfast nook provide for casual meals. The first-floor master suite has a bay window, perfect for a writing desk, and a garden tub in the bath. Versatile club quarters share the second floor with two additional bedrooms and a full bath. A large room with a walk-in closet is available as a fourth bedroom or home office.

DESIGN BY
©Living Concepts
Home Planning

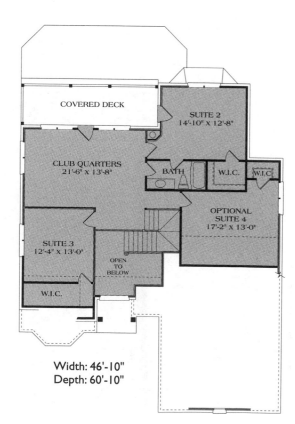

Width: 46'-10"
Depth: 60'-10"

Design 5537

Design 5537/5538

First Floor: 777/802 square feet
Second Floor: 720/757 square feet
Total: 1,497/1,559 square feet

DESIGN BY
© Home Planners

Width: 47'-0"
Depth: 34'-6"

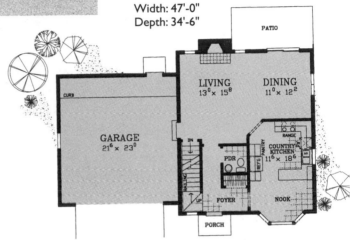

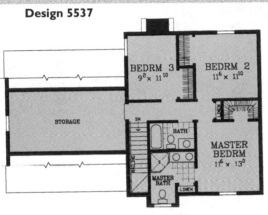

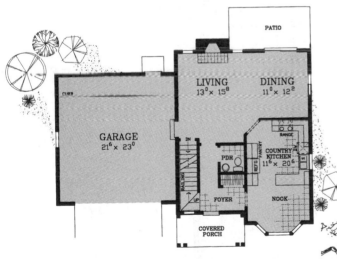

◆ Offering a smaller space while still providing today's neces-sary amenities, this two-story traditional home would be ideal for a corner lot. Inside, the foyer leads to all the living areas available on the first floor. The combination living/dining room features a large fireplace and access to the rear patio. The corner kitchen includes a pass-through to the breakfast nook that offers a bay window. Upstairs, two family bedrooms share a full hall bath while the master bedroom features its own bath. A large storage area on the second floor and a half-bath on the first floor complete this versatile plan.

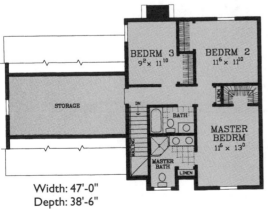

Width: 47'-0"
Depth: 38'-6"

Design 5538

Design F152

First Floor: 1,150 square feet
Second Floor: 939 square feet
Total: 2,089 square feet

Design By
©R.L. Pfotenhauer

◆ The exterior of this cottage has a distinctive European style. The combination of brick and stucco gives it a country look, as does the stickwork detailing, the cupola and the massive chimneys. Formal living and dining rooms fill the right side of the plan, which is enhanced by a bay window, a fireplace and decorative columns. In addition to a second fireplace, the family room boasts two French doors to the side patio. The L-shaped kitchen includes a cooktop island, a breakfast room and access to a rear patio. A laundry room and a powder room are located off the family room. The second floor holds three bedrooms, including a master suite with a compartmented bath and two closets.

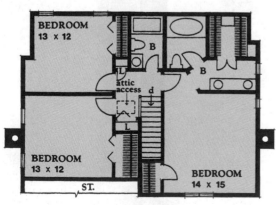

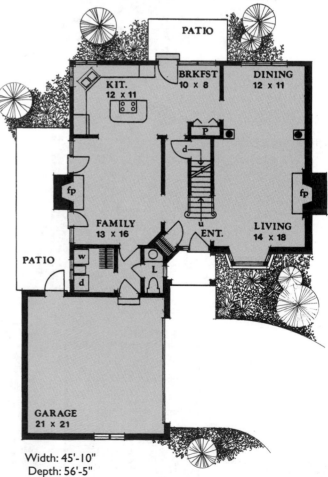

Width: 45'-10"
Depth: 56'-5"

◆ The well-balanced use of stucco and stone combined with box-bay window treatments and a covered entry make this English country home especially inviting. The two-story foyer opens on the right to the attractive living and dining rooms with large windows. The step-saving kitchen and breakfast area flow easily into the two-story great room and a media room with a through-fireplace. The second floor offers both open design and privacy. The opulent master suite includes a modified tray ceiling and a sitting area. The compartmented master bath offers two vanities, a separate shower and a walk-in closet. A double-bowl vanity enhances the full bath off the hall. Bedrooms 2 and 3 feature walk-in closets. This home is designed with a basement foundation.

Design T063

First Floor: 1,395 square feet
Second Floor: 1,210 square feet
Total: 2,605 square feet
Bonus Room: 225 square feet

DESIGN BY
Stephen Fuller

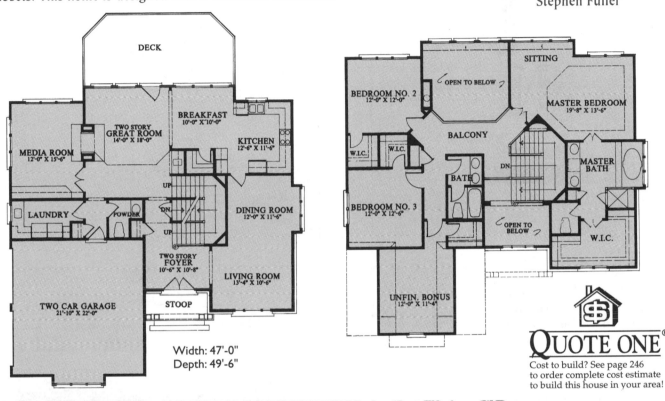

Width: 47'-0"
Depth: 49'-6"

Quote One®

Cost to build? See page 246
to order complete cost estimate
to build this house in your area!

© American Home Gallery, Ltd.

179

Design P172

First Floor: 1,290 square feet
Second Floor: 985 square feet
Total: 2,275 square feet
Bonus Room: 186 square feet

DESIGN BY
© Frank Betz
Associates, Inc.

◆ This elegant European country-style home is designed with room to grow. Formal living and dining rooms are defined by decorative columns and open from a two-story foyer, which leads to casual living space. A two-story family room offers a fireplace and shares a French door to the rear property with the breakfast room. A gallery hall with a balcony overlook connects two sleeping wings upstairs. The master suite boasts a vaulted bath, while the family hall leads to bonus space. Please specify basement, crawlspace or slab foundation when ordering.

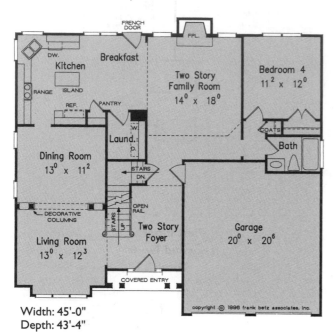

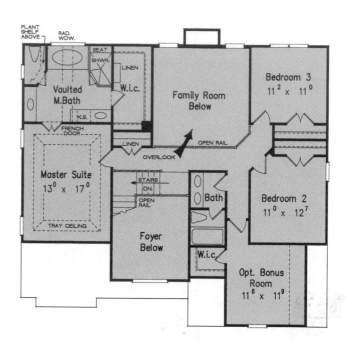

Width: 45'-0"
Depth: 43'-4"

copyright © 1996 frank betz associates, inc.

DESIGN BY
Donald A. Gardner Architects, Inc.

◆ Bricks, gables and shutters set a traditional tone for this sturdy, two-story home. The foyer opens up to all first-floor rooms and offers a coat closet and powder room. The kitchen easily serves the dining room, breakfast room and great room, which provides a fireplace and sliding glass doors to the wide deck that features a spa. Upstairs, three bedrooms, including the master suite, feature walk-in closets. The master bedroom enjoys a luxurious bath with a whirlpool tub, while the two family bedrooms share a bath. In addition to two linen closets on this floor, one bedroom opens to a storage/bonus area.

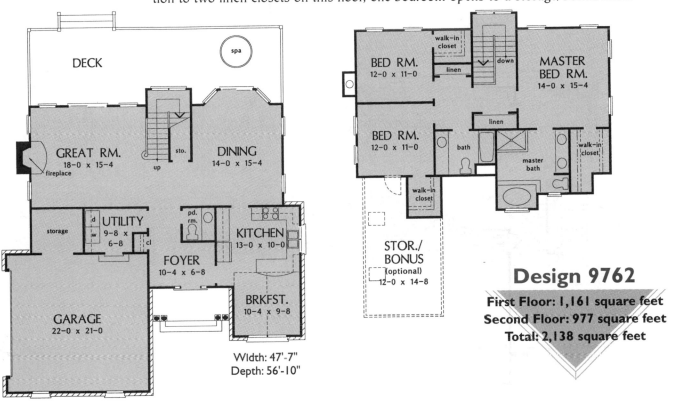

DECK
spa

GREAT RM.
18-0 x 15-4
fireplace

sto.
up

DINING
14-0 x 15-4

storage

UTILITY
9-8 x 6-8
d
w
cl

pd. rm.

KITCHEN
13-0 x 10-0

FOYER
10-4 x 6-8

BRKFST.
10-4 x 9-8

GARAGE
22-0 x 21-0

Width: 47'-7"
Depth: 56'-10"

© 1994 Donald A. Gardner Architects, Inc.

BED RM.
12-0 x 11-0

walk-in closet
linen
down

MASTER BED RM.
14-0 x 15-4

BED RM.
12-0 x 11-0

linen
bath
master bath
walk-in closet

walk-in closet

STOR./ BONUS
(optional)
12-0 x 14-8

Design 9762

First Floor: 1,161 square feet
Second Floor: 977 square feet
Total: 2,138 square feet

© 1994 Donald A. Gardner Architects, Inc.

B. NATHAN · © 1995 Donald A. Gardner Architects, Inc.

Design 9788

Square Footage: 1,302

DESIGN BY
**Donald A. Gardner
Architects, Inc.**

◆ Well designed for maximum efficiency and practical to build, this streamlined plan is big on popular innovations. A spacious cathedral ceiling expands the open great room, dining room and kitchen. A deck located off the kitchen amplifies the living and entertaining space. The versatile bedroom/study features a cathedral ceiling and shares a full skylit bath with another bedroom. The master bedroom is highlighted by a cathedral ceiling for extra volume and light. Its compartmented bath opens up with a skylight and includes a double-bowl vanity and garden tub. A walk-in closet adjacent to the bedroom completes the suite.

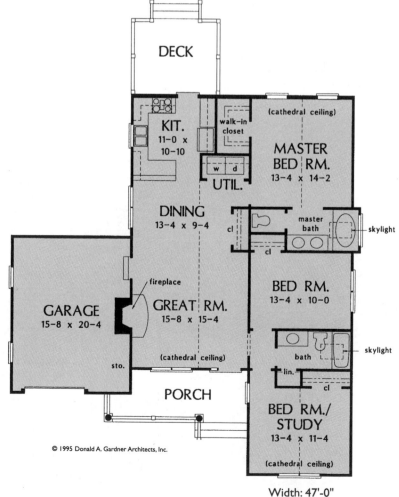

© 1995 Donald A. Gardner Architects, Inc.

Width: 47'-0"
Depth: 50'-4"

©1991 Donald A. Gardner Architects, Inc.

G·NATHAN

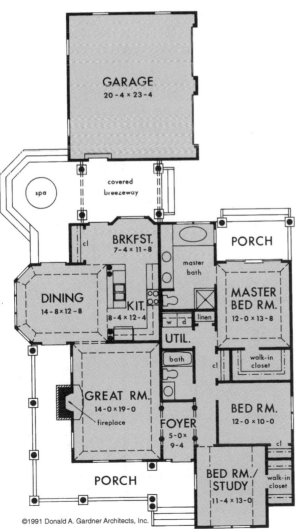

GARAGE
20-4 × 23-4

spa

covered breezeway

BRKFST.
7-4 × 11-8

cl

master bath

PORCH

DINING
14-8 × 12-8

KIT.
8-4 × 12-4

w d linen

MASTER BED RM.
12-0 × 13-8

UTIL.

bath

cl

walk-in closet

GREAT RM.
14-0 × 19-0

fireplace

FOYER
5-0 × 9-4

BED RM.
12-0 × 10-0

cl

PORCH

BED RM./ STUDY
11-4 × 13-0

walk-in closet

©1991 Donald A. Gardner Architects, Inc.

Design 9637

Square Footage: 1,608

<small>DESIGN BY</small>
Donald A. Gardner
Architects, Inc.

◆ This three-bedroom plan with arched windows and a wraparound porch offers a level of comfort uncommon to a plan of this size. The great room, dining room and master bedroom all boast tray ceilings, while the front bedroom features a vaulted ceiling to accentuate the arched window. An open kitchen design conveniently services the breakfast area, dining room and deck. The master suite has a private covered porch, a large walk-in closet and a master bath with a whirlpool tub.

Width: 45'-0"
Depth: 83'-8"

Design S121

First Floor: 1,367 square feet
Second Floor: 1,397 square feet
Total: 2,764 square feet

◆ A dramatic, steep-pitched, hip roof defines a stunning silhouette, while a multitude of windowpanes creates a surprising lightness. You will enjoy the view through the two-story foyer window each time you descend the stairway. The two-story formal living room and the adjoining dining room are lit by a dazzling wall of panes. Casual living areas span the rear of the home, from the kitchen with a snack bar, to the breakfast room, to the family room with a fireplace and built-in cabinets. The second floor is comprised of the sleeping quarters, including a loft bedroom. The master suite is a grand retreat with double doors, tray ceiling, fireplace, built-in shelves, His and Hers walk-in closets and an oversized oval tub.

DESIGN BY
©Archival Designs, Inc.

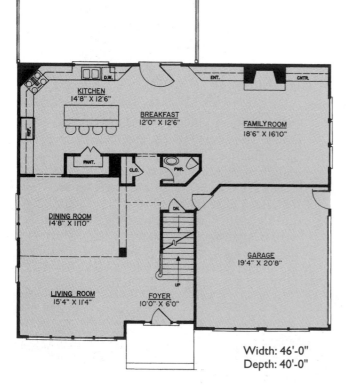

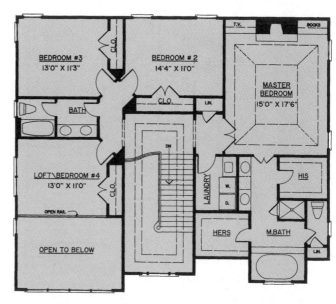

Width: 46'-0"
Depth: 40'-0"

DESIGN BY
Stephen Fuller

DECK

BREAKFAST
10'-4" X 10'-4"

MASTER SITTING
10'-4" x 6'-0"

GREAT ROOM
17'-0" X 17'-0"

MASTER BEDROOM
15'-4" X 13'-0"

KITCHEN
13'-4" X 11'-0"

MASTER BATH
12'-2" X 12'-8"

DINING ROOM
12'-10" X 10'-6"

FOYER
5'-0" X 13'-6"

POWDER

LAUNDRY
6'-0" X 8'-10"

W.I.C.

LIVING ROOM
11'-4" X 10'-8"

STOOP

TWO CAR GARAGE
21'-4" X 21'-4"

Width: 47'-10"
Depth: 63'-10"

ATTIC STORAGE

CLOSET

BEDROOM NO. 2
11'-2" X 13'-2"

OPEN TO BELOW

LOFT
8'-4" X 9'-2"

BATH

BEDROOM NO. 3
10'-8" X 14'-0"

CLOSET

Design T014

First Floor: 1,724 square feet
Second Floor: 700 square feet
Total: 2,424 square feet

◆ This cozy English cottage might be found hidden away in a European garden. All the charm of gables, stonework and multi-level rooflines combine to create this lovely exterior. To the left of the foyer, the sunlit dining room is highlighted by a dramatic tray ceiling and expansive windows with transoms. This room and the living room flow together to form one large entertainment area. The gourmet kitchen provides a work island, oversized pantry and a bright adjoining octagonal breakfast room with a gazebo ceiling. The great room features a pass-through wet bar, a fireplace and bookcases or an entertainment center. The master suite enjoys privacy at the rear of the home. An open-rail loft above the foyer leads to additional bedrooms with walk-in closets, private vanities and a shared bath. This home is designed with a basement foundation.

QUOTE ONE®

Cost to build? See page 246
to order complete cost estimate
to build this house in your area!

© American Home Gallery, Ltd.

185

Design 8773

First Floor: 1,226 square feet
Second Floor: 1,215 square feet
Total: 2,441 square feet

DESIGN BY
© Home Design
Services

◆ Stone accents, copper roofs and a balcony make this quaint two-story home hard to resist. The entry welcomes you into the foyer, which has a stone floor and a gently curving staircase. The formal living room adjoins the dining room through an arch framed by columns. A country kitchen with a work island and a bay window opens to the covered patio. The master suite dominates the second floor, with a balcony overlooking the front entry, a fireplace, a media wall, a private bath and a walk-in closet.

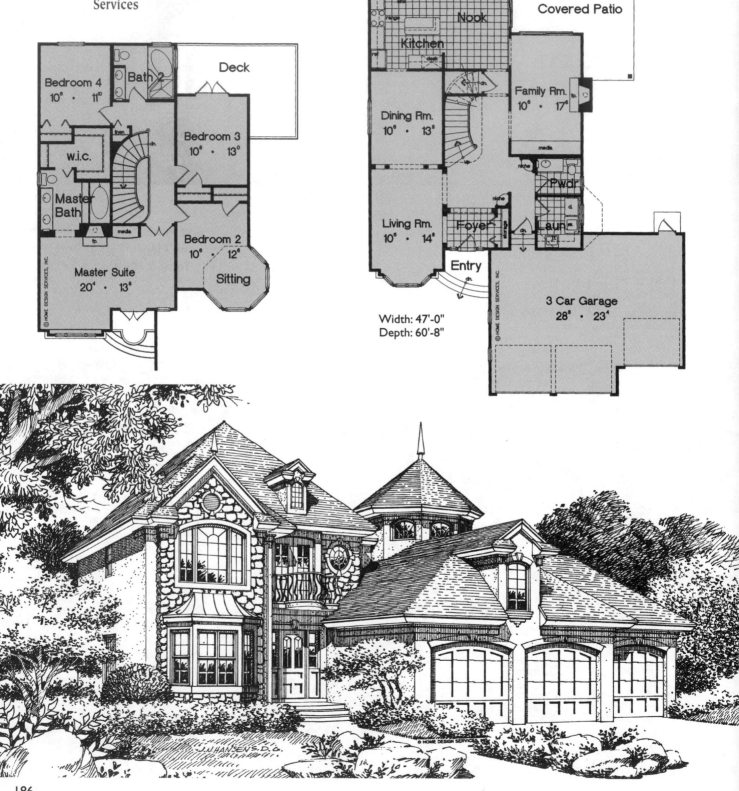

Bedroom 4
10⁶ · 11¹⁰

Bath 2

Deck

w.i.c.

linen

Bedroom 3
10⁶ · 13⁰

Master
Bath

media

fp.

Bedroom 2
10⁶ · 12⁶

Master Suite
20⁴ · 13⁸

Sitting

Nook

Covered Patio

Kitchen

range

ref

Dining Rm.
10⁶ · 13⁸

Family Rm.
10⁶ · 17⁶

media

Living Rm.
10⁶ · 14⁸

Foyer

Pwdr

Laun

niche

niche

storage

Entry

Width: 47'-0"
Depth: 60'-8"

3 Car Garage
28⁸ · 23⁴

186

Stately pilasters and a decorative balcony at a second-floor window adorn this ornate four-bedroom design. Inside the recessed entryway, columns define the formal dining room. Ahead is a great room with a fireplace, built-in bookshelves and access to the rear deck. A breakfast nook nestles in a bay window and joins an efficient island kitchen. The master suite on the first floor features a vaulted ceiling, walk-in closet and garden tub in the bath. Upstairs, a versatile loft, three additional bedrooms and two baths are connected by a hallway open to the great room below.

Design A133

First Floor: 1,751 square feet
Second Floor: 1,043 square feet
Total: 2,794 square feet

DESIGN BY
©Living Concepts
Home Planning

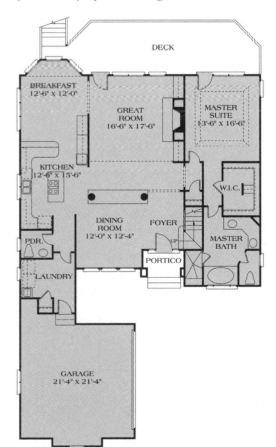

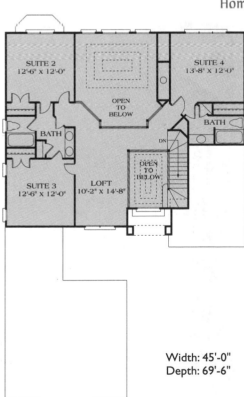

Width: 45'-0"
Depth: 69'-6"

Design S104

First Floor: 1,290 square feet
Second Floor: 1,241 square feet
Total: 2,531 square feet

◆ Varied rooflines and stone textures offset the stolidity of this impressive home, while the interior offers a grandeur to match the exterior. The raised covered entry opens to a two-story foyer, and beyond that there's abundant room for entertaining. A front parlor adjoins an elegant dining room through a wide archway. To the left, generous kitchen space includes a sink-top island. The morning room features a tray ceiling and built-in desk and opens to the spacious family room accented by a fireplace. The master suite is distinguished by details such as an octagonal tray ceiling, a bay window and double doors to the huge master bath that offers an oval tub, spacious twin vanities and a shower with a seat.

DESIGN BY
© Archival Designs, Inc.

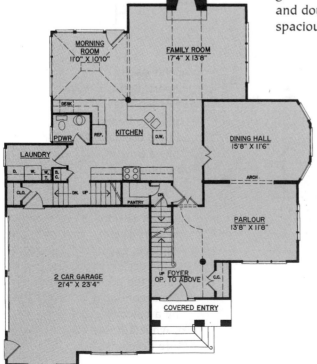

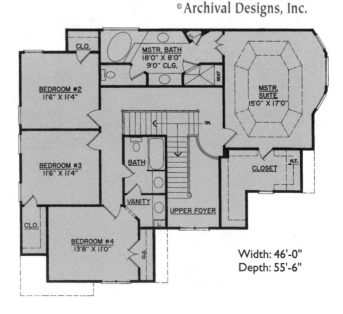

Width: 46'-0"
Depth: 55'-6"

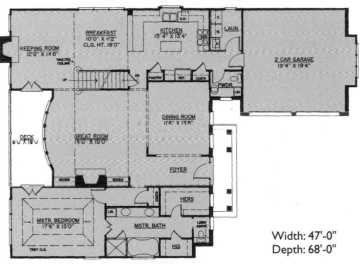

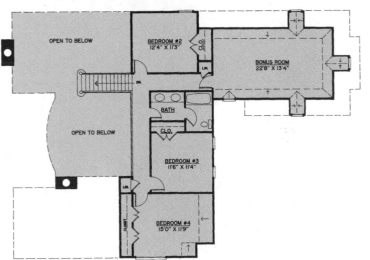

Width: 47'-0"
Depth: 68'-0"

Design S103

First Floor: 1,743 square feet
Second Floor: 762 square feet
Total: 2,505 square feet
Bonus Room: 361 square feet

DESIGN BY
©Archival Designs, Inc.

◆ The graceful sweep of the facade sets this home apart. Beneath the striking roofline is nestled a columned entry with double doors. The impressive floor plan is highlighted by a dramatic two-story great room that has a bow window overlooking the deck and built-in shelves flanking the fireplace. The kitchen provides a window sink and an island. The adjacent breakfast room features an 18-foot ceiling and flows into the two-story keeping room that offers a second fireplace, vaulted ceiling and double doors to the deck. The master bedroom also opens onto the deck through double doors. On the second floor, three bedrooms are joined by a balcony overlooking the great room, while a bonus room is available for future development.

Design M556

Square Footage: 2,139

DESIGN BY
©Andy McDonald
Design Group

◆ New Orleans gave this design its exterior charm and interior grandeur. Organized around a rear courtyard, the floor plan reflects a relaxed lifestyle. The entry opens into the foyer through double doors. The dining room, kitchen and family room are directly accessible. A work island, large pantry and breakfast area highlight the kitchen, while a fireplace, built-in shelves and double doors to the rear porch grace the family room. Three family bedrooms share a bath, with the laundry room and a linen closet nearby. The master bedroom extends past the courtyard and offers a compartmented bath and a walk-in closet.

Width: 47'-8"
Depth: 79'-0"

Design 7635
Square Footage: 1,417

Donald A. Gardner
Architects, Inc.

(optional)

GARAGE
20-8 x 22-0

storage

MASTER BED RM.
14-0 x 12-4

cl

skylight

master bath

walk-in closet

KITCHEN
13-4 x 9-0

w d lin. cl

walk-in closet

DINING
13-4 x 10-8

bath

BED RM.
10-4 x 12-4

BED RM.
10-4 x 11-0

cl

FOYER
6-0 x 5-8

GREAT RM.
13-4 x 17-0

fireplace

© 1996 Donald A. Gardner Architects, Inc.

PORCH

(cathedral ceiling)

Width: 46'-0"
Depth: 39'-0"

◆ Three box-bay windows dress up a hip roof on this stunning stucco exterior. A contemporary floor plan offers an open, airy feel with a cathedral ceiling and columns separating the dining room and great room. A fireplace warms this common area while two box-bay windows let in streams of natural light. The master suite boasts a U-shaped walk-in closet, a dressing area and a sensational private bath with a whirlpool tub and a skylight. A hall bath serves two family bedrooms—one with its own walk-in closet. The side-entry garage offers a service entrance to the kitchen and additional storage space.

B. NATHAN.

© 1996 Donald A. Gardner Architects, Inc.

191

Design B115

First Floor: 1,332 square feet
Second Floor: 454 square feet
Total: 1,786 square feet
Bonus Room: 209 square feet

DESIGN BY
©Greg Marquis
& Associates

◆ A touch of New Orleans is reflected in this brick and stucco facade with dramatic arched windows and a metal roof sheltering the front porch. Its strong architectural character continues inside with a great traffic flow. A large formal dining room welcomes guests just off the two-story foyer. The L-shaped kitchen is convenient to both this room and the breakfast room. A warming fireplace graces the spacious family room. The first-floor master suite is separated from the two family bedrooms located upstairs, providing a peaceful retreat. There's room to grow with the optional bonus room upstairs.

Width: 45'-0"
Depth: 40'-0"

◆ Fine stucco detailing, two Palladian windows and plenty of flexibility make this home stand out from the rest. Formal areas can be found to the right, starting with the spacious living area and flowing back to the formal dining room that displays a lovely bay window. Casual living takes place toward the back, with a large family room flooded with natural light from two walls of windows and warmed by a fireplace. The first-floor master suite provides privacy for the homeowners, while three upstairs bedrooms share a bath, a loft and a bonus room. Please specify basement, crawlspace or slab foundation when ordering.

Design X021

First Floor: 1,467 square feet
Second Floor: 846 square feet
Total: 2,313 square feet
Bonus Room: 489 square feet

DESIGN BY
© Jannis Vann &
Associates, Inc.

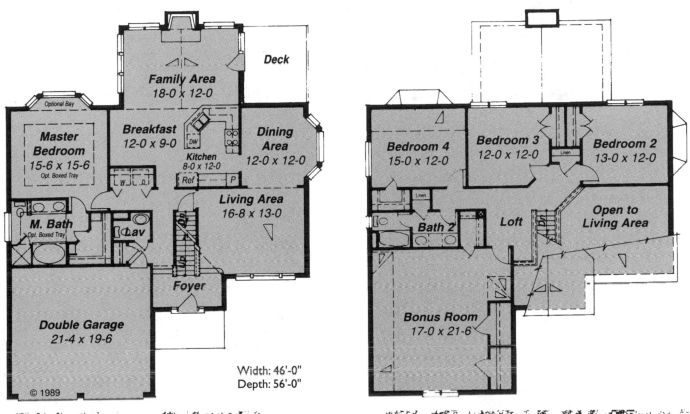

Family Area
18-0 x 12-0

Deck

Breakfast
12-0 x 9-0

Dining Area
12-0 x 12-0

Master Bedroom
15-6 x 15-6
Opt. Boxed Tray

Optional Bay

Kitchen
8-0 x 12-0

Ref | P

DW

Living Area
16-8 x 13-0

W | D

M. Bath
Opt. Boxed Tray

Lav

Foyer

Double Garage
21-4 x 19-6

© 1989

Width: 46'-0"
Depth: 56'-0"

Bedroom 4
15-0 x 12-0

Bedroom 3
12-0 x 12-0

Linen

Bedroom 2
13-0 x 12-0

Linen

Bath 2

Loft

Open to Living Area

Bonus Room
17-0 x 21-6

Design 7289

First Floor: 1,265 square feet
Second Floor: 395 square feet
Total: 1,660 square feet

DESIGN BY
©Design Basics, Inc.

◆ Gabled rooflines and a covered front porch create a welcoming elevation for this traditional design. The foyer opens to a formal dining room or optional parlor. The great room boasts a high ceiling, an extended-hearth fireplace and two transom windows. French doors open to the kitchen, which overlooks a convenient snack bar to share sunny views offered by the breakfast room. The master suite enjoys a secluded corner of the first-floor plan and offers a volume ceiling and a windowed whirlpool bath. Two secondary bedrooms upstairs share a full bath.

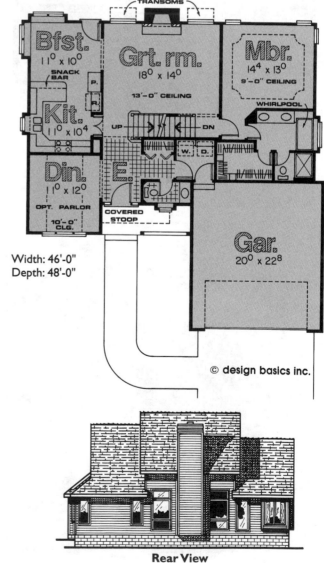

Width: 46'-0"
Depth: 48'-0"

© design basics inc.

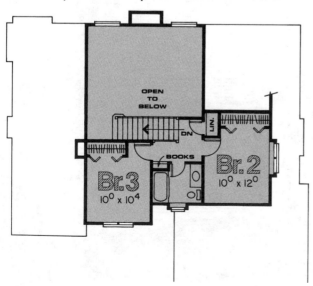

Rear View

Floor Plan Labels

Grt. rm. 14⁰ x 18⁰ — 10'-0" CEILING

Bfst. 11⁰ x 13⁰

TRANSOMS

SNACK BAR

Kit. 10² x 11⁰

PANT.

Mbr. 13⁰ x 15⁰ — 9'-6" CEILING

WHIRLPOOL

Din. 11⁰ x 13⁰

Gar. 21⁴ x 21⁸

COVERED STOOP

DN

UP

LIN.

Width: 46'-8"
Depth: 52'-4"

Br. 3 11⁰ x 12⁸

LINEN

Br. 2 12⁸ x 11⁰

SEAT

DN

PLANT SHELF

OPEN TO BELOW

Br. 4 11⁰ x 12⁸

DESIGN BY
© Design Basics, Inc.

Design 7330

First Floor: 1,406 square feet
Second Floor: 703 square feet
Total: 2,109 square feet

◆ Brick wing walls anchor this magnificent elevation while varying rooflines add a whimsical touch. The covered stoop opens to a two-story entry that provides a coat closet, a staircase and a powder room. A ten-foot ceiling, transom windows and a brick fireplace enhance the great room. The kitchen provides a corner sink, a large pantry, a snack bar and a breakfast room with a box-bay window and access to the back yard. The master suite includes a walk-in closet and a private bath that has a whirlpool tub and a double-bowl vanity. Three upstairs bedrooms share a full bath.

Rear View

Design Q323

Square Footage: 1,936

◆ Choose from two exteriors for this lovely home—details for both are included in the blueprints. The traditional version is brick veneer with horizontal wood siding. The alternate version is cool white stucco. Both versions encompass a light-filled floor plan. A transom window over the living room accentuates the vaulted ceiling, which stretches throughout the home. A pair of fluted columns crowned with a bridging plant shelf accents the entrance to the living room. Opposite are double doors to the covered deck and the patio. A glass-walled fireplace is shared by the living room and breakfast room. The L-shaped kitchen features a cooktop island. Bedrooms include a lovely master suite with a coffered ceiling, a sitting bay, deck access and a well appointed bath. Two family bedrooms and a full bath are to the front of the home.

DESIGN BY
©Select Home Designs

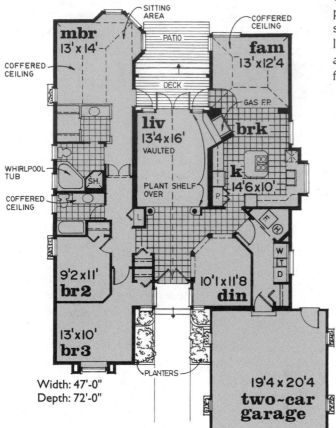

COFFERED CEILING

mbr 13' x 14'

SITTING AREA

PATIO

COFFERED CEILING

fam 13' x 12'4

COFFERED CEILING

DECK

GAS F.P.

liv 13'4 x 16' VAULTED

brk

WHIRLPOOL TUB

SH.

PLANT SHELF OVER

k 14'6 x 10'

P

COFFERED CEILING

L

F H

9'2 x 11'
br2

10'1 x 11'8
din

W T D

13' x 10'
br3

PLANTERS

19'4 x 20'4
two-car garage

Width: 47'-0"
Depth: 72'-0"

Alternate Elevation

Rear View

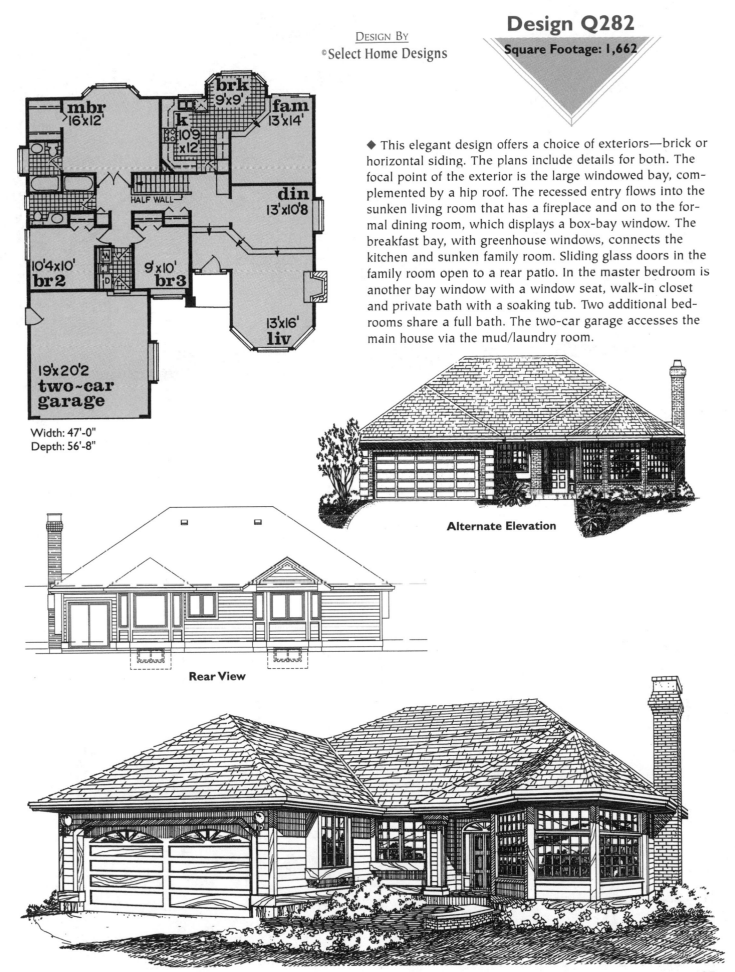

DESIGN BY
©Select Home Designs

Design Q282

Square Footage: 1,662

mbr 16x12'

brk 9'x9'

k 10'9 x12'

fam 13'x14'

din 13'x10'8

HALF WALL

10'4x10' **br2**

9'x10' **br3**

13'x16' **liv**

19'x20'2 **two-car garage**

Width: 47'-0"
Depth: 56'-8"

◆ This elegant design offers a choice of exteriors—brick or horizontal siding. The plans include details for both. The focal point of the exterior is the large windowed bay, complemented by a hip roof. The recessed entry flows into the sunken living room that has a fireplace and on to the formal dining room, which displays a box-bay window. The breakfast bay, with greenhouse windows, connects the kitchen and sunken family room. Sliding glass doors in the family room open to a rear patio. In the master bedroom is another bay window with a window seat, walk-in closet and private bath with a soaking tub. Two additional bedrooms share a full bath. The two-car garage accesses the main house via the mud/laundry room.

Alternate Elevation

Rear View

Design U182

First Floor: 1,176 square feet
Second Floor: 1,093 square feet
Total: 2,269 square feet

◆ Space abounds in this roomy, two-story plan. The entry offers access to all the first floor rooms, either directly or through the breakfast nook. The powder room is off the family room, which boasts a fireplace flanked by built-in shelves. The kitchen presents a box-bay window sink, an eating bar and a planning desk. The dining room and living room are open for easy entertaining. Upstairs, four bedrooms include the master suite and three family bedrooms that share a bath.

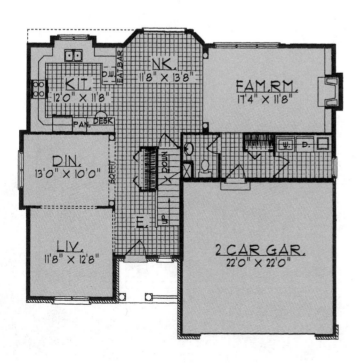

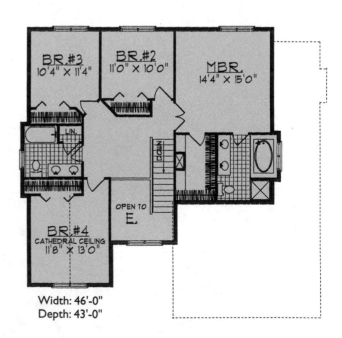

Width: 46'-0"
Depth: 43'-0"

Plan 5507

◆ This cozy one-story home fits comfortably on both narrow and corner lots. The covered front porch provides entrance into a combination living room and dining room that features a fireplace with a tiled hearth and a bay window. The central kitchen includes a large pantry and a snack bar to the family room, which offers a bay window and rear porch access. The two-car garage is built to shield the family bedrooms from street noise. While the secondary bedrooms share a full bath, the master bedroom includes its own bath, complete with a separate tub and shower, a double-bowl vanity and a large walk-in closet. The laundry room is conveniently located near all the bedrooms.

Width: 45'-0"
Depth: 64'-0"

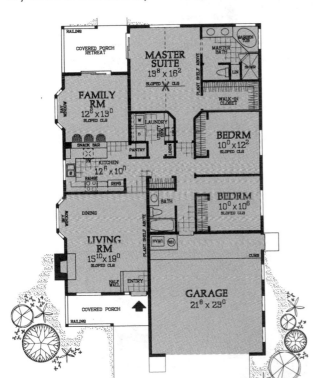

Width: 41'-0"
Depth: 64'-0"

Design 5507/5508

Square Footage: 1,676

Plan 5508

COPYRIGHT LARRY E. BELK

Design 8107

First Floor: 1,745 square feet
Second Floor: 708 square feet
Total: 2,453 square feet

◆ This lovely home features a traditional brick exterior. A large family room warmed by a fireplace provides access to the rear yard. The kitchen features an efficient work space containing a prep island, an eating bar and a corner walk-in pantry. An adjacent multi-window breakfast room provides a sunny space for casual meals. Two walk-in closets, a double vanity with seating, a corner whirlpool tub and a separate shower make the master suite an outstanding private retreat. Two family bedrooms and a full bath complete the second floor. Please specify crawlspace or slab foundation when ordering.

DESIGN BY
©Larry E. Belk
Designs

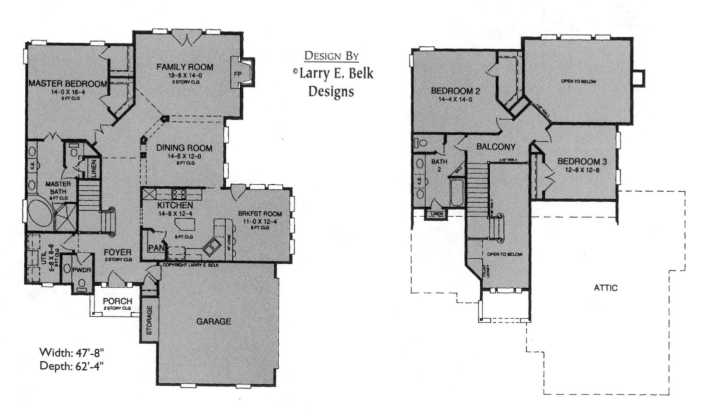

Width: 47'-8"
Depth: 62'-4"

◆ The grandeur of this stunning entry reflects the elegant comfort found inside the home. The dining room and two-story living room share a through fireplace. The kitchen offers a window seat and a pass-through to the dining room. The master bedroom provides a walk-in closet and a bath that has separate vanities. An angled staircase leads to the second floor, where a loft overlooks the living room and the foyer. Two bedrooms off the loft share a bath. Behind the closet of Bedroom 2, there's a secret storage room.

Design 8237

First Floor: 1,330 square feet
Second Floor: 698 square feet
Total: 2,028 square feet

DESIGN BY
© Larry E. Belk
Designs

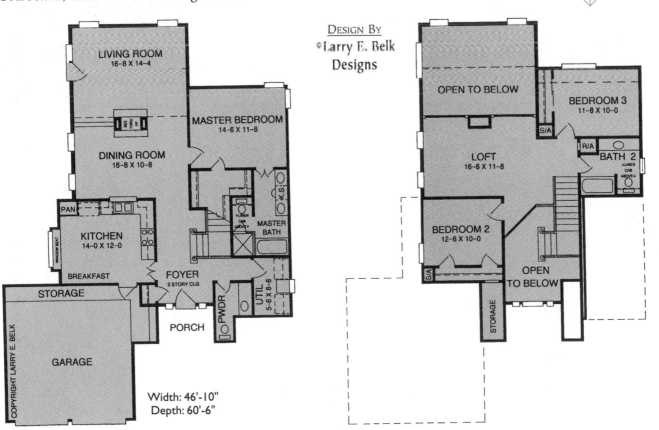

Width: 46'-10"
Depth: 60'-6"

Design Q473

First Floor: 852 square feet
Second Floor: 829 square feet
Total: 1,681 square feet
Bonus Room: 374 square feet

DESIGN BY
©Select Home Designs

◆ Options in this three-bedroom home include two elevations—both are included in the floor plans. There is also an optional two-car garage. The bonus room, which sits over the garage, may be finished at the initial building stages or left for future development. The main entry opens to a great room that has a nine-foot ceiling, corner gas fireplace and media-center alcove. A covered porch and sun deck in the rear are reached through a French door in the family room. Skylights brighten the upper hall.

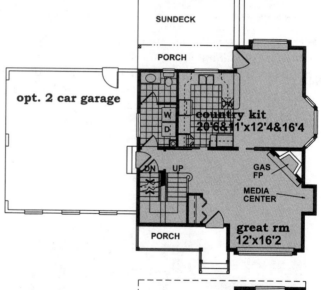

SUNDECK

PORCH

opt. 2 car garage

W
D

DW
country kit
20'6&11'x12'4&16'4

GAS
FP

MEDIA
CENTER

DN   UP

PORCH

great rm
12'x16'2

br3
10'X10'

br2
11'X10'

8' CLG
optional bonus rm
21'6X15'8

8' CLG

SKYLIGHT

DN

LIN   ST

WIC

mbr
12'X14'

Alternate Elevation

Rear View

Width: 50'-0"
Depth: 36'-0"

Rear View

DESIGN BY
©The Sater
Design Collection

Design 6698

First Floor: 1,684 square feet
Second Floor: 1,195 square feet
Total: 2,879 square feet
Bonus Space: 674 square feet

◆ Stunning New South charm flavors this reinterpretation of Key West island style. Asymmetrical rooflines set off a grand turret and a two-story bay that allows glorious views. Glass doors open the great room to a deck, while arch-top clerestory windows enhance the casual atmosphere with natural light. The gourmet kitchen boasts a center island with an eating bar for easy meals. A winding staircase leads to a luxurious master suite that features a morning kitchen and opens onto a private balcony. The gallery hall leads to a study, which enjoys wide views.

© The Sater Group, Inc.

covered veranda 22'-0" x 12'-0" avg.

sundeck 20'-0" x 8'-0" avg.

down

great room 21'-0" x 17'-0" 17'-4" clg.

corner fireplace

dining 12'-0" x 14'-0" 8'-0" clg.

kitchen

eating bar

10' x 18'

wetbar

arch   arch

guest 13'-0" x 16'-0" 8'-0" clg.

dn.   up

mid level foyer   util.

guest 13'-0" x 11'-6" avg. 8'-0" clg.

covered entry

Width: 45'-0"
Depth: 52'-0"

master balcony

© The Sater Group, Inc.

master 21'-0" x 20'-0" vaulted clg.

open to grand room below

am kitchen

overlook

2 sided fireplace

hers

dn.

hers

study 13'-0" x 18'-0" 8'-0" clg.

his

his

window seat

covered veranda 41'-0" x 12'-0" avg.

bonus room 24'-0 x 17'-6"

garage 19'-6" x 30'-0" avg.

tower foyer   up

bonus/ stor. 12'-8" x 20'-0"

© The Sater Group, Inc.

bike storage/ workshop

up

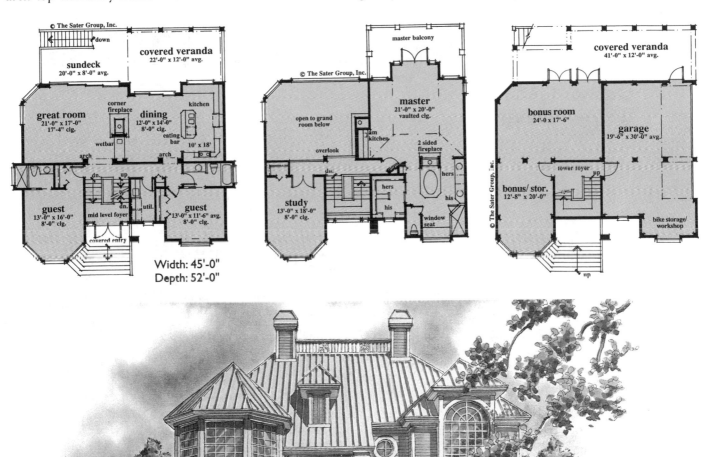

Design M186

Square Footage: 2,654

DESIGN BY
**©Fillmore
Design Group**

◆ This creative floor plan offers elegance, comfort and whimsy all at once! The main entry, at the side of the plan, opens to a gallery that leads to a delightful dining room/living room combination. This part of the floor plan flows from room to room at odd angles, giving options for creative furniture placement. A patio off the living room plays second fiddle to the adjacent conservatory that features a corner fireplace and two walls of windows. Another patio is accessed through the dining area. The triangular master bedroom enjoys a compartmented bath and a walk-in closet. Toward the front of the plan, a study opens through French doors and shares a bath with the second bedroom.

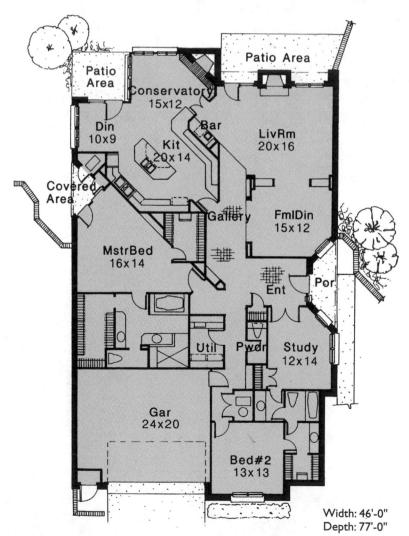

Width: 46'-0"
Depth: 77'-0"

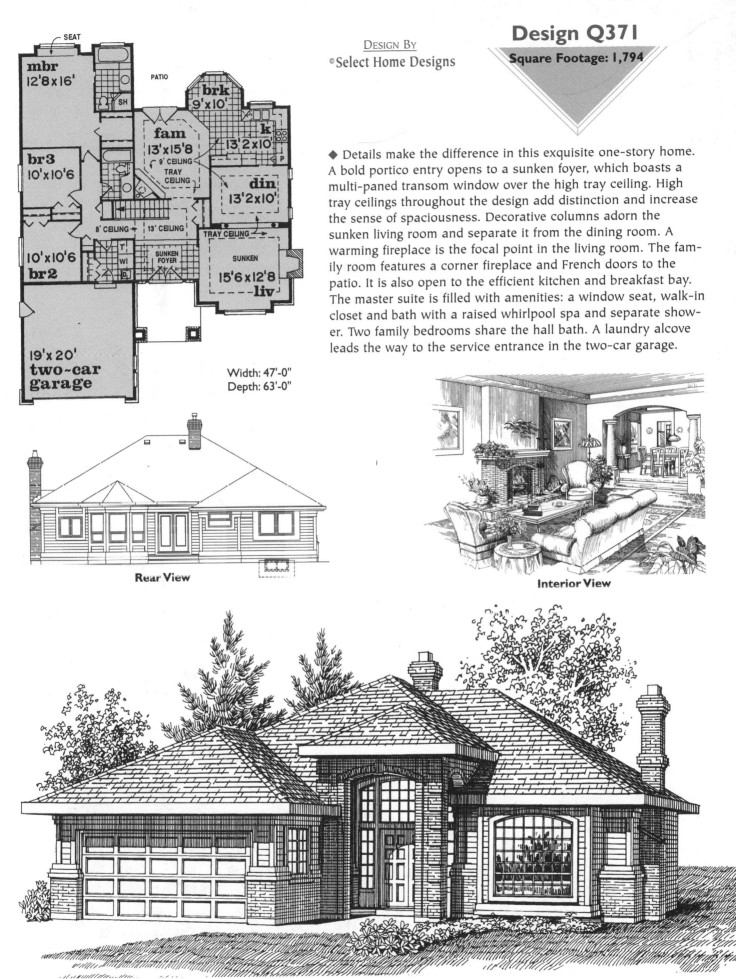

SEAT

mbr
12'8 x 16'

PATIO

brk
9' x 10'

fam
13' x 15'8

9' CEILING
TRAY
CEILING

k
13'2 x 10

P

br3
10' x 10'6

din
13'2 x 10

8' CEILING · 13' CEILING

TRAY CEILING

br2
10' x 10'6

WI

SUNKEN
FOYER

SH

SUNKEN
15'6 x 12'8
liv

19' x 20'
**two-car
garage**

Width: 47'-0"
Depth: 63'-0"

DESIGN BY
©Select Home Designs

Design Q371

Square Footage: 1,794

◆ Details make the difference in this exquisite one-story home. A bold portico entry opens to a sunken foyer, which boasts a multi-paned transom window over the high tray ceiling. High tray ceilings throughout the design add distinction and increase the sense of spaciousness. Decorative columns adorn the sunken living room and separate it from the dining room. A warming fireplace is the focal point in the living room. The family room features a corner fireplace and French doors to the patio. It is also open to the efficient kitchen and breakfast bay. The master suite is filled with amenities: a window seat, walk-in closet and bath with a raised whirlpool spa and separate shower. Two family bedrooms share the hall bath. A laundry alcove leads the way to the service entrance in the two-car garage.

Rear View

Interior View

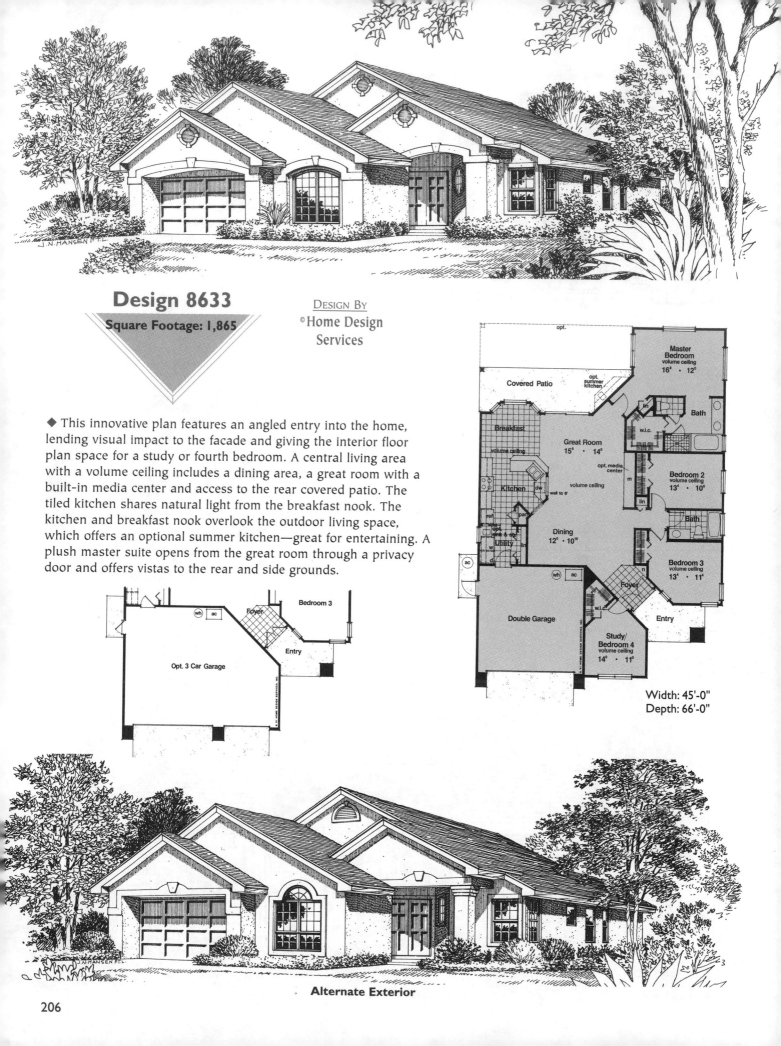

Design 8633

Square Footage: 1,865

DESIGN BY
© Home Design
Services

◆ This innovative plan features an angled entry into the home, lending visual impact to the facade and giving the interior floor plan space for a study or fourth bedroom. A central living area with a volume ceiling includes a dining area, a great room with a built-in media center and access to the rear covered patio. The tiled kitchen shares natural light from the breakfast nook. The kitchen and breakfast nook overlook the outdoor living space, which offers an optional summer kitchen—great for entertaining. A plush master suite opens from the great room through a privacy door and offers vistas to the rear and side grounds.

Opt. 3 Car Garage

Foyer
Bedroom 3
Entry
wh
ac

Covered Patio
opt.
opt. summer kitchen
Master Bedroom
volume ceiling
16⁸ · 12⁰
Bath
w.i.c.
Breakfast
volume ceiling
Great Room
15⁸ · 14⁰
opt. media center
Bedroom 2
volume ceiling
13⁴ · 10⁰
Kitchen
dw
wall to 8'
volume ceiling
m
lin
Bath
ref
opt. sink & etc.
pan
Dining
12⁰ · 10¹⁰
Bedroom 3
volume ceiling
13⁴ · 11⁴
Utility
lin
Foyer
wh
ac
w.i.c.
Double Garage
Study/
Bedroom 4
volume ceiling
14⁰ · 11⁰
Entry
ac

Width: 45'-0"
Depth: 66'-0"

Alternate Exterior

SPACIOUS DESIGNS FOR NARROW LOTS

Design 9621

First Floor: 1,325 square feet
Second Floor: 453 square feet
Total: 1,778 square feet

DESIGN BY
Donald A. Gardner
Architects, Inc.

◆ Here's a compact design with all the amenities available in larger plans but with little wasted space. In addition, a wraparound covered porch, a front Palladian window, dormers and rear arched windows provide exciting visual elements to the exterior. The spacious great room offers a fireplace, a cathedral ceiling and clerestory windows. A second-level balcony overlooks this gathering area. The kitchen is centrally located and features a pass-through to the great room. Besides the generous master suite with a full bath, two family bedrooms are located on the second level. They share a full bath that has a double vanity. Please specify basement or crawlspace foundation when ordering.

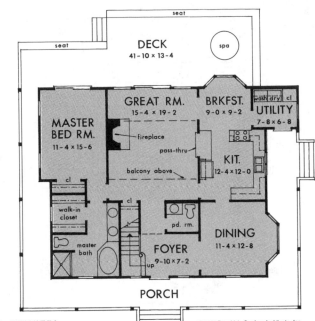

© 1991 Donald A. Gardner Architects, Inc.

Rear View

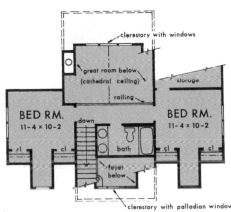

Width: 48'-4"
Depth: 51'-10"

© 1991 Donald A. Gardner Architects, Inc.

© 1992 Donald A. Gardner Architects, Inc.

Design 9693

Square Footage: 1,677

DESIGN BY
**Donald A. Gardner
Architects, Inc.**

Width: 49'-10"
Depth: 89'-6"

◆ Arched windows and a wraparound porch display a sense of elegance not usually seen in a plan this size. Cathedral ceilings grace both the great room and the bedroom/study, while tray ceilings appear in the dining room and master bedroom. The open kitchen design allows for a serving island, which is convenient to the breakfast area, dining room and rear porch. The master suite has direct access to the deck and features a walk-in closet and a master bath with a double-bowl vanity, shower and whirlpool tub. A covered breezeway connects the garage to the house.

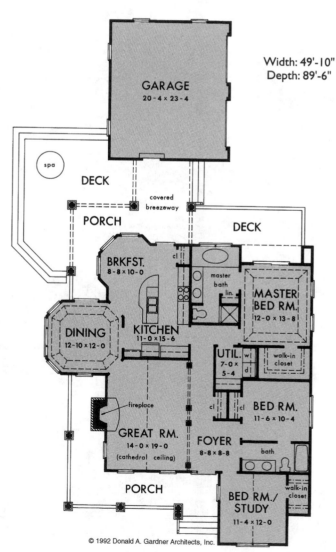

© 1992 Donald A. Gardner Architects, Inc.

© 1995 Donald A. Gardner Architects, Inc.

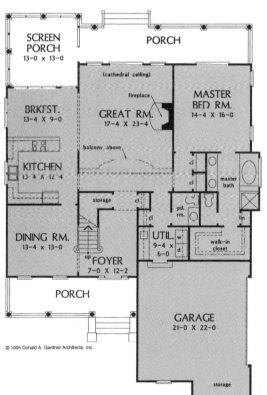

SCREEN PORCH
13-0 x 13-0

PORCH

(cathedral ceiling)

BRKFST.
13-4 x 9-0

GREAT RM.
17-4 X 23-4

fireplace

MASTER BED RM.
14-4 x 16-0

balcony above

KITCHEN
13-4 X 12-4

cl

cl

master bath

storage

cl

pd. rm.

lin

DINING RM.
13-4 x 13-0

up

FOYER
7-0 X 12-2

UTIL.
9-4 x 6-0

w
d

walk-in closet

PORCH

GARAGE
21-0 X 22-0

storage

© 1995 Donald A. Gardner Architects, Inc.

Width: 48'-0"
Depth: 71'-4"

◆ Indoor and outdoor living are a pure delight with this two-story farmhouse. Front and rear covered porches are further complemented by a separate screened porch off the breakfast area. The large great room is graced by a fireplace and has access to the rear porch. A spacious U-shaped kitchen separates formal and informal dining areas. Also located on the first floor is the luxurious master bedroom. It provides abundant closet space, a separate shower and tub and access to the rear porch. Upstairs, two family bedrooms share a full bath. The large bonus room could be a future guest suite or games room.

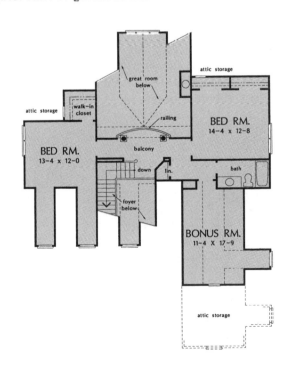

great room below

attic storage

attic storage

walk-in closet

railing

BED RM.
14-4 x 12-8

BED RM.
13-4 x 12-0

balcony

down

lin.

bath

stairs

down

foyer below

BONUS RM.
11-4 x 17-9

attic storage

DESIGN BY
Donald A. Gardner
Architects, Inc.

Design 9777

First Floor: 1,732 square feet
Second Floor: 758 square feet
Total: 2,490 square feet

Design 7613

First Floor: 1,116 square feet
Second Floor: 442 square feet
Total: 1,558 square feet

DESIGN BY
Donald A. Gardner
Architects, Inc.

◆ This two-story design is a great starter home for a young family with plans to grow or for empty-nesters with a need for guest rooms. The two secondary bedrooms and shared bath on the second floor could also be used as office space. Additional attic storage is available as family needs expand. On the first floor, the front porch is perfect for relaxing. Inside, the foyer opens through a columned entrance to the large great room with its cathedral ceiling and fireplace. A tray-ceilinged dining room offers access to both the deck and the central kitchen. The laundry room and a powder room are nearby. The master bedroom is located at the rear of the home for privacy and features a walk-in closet and a corner whirlpool tub.

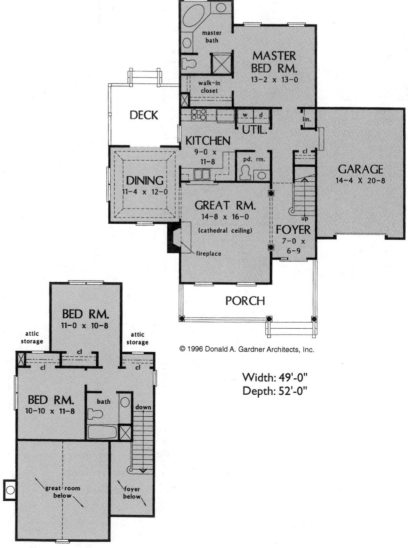

© 1996 Donald A. Gardner Architects, Inc.

Width: 49'-0"
Depth: 52'-0"

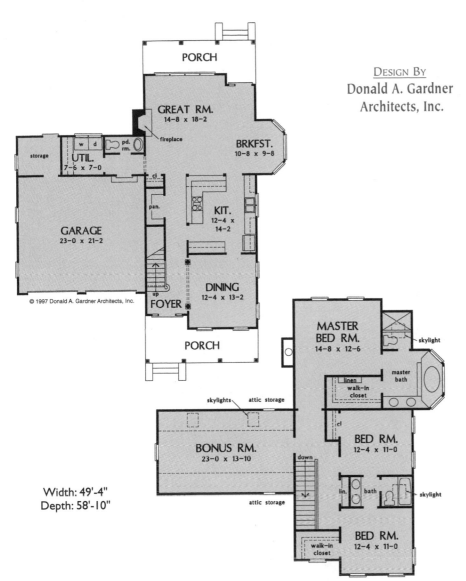

PORCH

GREAT RM.
14-8 x 18-2

fireplace

BRKFST.
10-8 x 9-8

storage

UTIL.
7-6 x 7-0

w d

pd. rm.

cl

GARAGE
23-0 x 21-2

pan.

KIT.
12-4 x 14-2

DINING
12-4 x 13-2

up

FOYER

PORCH

© 1997 Donald A. Gardner Architects, Inc.

MASTER BED RM.
14-8 x 12-6

skylight

linen
walk-in closet

master bath

skylights   attic storage

cl

BED RM.
12-4 x 11-0

BONUS RM.
23-0 x 13-10

down

lin.   bath   skylight

attic storage

BED RM.
12-4 x 11-0

walk-in closet

Width: 49'-4"
Depth: 58'-10"

DESIGN BY
Donald A. Gardner
Architects, Inc.

Design 7642

First Floor: 1,113 square feet
Second Floor: 960 square feet
Total: 2,073 square feet
Bonus Room: 338 square feet

◆ A perfect blend of country and traditional, this family home provides a compact floor plan. Columns define the entry to the dining room, while the kitchen, breakfast bay and great room remain open for a casual atmosphere. A wonderful walk-in pantry is included in the kitchen. A fireplace, a wall of windows and access to the rear porch highlight the great room. A half-bath and utility room are conveniently located nearby. Upstairs, the master suite has a luxurious bath with a bay window. Two additional bedrooms share a bath. Both baths are brightened by skylights.

© 1997 Donald A. Gardner Architects, Inc.

Design B152

First Floor: 1,128 square feet
Second Floor: 631 square feet
Total: 1,759 square feet

◆ Three columns introduce an elegant entry that leads to the spacious family room in this three-bedroom home. The family room offers a warming fireplace and a curving staircase to the second floor. The L-shaped kitchen is enhanced by a window sink, a work island, direct access to the dining area and a door to the rear porch. Located on the main level for privacy, the master bedroom presents a walk-in closet and a private bath with a skylight. Upstairs, a loft is available for studying or reading, while two secondary bedrooms share a bath. Note the bonus area off the loft.

DESIGN BY
©Greg Marquis
& Associates

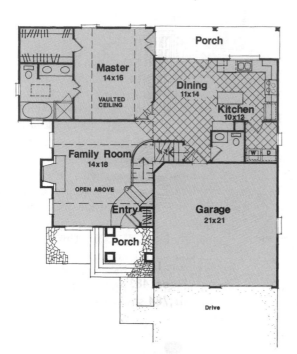

Porch
Master
14x16
VAULTED CEILING
Dining
11x14
Kitchen
10x12
Family Room
14x18
OPEN ABOVE
W D
Entry
Garage
21x21
Porch
Drive

Width: 46'-0"
Depth: 46'-0"

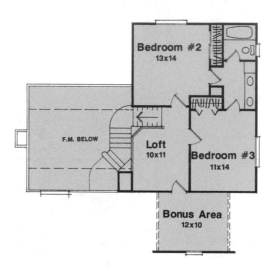

Bedroom #2
13x14
F.M. BELOW
Loft
10x11
Bedroom #3
11x14
Bonus Area
12x10

B. NATHAN.

DESIGN BY
**Donald A. Gardner
Architects, Inc.**

Design 9768

**First Floor: 1,301 square feet
Second Floor: 483 square feet
Total: 1,784 square feet**

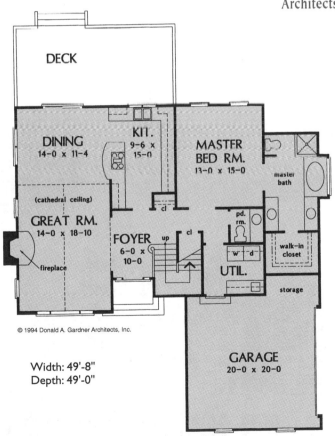

DECK

DINING
14-0 x 11-4

KIT.
9-6 x 15-0

MASTER BED RM.
13-0 x 15-0

master bath

(cathedral ceiling)

GREAT RM.
14-0 x 18-10

fireplace

FOYER
6-0 x 10-0

up

cl

cl

pd. rm.

w / d

walk-in closet

UTIL.

storage

GARAGE
20-0 x 20-0

Width: 49'-8"
Depth: 49'-0"

◆ Horizontal siding and arched windows dress up this compact traditional home. To the left of the foyer is a great room enhanced by a cheerful fireplace and a cathedral ceiling. The adjacent dining room and kitchen make this casual living space ideal for formal and informal gatherings. The master suite is located on the first floor for privacy and features a walk-in closet and a luxurious bath with a double vanity, a whirlpool tub and a separate shower. A utility room and a powder room complete the first floor. Upstairs, two bedrooms—each with a walk-in closet—share a full bath.

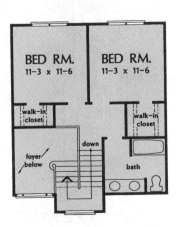

BED RM.
11-3 x 11-6

BED RM.
11-3 x 11-6

walk-in closet

walk-in closet

foyer below

down

bath

213

Design 2864
Square Footage: 1,387

LD

◆ Projecting the garage to the front of a house is economical in two ways. One, it reduces the required lot size, and two, it protects the interior from street noise. Many other characteristics of this design also deserve mention. The interior kitchen has an adjacent breakfast room and a snack bar, while the study offers a wet bar. The gathering room—with a sloped ceiling—features a warming fireplace. Sliding glass doors in the formal dining room, study and master suite open to the terrace. Skylights add cheer to the hall bath and the master bath, which is designed to pamper the homeowners.

QUOTE ONE®

Cost to build? See page 246
to order complete cost estimate
to build this house in your area!

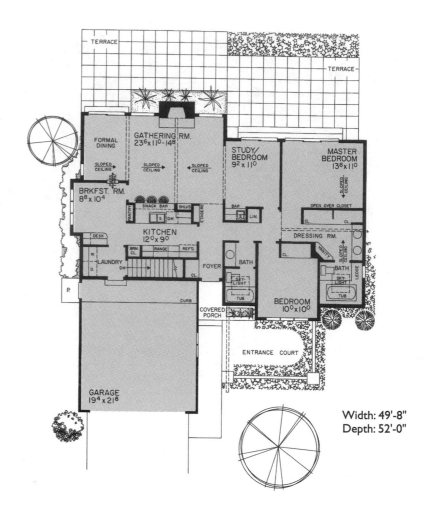

Width: 49'-8"
Depth: 52'-0"

Design 9403

Design 9403/9403A

Square Footage: 1,565

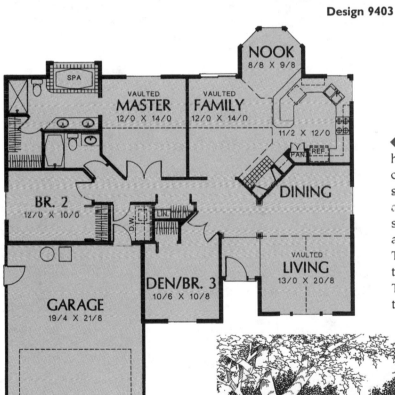

NOOK
8/8 X 9/8

SPA

VAULTED
MASTER
12/0 X 14/0

VAULTED
FAMILY
12/0 X 14/0

11/2 X 12/0

REF.
PAN.

DINING

BR. 2
12/0 X 10/0

D.W. LIN.

VAULTED
LIVING
13/0 X 20/8

DEN/BR. 3
10/6 X 10/8

GARAGE
19/4 X 21/8

Width: 50'-0"
Depth: 52'-10"

DESIGN BY
© Alan Mascord
Design Associates, Inc.

◆ If you're looking for a traditional-styled ranch home, this one with front-facing gables and a combination of cedar shingles and vertical cedar siding may be just right for you. Or chose the alternate elevation with a hip roof and horizontal siding. The vaulted living room faces the street and is set off with a gorgeous Palladian window. The family room—with an angled fireplace—and the master bedroom also feature vaulted ceilings. Through French doors near the entry is a den that could be used as a third bedroom.

Design 9403A

Design Y021

Square Footage: 1,654

DESIGN BY
© The Nelson
Group, Inc.

◆ Varying rooflines and a multi-pane arched window turn this compact design into a neighborhood showplace. The arched window belongs to the great room, which opens through a pair of columns off the foyer. The kitchen—with a snack bar—is straight ahead and beyond it is the dining room with a wall of windows and access to the rear porch. The master suite is on the right of the plan along with the laundry room, a service entrance to the garage and storage space. Two family bedrooms on the opposite side of the plan share a bath and a linen closet. Please specify crawl-space or slab foundation when ordering.

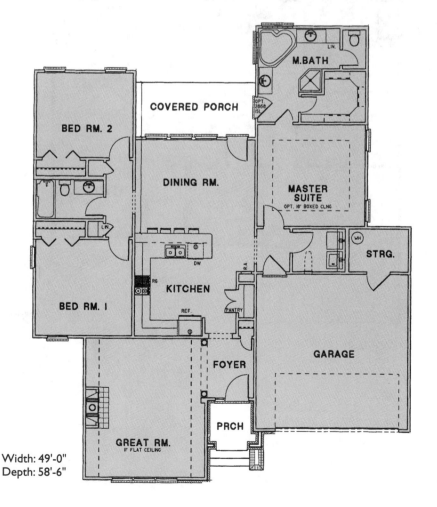

Width: 49'-0"
Depth: 58'-6"

© American Home Gallery, Ltd.

R.DENTRI

DESIGN BY
Stephen Fuller

Design T093
Square Footage: 1,770

BREAKFAST
10'-10" X 9'-4"

MASTER BATH

KITCHEN
0'-10" X 11'-0"

MASTER BEDROOM
13'-0" X 15'-6"

FAMILY ROOM
14'-0" X 19'-0"

W.I.C.

BEDROOM NO.2
12'-0" X 10'-6"

BATH

FOYER
7'-6" X 18'-0"

DINING ROOM
13'-6" X 10'-6"

BEDROOM NO.1
12'-0" X 10'-0"

STOOP

Width: 49'-6"
Depth: 47'-0"

◆ Perfect for a hillside lot, this split-level plan has three distinct levels: basement, sleeping and living. The basement is undeveloped space but could be used for any number of activities if needed. The sleeping level holds two family bedrooms and a master suite with plenty of amenities. Its bath is truly opulent with a corner tub, double bowl vanity, walk-in closet and separate shower. The family bedrooms each have a walk-in closet and share a full bath. The living areas include a formal dining room, family room and kitchen with a wide breakfast bay. Special items include the fireplace in the family room and the decorative columns that separate the dining and family rooms. This home is designed with a basement foundation.

© American Home Gallery, Ltd.

Design T141

First Floor: 1,921 square feet
Second Floor: 716 square feet
Total: 2,637 square feet

DESIGN BY
Stephen Fuller

◆ Gracious living possibilities are evident in this delightful two-story home. A front porch framed by columns offers passage into the foyer. To the right, a well proportioned living room combines with a rear-facing dining room to provide fine formal living. An angled kitchen easily serves the dining room as well as the informal areas. Sleeping accommodations include a private master suite located at the front. It enjoys a smartly zoned bath with two walk-in closets, a double-bowl vanity, a compartmented toilet and a separate tub and shower. Upstairs, two family bedrooms have private access to a sectioned bath. This home is designed with a basement foundation.

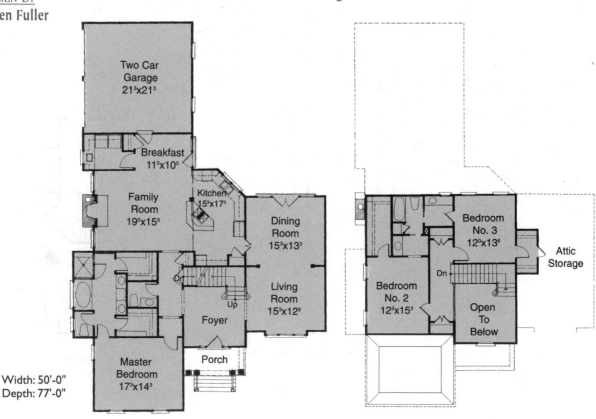

Width: 50'-0"
Depth: 77'-0"

Design P454

First Floor: 1,306 square feet
Second Floor: 1,276 square feet
Total: 2,582 square feet

DESIGN BY
©Frank Betz
Associates, Inc.

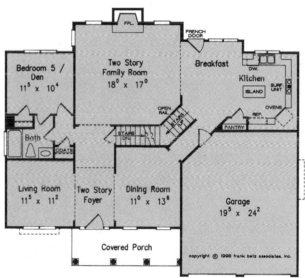

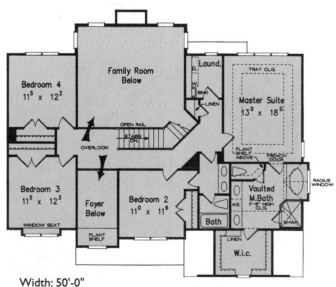

♦ A two-story family room with a balcony overlook is the stamp of a luxurious life-style. This floor plan also includes a fireplace in the family room and an overlook to the two-story foyer. The living room and dining room are to the front of the plan with a gallery hall that leads back to the breakfast room and U-shaped kitchen. One family bedroom is on the first floor with private access to a hall bath. The laundry room is on the second floor, where the master suite includes a compartmented bath that offers separate vanities. Three family bedrooms share a compartmented hall bath that contains a double-bowl vanity. Please specify basement, crawlspace or slab foundation when ordering.

Width: 50'-0"
Depth: 45'-4"

Design T078

Square Footage: 1,770

DESIGN BY
Stephen Fuller

Width: 48'-0"
Depth: 47'-0"

QUOTE ONE®

Cost to build? See page 246
to order complete cost estimate
to build this house in your area!

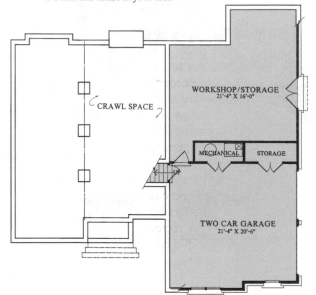

◆ The country-cottage styling of this stately brick home includes brick detailing framing the front entry and windows. Gables and a multi-level roof help create the soft charm of this design. The foyer provides views into the large great room, with a warming hearth, and the dining room that has a vaulted ceiling. From the great room, enter the kitchen and adjacent breakfast room. The second level, up a half flight of stairs, offers two bedrooms that share a bath. The master bedroom is entered through double doors and features a tray ceiling and French doors leading to a private deck. The generous master bath is complete with His and Hers vanities, a garden tub and a walk-in closet. This home is designed with a basement foundation.

© American Home Gallery, Ltd.

Design T109

Square Footage: 1,770

BREAKFAST
11'-4" X 7'-4"

GREAT ROOM
14'-0" X 19'-6"

DECK

DN

W.I.C.

MASTER
BEDROOM
12'-6" X 16'-0"

MASTER
BATH

KITCHEN
11'-4" X 12'-0"

W.I.C.

W.I.C.

UP

DN

FOYER
5'-0" X 8'-8"

POWDER

LAUNDRY

BEDROOM NO. 3
12'-0" X 11'-0"

DINING ROOM
11'-4" X 12'-6"

COAT

STOOP

BATH

BEDROOM NO. 2
12'-9" X 11'-9"

QUOTE ONE®
Cost to build? See page 246
to order complete cost estimate
to build this house in your area!

Width: 48'-0"
Depth: 47'-5"

DESIGN BY
Stephen Fuller

◆ Perfect for a sloping lot, this European one-story plan offers privacy for the sleeping quarters by placing them a few steps up from the living area. The master suite is secluded off the central hallway, partitioned by double doors, which are echoed by lovely French doors to the rear deck and by doors leading to a sumptuous bath with a garden tub. Secondary bedrooms or guest quarters share a full bath that provides a double-bowl vanity. A spacious great room with a centered fireplace offers rear deck access and opens to the breakfast room that displays a box-bay window. The well-appointed U-shaped kitchen easily serves both formal and casual eating areas. The lower level offers bonus space that may be developed for recreational use. This home is designed with a basement foundation.

© American Home Gallery, Ltd.

Design X031

First Floor: 1,268 square feet
Second Floor: 1,333 square feet
Total: 2,601 square feet

◆ Visual delight in this European-style home includes a high hip roof, multi-pane windows and a glass entry with a transom. Formal elegance is captured in the two-story living area featuring a warming fireplace and deck access. The open kitchen and breakfast area is accented by a bay window. One family bedroom with a full bath is on the first floor. Two other family bedrooms are on the second floor where they share a bath, a loft and a linen cloet. The luxurious master suite includes a private bath and two walk-in closets.

DESIGN BY
©Jannis Vann & Associates, Inc.

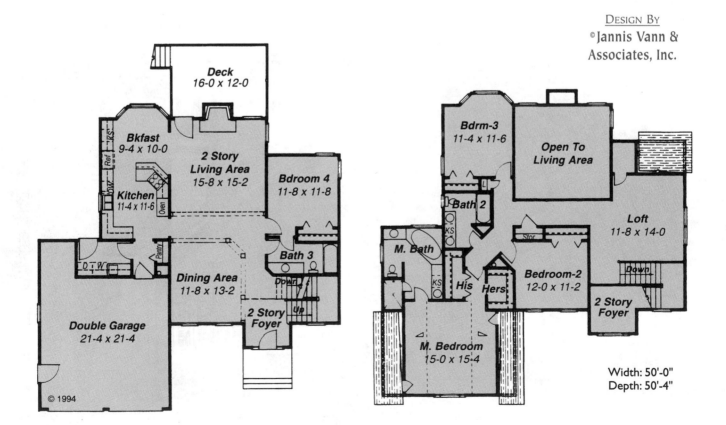

Width: 50'-0"
Depth: 50'-4"

Sundeck
28-0 x 12-0

Sundeck
22-0 x 12-0

Dining Rm.
13-0 x 12-6

Family Rm.
14-6 x17-6

Kitchen
11-0 x 14-6

Brkfst.
10-6 x 12-6

Stor. Pant. Desk Ref.

Lnd.

W. D. Lav. Cls.

Two Story Foyer
13-0 x 15-6

Line of Balcony

Living Rm.
14-6 x 11-6

Double Garage
21-4 x 26-8

© Jannis Vann & Associates, Inc. 19900

Width: 50'-0"
Depth: 67'-0"

Bdrm. 4
13-0 x 10-2

Bdrm.3
11-6 x 12-6

Bath 2

Open to Foyer

Bdrm.2
11-6 x 11-0

Balcony

Master Bdrm.
21-4 x 14-6

M.Bath
w/ Barrel Ceil.

Design X047

First Floor: 1,348 square feet
Second Floor: 1,303 square feet
Total: 2,651 square feet

DESIGN BY
©Jannis Vann &
Associates, Inc.

◆ With the wonderful sun deck across the back of this home, you won't have to move to the Mediterranean to get your fill of sunshine. The stucco exterior, keystone arches and hip roof add to the European flavor of the design. The living room opens off the two-story foyer, which also provides access to the family room and the dining room. A through-fireplace and built-ins separate and enhance the family and living rooms. Informal meals will be enjoyed in the large breakfast area or on the sun deck, which is accessible from all three rooms at the rear of the house. A stairway in the two-story foyer leads to the second floor, which houses three family bedrooms and a master suite that presents a whirlpool tub, separate vanities, two closets and a small private balcony.

Design B556

First Floor: 1,036 square feet
Second Floor: 861 square feet
Total: 1,897 square feet

DESIGN BY
©Studer Residential
Designs, Inc.

◆ The refined exterior of this distinctive plan introduces a charming and liveable home. Highlights of the floor plan include a furniture alcove in the formal dining room, a high ceiling and French doors topped with arched windows in the great room, a wood rail at the split stairs, a walk-in pantry in the kitchen and a laundry room that's roomy enough to do a family-size laundry with helpers. The view from the foyer through the great room to the rear yard enhances indoor-outdoor entertaining, while the spacious kitchen and breakfast area encourage relaxed gatherings. The second floor features a window seat at the top of the stairs and a computer desk in the extra-large hallway. For your relaxation, the deluxe master suite offers a whirlpool tub, separate vanities, a shower stall and a spacious walk-in closet.

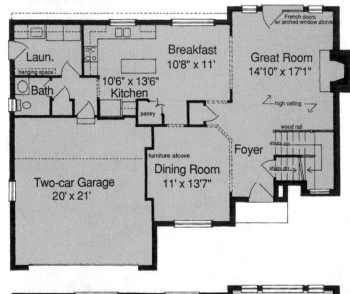

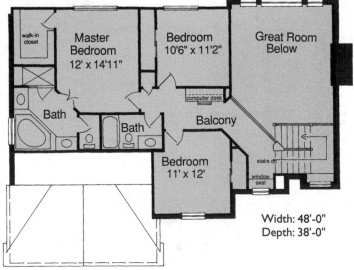

Width: 48'-0"
Depth: 38'-0"

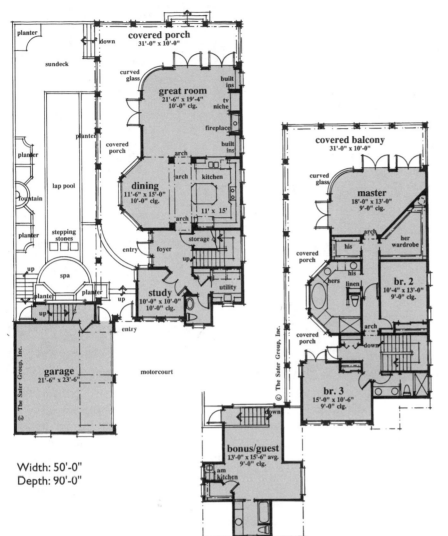

Design 6688

First Floor: 1,293 square feet
Second Floor: 1,154 square feet
Total: 2,447 square feet
Bonus Room: 426 square feet

DESIGN BY
©The Sater
Design Collection

◆ This home is a water-lover's dream. Spend long summer hours on the sun deck and in the pool and spa, surrounded by fountains and planters. The covered porch and balcony offer additional outdoor retreats. Distinctive arches, sturdy columns and cornice detailing characterize the exterior. To the right of the entry foyer are the study and powder room; to the left are the kitchen and formal living areas. The dining room is open to the kitchen through archways. Arches also accent the threshold to the great room, where the main interest is an unusual curved window. Upstairs, a second curved window accents the master suite, which also features double doors and two walk-in closets.

Width: 50'-0"
Depth: 90'-0"

Design 8008

First Floor: 1,700 square feet
Second Floor: 668 square feet
Total: 2,368 square feet

◆ Designed for a narrow, golf-course lot, this two-story home mixes wood shingles, brick and a swoop roof to achieve a bungalow look. The garage location can be moved to the right to open up the elevation and make the home appear larger from the curb. Ten-foot ceilings downstairs and the use of glass across the rear make an open and spacious floor plan. The large master suite on the left of the home includes an enormous walk-in closet perfect for built-ins. Upstairs, two bedrooms and a bath complete the plan. Please specify basement or crawlspace foundation when ordering.

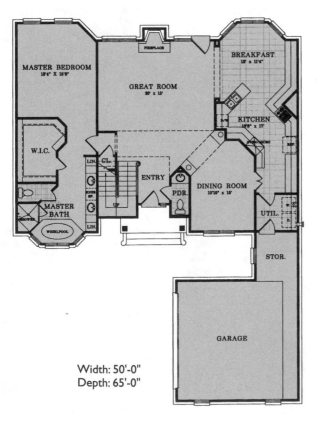

Width: 50'-0"
Depth: 65'-0"

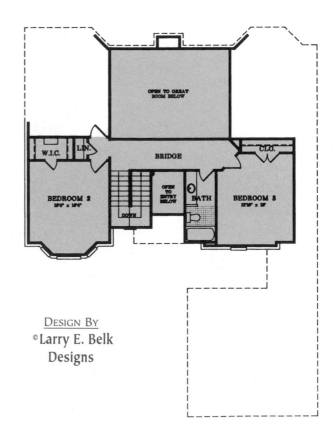

DESIGN BY
©Larry E. Belk
Designs

◆ A tower, variable rooflines and a covered front porch combine to give this home a wonderful ambiance. Enter through the mid-level foyer and head either up to the main floor or down to the garage. On the main level, a spacious, light-filled great room shares a fireplace with the dining room. A study offers access to the rear covered veranda. The efficient island kitchen is open to the dining room, offering ease in entertaining. A guest suite with a private full bath completes this level. Upstairs, a second guest room, with its own bath, and a deluxe master suite, with a covered balcony, sun deck, walk-in closet and lavish bath, complete this wonderful plan.

Design 6682

First Floor: 1,617 square feet
Second Floor: 991 square feet
Total: 2,608 square feet
Bonus Room: 532 square feet

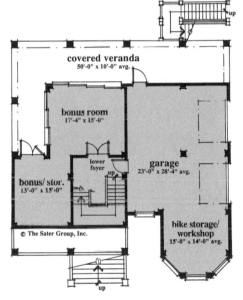

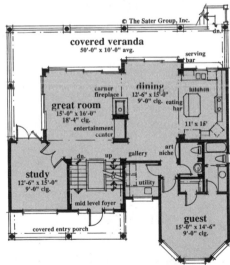

DESIGN BY
©The Sater
Design Collection

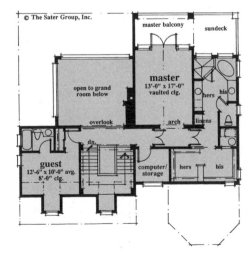

Width: 50'-0"
Depth: 53'-0"

Rear View

227

Design S144

First Floor: 1,396 square feet
Second Floor: 1,584 square feet
Total: 2,980 square feet

DESIGN BY
©Archival Designs, Inc.

◆ Classic symmetry and four elegant columns make this home a gem that others will stop to admire. Inside, luxury is evident by the dimensions of each room. The foyer is flanked by a large, yet cozy library to the right and a gracefully formal living room to the left. It's just a couple of steps up into the formal dining room, making this area fine for entertaining. Casual-living areas are located toward the rear of the home, with a huge family room connecting to an interestingly shaped breakfast room and near an efficient kitchen. The bedrooms upstairs include a deluxe master suite with a sumptuous private bath.

Width: 48'-0"
Depth: 52'-0"

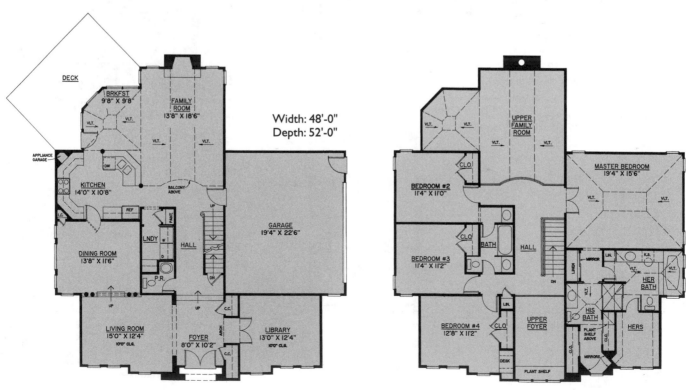

♦ If ever a home was designed with a Fifth Avenue address in mind, this is it. The grand entry opens to a wide foyer that presents two coat closets and angled stairs to the second floor. Through a pair of columns to the left, enter the dining room. Or go to the right into the formal living room that has an elegant bay window. The angled kitchen opens to the breakfast room and two-story great room. Stairs to the second floor go up to the wide loft that overlooks the great room. The laundry room on this floor serves the three family bedrooms with their two baths and the master suite.

Design S141

First Floor: 1,332 square feet
Second Floor: 1,331 square feet
Total: 2,663 square feet

DESIGN BY
© Archival Designs, Inc.

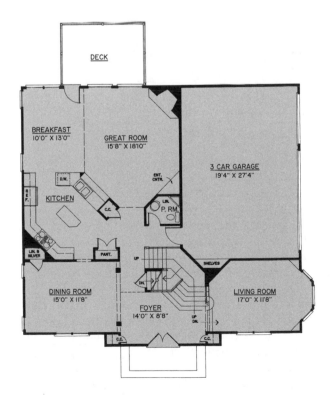

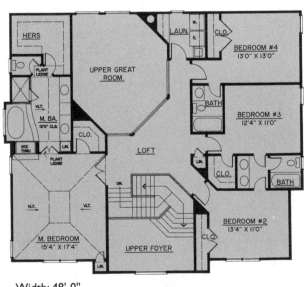

Width: 48'-0"
Depth: 42'-0"

© American Home Gallery, Ltd.

Design T148

First Floor: 1,540 square feet
Second Floor: 1,430 square feet
Total: 2,970 square feet

DESIGN BY
Stephen Fuller

Width: 49'-3"
Depth: 69'-3"

Two Car Garage
21³x21³

Family Room
20⁰x14⁶

Breakfast
13³x14⁶

Kitchen
13³x13⁹

Living Room
14³x11⁹

Foyer

Dining Room
14⁰x12⁶

Porch

Dn

Up

Master Bedroom
14⁶x14⁶

Dn

Bedroom No. 2
14³x11⁹

Bedroom No. 3
14⁰x12⁶

◆ Wood siding, shutters and a columned front porch add Colonial touches to this two-story home. From the foyer, pairs of columns frame openings to the formal living room on the left and the formal dining room on the right. The family room is located to the rear of the plan and combines well with the breakfast room and the kitchen for a spacious informal gathering area. The second floor contains the sleeping areas: a master suite and two secondary bedrooms that share a full bath. The master bedroom features two walk-in closets and a master bath with separate vanities, a whirlpool tub and a separate shower. This home is designed with a basement foundation.

Two Car
Garage
21³x21³

Storage

Kitchen
12⁵x13⁶

Breakfast
15⁹x9³

Family
Room
16⁰x19³

Office

Dn

Up

Dining
Room
12⁵x15⁹

Foyer

Living
Room
13⁶x13⁹

Porch

Design T150

First Floor: 1,601 square feet
Second Floor: 1,520 square feet
Total: 3,121 square feet

DESIGN BY
Stephen Fuller

Master
Bedroom
14³x21³

Bedroom
No. 4
13⁹x12⁹

Dn

Bedroom
No. 2
12⁶x13⁶

Bedroom
No. 3
13⁹x11³

Width: 49'-3"
Depth: 74'-3"

◆ George Washington slept here. Not really, but he may have slept in a home with a Georgian exterior such as this. The amenity-filled interior begins through the front entry—flanked by columns—to the formal dining room on the left and the formal living room on the right. Adjacent to the living room is the family room. An L-shaped kitchen is highlighted by a center cooktop island and access to an office tucked behind the powder room. The second floor contains three family bedrooms, two full baths and the master suite. This home is designed with a basement foundation.

© American Home Gallery, Ltd.

Plan 5504

Design 5504/5505
First Floor: 1,147/1,160 square feet
Second Floor: 877 square feet
Total: 2,024/2,037 square feet
Bonus Room: 193 square feet

DESIGN BY
© Home Planners

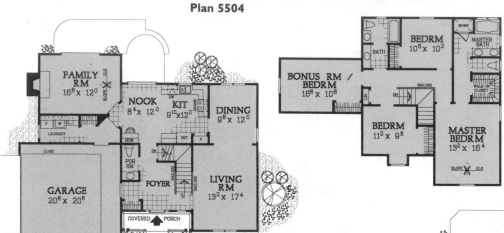

Width: 50'-0"
Depth: 41'-10"

QUOTE ONE®
Cost to build? See page 246
to order complete cost estimate
to build this house in your area!

◆ Subtle differences distinguish these two homes. Design 5504 features a covered porch that bids welcome into an interior that lends itself to quiet casual living or to entertaining with style. Design 5505 offers two bay windows that bathe the foyer with natural light, setting the tone for the warmth and comfort found throughout. Both floor plans offer a large living room that leads to the rear dining room and kitchen. A large family room with a fireplace and a convenient laundry room are nearby. On the second floor, the master bedroom features an amenity-filled bath with a separate shower and tub, a double-bowl vanity and a walk-in closet. Three family bedrooms—or two bedrooms and a bonus room—share a full bath that has separate vanities.

Width: 50'-0"
Depth: 43'-6"

Plan 5505

DECK

BREAKFAST
11'-4" X 7'-6"

GREAT ROOM
14'-0" X 16'-0"

KITCHEN
11'-4" X 12'-0"

W.I.C.

MASTER
BEDROOM
12'-6" X 16'-0"

MASTER
BATH

W.I.C.

W.I.C.

UP

DN.

FOYER
5'-0" X
8'-6"

LNDR.

POWDER

BEDROOM NO. 3
12'-0" X 11'-0"

DINING ROOM
11'-4" X 13'-6"

BATH

BEDROOM NO. 2
12'-4" X 11'-4"

Width: 48'-0"
Depth: 47'-5"

Design T137

Square Footage: 1,770

DESIGN BY
Stephen Fuller

◆ A wood frame, weatherboard siding
and stacked stone give this home its
country-cottage appeal. The concept
is reinforced by the double arches
over the front porch, the Colonial
balustrade and the roof-vent dormer.
Inside, the foyer leads to the great
room and the dining room. The well-
planned kitchen easily serves the
breakfast room. A rear deck makes
outdoor living extra-enjoyable. Three
bedrooms include a master suite with
a tray ceiling and a luxurious bath.
The two secondary bedrooms share a
compartmented bath. This home is
designed with a basement foundation.

233

Design P458

First Floor: 1,559 square feet
Second Floor: 475 square feet
Total: 2,034 square feet
Bonus Room: 321 square feet

DESIGN BY
©Frank Betz
Associates, Inc.

◆ Not quite seven gables, this home will end up being named "The House of the Five Gables." In spite of the historical image brought up by the many gables, this is an up to-date plan with the latest amenities in home design. The great room and dining room are both vaulted and separated by the bright breakfast room and the gourmet kitchen. The master bedroom's tray ceiling adds a sense of space, which already exists in the compartmented master bath. Bedroom 4, next to a full bath, could be a study or home office. The laundry room is nearby as is a staircase to the second floor, where there are two bedrooms, a bath and an optional bonus room. Please specify basement or crawlspace foundation when ordering.

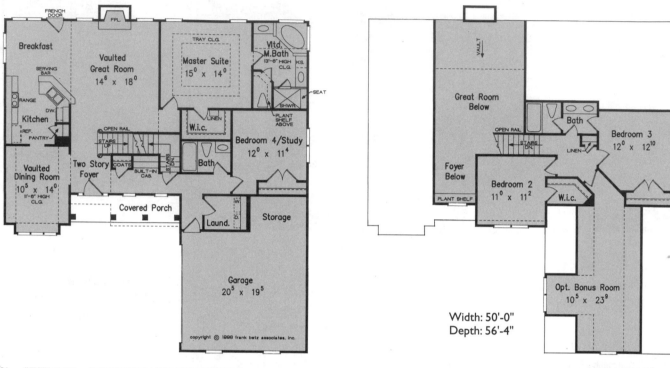

Width: 50'-0"
Depth: 56'-4"

© American Home Gallery, Ltd.

◆ The Country French charm of the gambrel roof, combined use of stone and wood and the segmented arch window detailing is irresistible. The two-story foyer with staircase and tray ceiling gives a first impression of space and style. The living and dining rooms are complemented by large window areas, a fireplace and detailed columns. The art of cooking is emphasized in the kitchen, with a work island and charming breakfast bay that opens into a large family room featuring a fireplace and wet bar. A second staircase from the family room allows easy access to the second floor. On the upper level, the hallway leads to two bedrooms, both with large closets and a shared bath. A fourth bedroom has a walk-in closet and private bath. The master suite includes a wide sitting bay, a luxurious master bath, an extensive walk-in closet and an exercise room or hideaway.

Design T059

First Floor: 1,530 square feet
Second Floor: 1,515 square feet
Total: 3,045 square feet

DESIGN BY
Stephen Fuller

Width: 49'-8"
Depth: 57'-4"

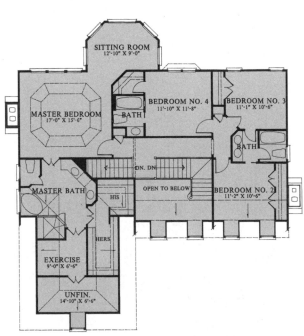

Design 2657

First Floor: 1,217 square feet
Second Floor: 868 square feet
Total: 2,085 square feet

L

DESIGN BY
©Home Planners

◆ Deriving its design from traditional Cape Cod style, this facade features clapboard siding, small-pane windows and a transom-lit entrance flanked by carriage lamps. A central chimney services two fireplaces, one in the country kitchen and the other in the formal living room, which is removed from the flow of traffic. The master suite is located to the left of the upstairs landing. Two family bedrooms and a full bathroom complete the second floor.

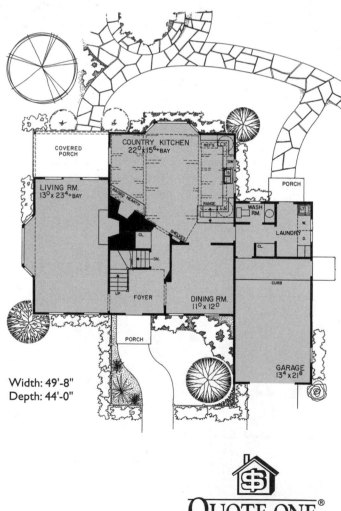

Width: 49'-8"
Depth: 44'-0"

Cost to build? See page 246
to order complete cost estimate
to build this house in your area!

236

Design S163

First Floor: 1,296 square feet
Second Floor: 468 square feet
Total: 1,764 square feet
Bonus Room: 169 square feet

DESIGN BY
© Archival Designs, Inc.

Width: 49'-0"
Depth: 46'-0"

◆ Don't let the simple exterior design of this home fool you—the interior opens up with sophisticated flair. The dining room is defined from the foyer and grand salon by a series of decorative columns. The great room, with a vaulted ceiling and fireplace, shares a snack bar with the kitchen. The octagonal breakfast room will be flooded with natural light. A laundry room, huge walk-in pantry and powder room complete this side of the first floor. The master suite takes up the opposite side and features a bath and a walk-in closet. Two bedrooms on the second floor share a bath.

Design 2707

Square Footage: 1,267

L|D

DESIGN BY
©Home Planners

◆ Here is a charming Early American adaptation that will serve as a picturesque and practical retirement or starter home. The design has an efficient floor plan and can be built economically. The living area, highlighted by the raised-hearth fireplace, is spacious. The kitchen features eating space and easy access to the garage and basement. The dining room is adjacent to the kitchen and views the rear yard. The bedroom wing offers three bedrooms and two full baths. Don't miss the sliding doors to the terrace from the living room and the master bedroom. Plentiful storage units include a pantry cabinet in the eating area of the kitchen.

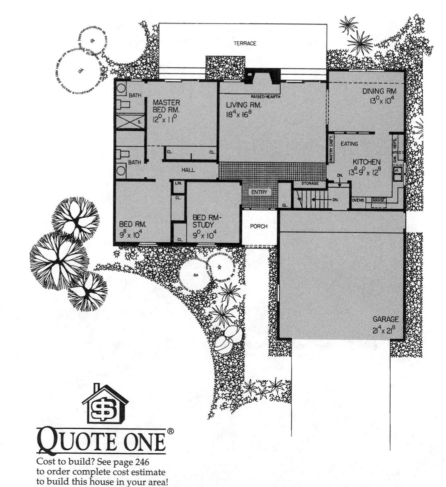

QUOTE ONE®

Cost to build? See page 246
to order complete cost estimate
to build this house in your area!

Width: 46'-0"
Depth: 50'-0"

PLAY TERRACE

DINING TERRACE

FAMILY RM. 19⁴ x 12⁰
BEAMED CEILING

BREAKFAST 8⁰ x 11⁰

SINK   D.W.
KIT. 10²x11⁰
RANGE

DINING RM. 11⁰ x 11⁰

DN.

BOOKS

GARAGE 19⁴ x 21⁰

REF'G OVEN
PANTRY

DN
CL.
PDR. RM.
CL.

ENTRY
UP

LIVING RM. 18⁰ x 13⁰

PORCH

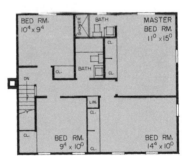

BED RM. 10⁴ x 9⁴
SHOWER BATH
MASTER BED RM. 11⁰ x15⁰
CL.
DN
BATH
CL.
CL.
LIN.
CL.
BED RM. 9⁴ x 10⁰
CL.
BED RM. 14⁴ x 10⁰

Width: 50'-0"
Depth: 34'-10"

DESIGN BY
©Home Planners

Design 1957

First Floor: 1,042 square feet
Second Floor: 780 square feet
Total: 1,822 square feet

L D

◆ When you order blueprints for this design, you will receive details for the construction of all three exteriors pictured. Whichever exterior you decide to build, the floor plan will be essentially the same except for the location of the windows. The first floor contains a living room, dining room and U-shaped kitchen with a breakfast area. A beamed ceiling and a fireplace highlight the family room. Both the family room and dining room access the terrace through sliding glass doors. There's also a powder room on this floor. Four bedrooms and two full baths—one with a stall shower—are upstairs.

Alternate Exterior

QUOTE ONE®

Cost to build? See page 246 to order complete cost estimate to build this house in your area!

Alternate Exterior

Design 5514/5515

First Floor: 718 square feet
Second Floor: 691/700 square feet
Total: 1,409/1,418 square feet

DESIGN BY
© Home Planners

◆ This narrow-lot design utilizes every square foot and provides plenty of flexibility and room for growth. Perhaps the country warmth supplied by the dormers and covered front porch of Design 5514 makes this home everything you've ever wanted. Or maybe the Colonial appeal of Design 5515 speaks to your strong, independent spirit. Whichever you choose, the combination living/dining room provides ample room for entertaining, both formal and informal. The L-shaped kitchen serves this living area with ease. Upstairs, two family bedrooms share a full bath, while the master bedroom features a private bath, a walk in closet and a bayed sitting area.

Design 5514

Width: 49'-8"
Depth: 34'-0"

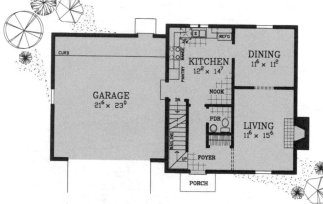

Width: 49'-8"
Depth: 32'-6"

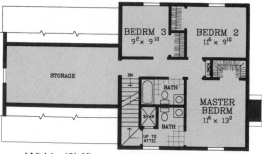

Design 5515

240

◆ Brick and siding combine with gabled rooflines and a graceful covered wraparound porch to capture your imagination. Inside, the foyer is flanked by a formal dining room and a formal living room. Casual living takes place to the rear of the home, with a spacious family room featuring a fireplace and access to the rear sun deck. The efficient L-shaped kitchen offers a walk-in pantry and an adjacent breakfast bay. Upstairs is the sleeping zone, complete with a large master suite, designed to pamper the homeowners, and three secondary bedrooms that share a full hall bath.

Design X017
First Floor: 1,038 square feet
Second Floor: 1,034 square feet
Total: 2,072 square feet

DESIGN BY
©Jannis Vann &
Associates, Inc.

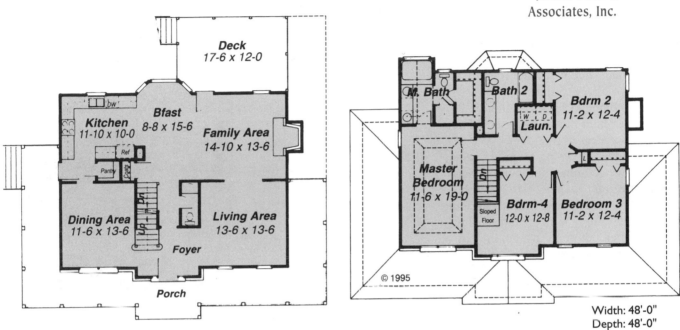

Width: 48'-0"
Depth: 48'-0"

Design Y022
Square Footage: 1,598

DESIGN BY
© The Nelson
Group, Inc.

◆ Multi-pane windows and a brick exterior with stone trim give a textured effect to this appealing plan. The two-car garage houses both a storage room and laundry room, which opens to the L-shaped kitchen. A combination work island and snack bar adds to the kitchen's efficiency, and there's access to the rear patio and a breakfast bay. The dining room is defined by decorative columns, but is otherwise open to the great room, which gives the option of a boxed ceiling. The master suite also opens to the rear patio and includes a compartmented bath. Two family bedrooms share a hall bath.

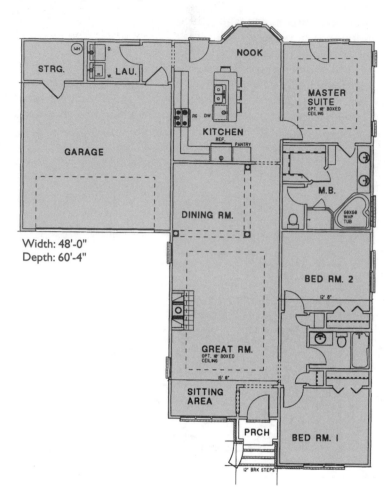

Width: 48'-0"
Depth: 60'-4"

FREILING

◆ A transitional design, this home superbly presents an elegantly gabled entry and contemporty windows. The entry offers a coat closet, a staircase and a wide opening to the living room, where there's a fireplace flanked by narrow windows. Along a short hallway, there's a powder room and a laundry room. The country kitchen and family room open through double doors to a screened porch—just right for outdoor dining. Sleeping quarters are upstairs and include a master suite and two family bedrooms that share a hall bath.

Design U220

First Floor: 1,132 square feet
Second Floor: 797 square feet
Total: 1,929 square feet

DESIGN BY
©Ahmann Design, Inc.

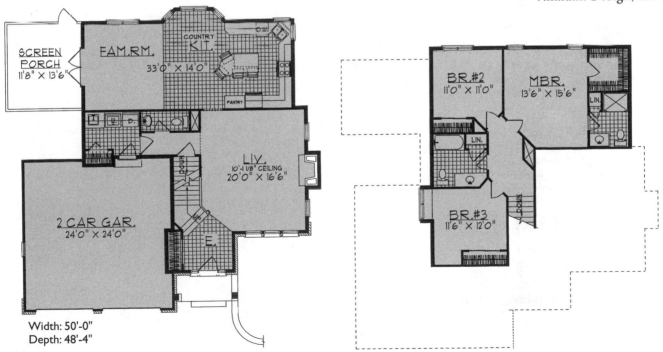

SCREEN PORCH
11'8" X 13'6"

FAM. RM.

COUNTRY KIT.
33'0" X 14'0"

PANTRY

LIV.
10'-1 1/8" CEILING
20'0" X 16'6"

2 CAR GAR.
24'0" X 24'0"

Width: 50'-0"
Depth: 48'-4"

BR. #2
11'0" X 11'0"

MBR.
13'6" X 15'6"

LIN.

BR. #3
11'6" X 12'0"

When You're Ready To Order . . .

Let Us Show You Our Home Blueprint Package.

Building a home? Planning a home? Our Blueprint Package has nearly everything you need to get the job done right, whether you're working on your own or with help from an architect, designer, builder or subcontractors. Each Blueprint Package is the result of many hours of work by licensed architects or professional designers.

QUALITY

Hundreds of hours of painstaking effort have gone into the development of your blueprint set. Each home has been quality-checked by professionals to insure accuracy and buildability.

VALUE

Because we sell in volume, you can buy professional-quality blueprints at a fraction of their development cost. With our plans, your dream home design costs only a few hundred dollars, not the thousands of dollars that custom architects charge.

SERVICE

Once you've chosen your favorite home plan, you'll receive fast, efficient service whether you choose to mail or fax your order to us or call us toll free at 1-800-521-6797. For customer service, call toll free 1-888-690-1116.

SATISFACTION

Over 50 years of service to satisfied home plan buyers provide us unparalleled experience and knowledge in producing quality blueprints. What this means to you is satisfaction with our product and performance.

ORDER TOLL FREE 1-800-521-6797

After you've looked over our Blueprint Package and Important Extras on the following pages, simply mail the order form on page 221 or call toll free on our Blueprint Hotline: 1-800-521-6797. We're ready and eager to serve you. For customer service, call toll free 1-888-690-1116.

Each set of blueprints is an interrelated collection of detail sheets which includes components such as floor plans, interior and exterior elevations, dimensions, cross-sections, diagrams and notations. These sheets show exactly how your house is to be built.

Among the sheets included may be:

Frontal Sheet
This artist's sketch of the exterior of the house gives you an idea of how the house will look when built and landscaped. Large ink-line floor plans show all levels of the house and provide an overview of your new home's livability, as well as a handy reference for deciding on furniture placement.

Foundation Plan
This sheet shows the foundation layout

SAMPLE PACKAGE

including support walls, excavated and unexcavated areas, if any, and foundation notes. If slab construction rather than basement, the plan shows footings and details for a monolithic slab. This page, or another in the set, may include a sample plot plan for locating your house on a building site.

Detailed Floor Plans
These plans show the layout of each floor of the house. Rooms and interior spaces are carefully dimensioned and keys are given for cross-section details provided later in the plans. The positions of electrical outlets and switches are shown.

House Cross-Sections
Large-scale views show sections or cut-aways of the foundation, interior walls, exterior walls, floors, stairways and roof details. Additional cross-sections may show important changes in floor, ceiling or roof heights or the relationship of one level to another. Extremely valuable for construction, these sections show exactly how the various parts of the house fit together.

Interior Elevations
Many of our drawings show the design and placement of kitchen and bathroom cabinets, laundry areas, fireplaces, bookcases and other built-ins. Little "extras," such as mantelpiece and wainscoting drawings, plus moulding sections, provide details that give your home that custom touch.

Exterior Elevations
These drawings show the front, rear and sides of your house and give necessary notes on exterior materials and finishes. Particular attention is given to cornice detail, brick and stone accents or other finish items that make your home unique.

Frontal Sheet

Foundation Plans

Detailed Floor Plans

Exterior Elevations

Interior Elevations

House Cross-Sections

245

*I*mportant Extras To Do The Job Right!

Introducing eight important planning and construction aids developed by our professionals to help you succeed in your home-building project.

MATERIALS LIST

(Note: Because of the diversity of local building codes, our Materials List does not include mechanical materials.)

For many of the designs in our portfolio, we offer a customized materials take-off that is invaluable in planning and estimating the cost of your new home. This Materials List outlines the quantity, type and size of materials needed to build your house (with the exception of mechanical system items). Included are framing lumber, windows and doors, kitchen and bath cabinetry, rough and finish hardware, and much more. This handy list helps you or your builder cost out materials and serves as a reference sheet when you're compiling bids. A Materials List cannot be ordered before blueprints are ordered.

SPECIFICATION OUTLINE

This valuable 16-page document is critical to building your house correctly. Designed to be filled in by you or your builder, this book lists 166 stages or items crucial to the building process. It provides a comprehensive review of the construction process and helps in, choosing materials. When combined with the blueprints, a signed contract, and a schedule, it becomes a legal document and record for the building of your home.

QUOTE ONE®

Summary Cost Report / Materials Cost Report

A new service for estimating the cost of building select designs, the Quote One® system is available in two separate stages: The Summary Cost Report and the Materials Cost Report.

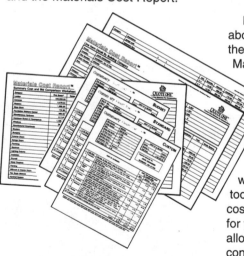

The Summary Cost Report is the first stage in the package and shows the total cost per square foot for your chosen home in your zip-code area and then breaks that cost down into various categories showing the costs for building materials, labor and installation. The total cost for the report (which includes three grades: Budget, Standard and Custom) is just $19.95 for one home, and additionals are only $14.95. These reports allow you to evaluate your building budget and compare the costs of building a variety of homes in your area.

Make even more informed decisions about your home-building project with the second phase of our package, our Materials Cost Report. This tool is invaluable in planning and estimating the cost of your new home. The material and installation (labor and equipment) cost is shown for each of over 1,000 line items provided in the Materials List (Standard grade), which is included when you purchase this estimating tool. It allows you to determine building costs for your specific zip-code area and for your chosen home design. Space is allowed for additional estimates from contractors and subcontractors, such as for mechanical materials, which are not included in our packages. This invaluable tool is available for a price of $110 ($120 for a Schedule E plan), which includes a Materials List. A Materials Cost Report cannot be ordered before blueprints are ordered.

The Quote One® program is continually updated with new plans. If you are interested in a plan that is not indicated as Quote One®, please call and ask our sales reps. They will be happy to verify the status for you. To order these invaluable reports, use the order form on page 221 or call 1-800-521-6797.

CONSTRUCTION INFORMATION

If you want to know more about techniques—and deal more confidently with subcontractors—we offer these useful sheets. Each set is an excellent tool that will add to your understanding of these technical subjects.

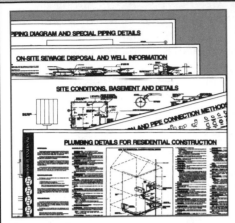

PLUMBING

The Blueprint Package includes locations for all the plumbing fixtures in your new house, including sinks, lavatories, tubs, showers, toilets, laundry trays and water heaters. However, if you want to know more about the complete plumbing system, these 24x36-inch detail sheets will prove very useful. Prepared to meet requirements of the National Plumbing Code, these six fact-filled sheets give general information on pipe schedules, fittings, sump-pump details, water-softener hookups, septic system details and much more. Color-coded sheets include a glossary of terms.

ELECTRICAL

The locations for every electrical switch, plug and outlet are shown in your Blueprint Package. However, these Electrical Details go further to take the mystery out of household electrical systems. Prepared to meet requirements of the National Electrical Code, these comprehensive 24x36-inch drawings come packed with helpful information, including wire sizing, switch-installation schematics, cable-routing details, appliance wattage, door-bell hook-ups, typical service panel circuitry and much more. Six sheets are bound together and color-coded for easy reference. A glossary of terms is also included.

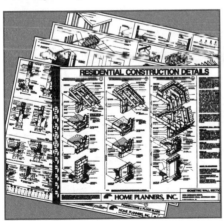

CONSTRUCTION

The Blueprint Package contains everything an experienced builder needs to construct a particular house. However, it doesn't show all the ways that houses can be built, nor does it explain alternate construction methods. To help you understand how your house will be built—and offer additional techniques—this set of drawings depicts the materials and methods used to build foundations, fireplaces, walls, floors and roofs. Where appropriate, the drawings show acceptable alternatives. These six sheets will answer questions for the advanced do-it-yourselfer or home planner.

MECHANICAL

This package contains fundamental principles and useful data that will help you make informed decisions and communicate with subcontractors about heating and cooling systems. The 24x36-inch drawings contain instructions and samples that allow you to make simple load calculations and preliminary sizing and costing analysis. Covered are today's most commonly used systems from heat pumps to solar fuel systems. The package is packed full of illustrations and diagrams to help you visualize components and how they relate to one another.

Plan-A-Home®

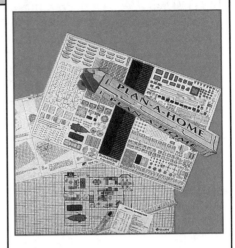

Plan-A-Home® is an easy-to-use tool that helps you design a new home, arrange furniture in a new or existing home, or plan a remodeling project. Each package contains:

- **More than 700 reusable peel-off planning symbols** on a self-stick vinyl sheet, including walls, windows, doors, all types of furniture, kitchen components, bath fixtures and many more.

- **A reusable, transparent, 1/4-inch scale planning grid** that matches the scale of actual working drawings (1/4-inch equals 1 foot). This grid provides the basis for house layouts of up to 140x92 feet.

- **Tracing paper** and a protective sheet for copying or transferring your completed plan.

- **A felt-tip pen,** with water-soluble ink that wipes away quickly.

Plan-A-Home® lets you lay out areas as large as a 7,500 square foot, six-bedroom, seven-bath house.

To Order, Call Toll Free 1-800-521-6797

To add these important extras to your Blueprint Package, simply indicate your choices on the order form on page 221 or call us Toll Free 1-800-521-6797 and we'll tell you more about these exciting products. For customer service, call toll free 1-888-690-1116.

D *The Deck Blueprint Package*

Many of the homes in this book can be enhanced with a professionally designed Home Planners Deck Plan. Those home plans highlighted with a D have a matching or corresponding deck plan available which includes a Deck Plan Frontal Sheet, Deck Framing and Floor Plans, Deck Elevations and a Deck Materials List. A Standard Deck Details Package, also available, provides all the how-to information necessary for building *any* deck. Our Complete Deck Building Package contains one set of Custom Deck Plans of your choice, plus one set of Standard Deck Building Details all for one low price. Our plans and details are carefully prepared in an easy-to-understand format that will guide you through every stage of your deck-building project. This page contains a sampling of 12 of the 25 different Deck layouts to match your favorite house. See page 186 for prices and ordering information.

SPLIT-LEVEL SUN DECK
Deck Plan D100

BI-LEVEL DECK WITH COVERED DINING
Deck Plan D101

WRAPAROUND FAMILY DECK
Deck Plan D104

DECK FOR DINING AND VIEWS
Deck Plan D107

TREND SETTER DECK
Deck Plan D110

TURN-OF-THE-CENTURY DECK
Deck Plan D111

WEEKEND ENTERTAINER DECK
Deck Plan D112

CENTER-VIEW DECK
Deck Plan D114

KITCHEN-EXTENDER DECK
Deck Plan D115

SPLIT-LEVEL ACTIVITY DECK
Deck Plan D117

TRI-LEVEL DECK WITH GRILL
Deck Plan D119

CONTEMPORARY LEISURE DECK
Deck Plan D120

▣ *The Landscape Blueprint Package*

For the homes marked with an ▣ in this book, Home Planners has created a front-yard landscape plan that matches or is complementary in design to the house plan. These comprehensive blueprint packages include a Frontal Sheet, Plan View, Regionalized Plant & Materials List, a sheet on Planting and Maintaining Your Landscape, Zone Maps and Plant Size and Description Guide. These plans will help you achieve professional results, adding value and enjoyment to your property for years to come. Each set of blueprints is a full 18" x 24" in size with clear, complete instructions and easy-to-read type. Six of the forty front yard Landscape Plans to match your favorite house are shown below.

Regional Order Map

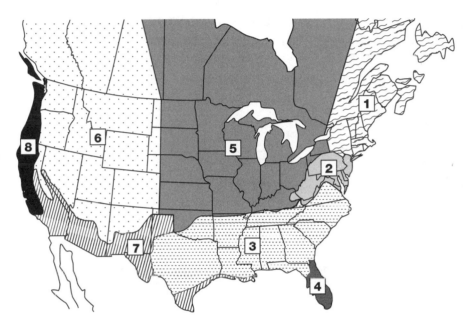

Most of the Landscape Plans shown on these pages are available with a Plant & Materials List adapted by horticultural experts to 8 different regions of the country. Please specify Geographic Region when ordering your plan. See page 250 for prices, ordering information and regional availability.

Region	1	Northeast
Region	2	Mid-Atlantic
Region	3	Deep South
Region	4	Florida & Gulf Coast
Region	5	Midwest
Region	6	Rocky Mountains
Region	7	Southern California & Desert Southwest
Region	8	Northern California & Pacific Northwest

CAPE COD COTTAGE
Landscape Plan L202

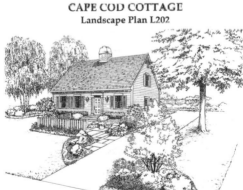

GAMBREL-ROOF COLONIAL
Landscape Plan L203

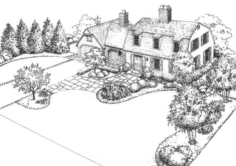

CENTER-HALL COLONIAL
Landscape Plan L204

CLASSIC NEW ENGLAND COLONIAL
Landscape Plan L205

COUNTRY-STYLE FARMHOUSE
Landscape Plan L207

TRADITIONAL SPLIT-LEVEL
Landscape Plan L228

Price Schedule & Plans Index

House Blueprint Price Schedule
(Prices guaranteed through December 31, 1999)

Tier	1-set Study Package	4-set Building Package	8-set Building Package	1-set Reproducible Sepias	Home Customizer® Package
A	$390	$435	$495	$595	$645
B	$430	$475	$535	$655	$705
C	$470	$515	$575	$715	$765
D	$510	$555	$615	$775	$825
E	$630	$675	$735	$835	$885

Prices for 4- or 8-set Building Packages honored only at time of original order.

Reverse blueprints (mirror image) with 4- or 8-set order.........$50 fee per order
Additional identical blueprints (standard or reverse) in same order....$50 per set
Additional sets ordered within one year of original purchase..........$50 per set
Specification Outlines ....$10 each
Materials Lists ....$50 or $75 each

Materials Lists for "E" price plans are an additional $10.

Deck Plans Price Schedule

CUSTOM DECK PLANS

Price Group	Q	R	S
1 Set Custom Plans	$25	$30	$35
Additional identical sets	$10 each		
Reverse sets (mirror image)	$10 each		

STANDARD DECK DETAILS
1 Set Generic Construction Details ....$14.95 each

COMPLETE DECK BUILDING PACKAGE

Price Group	Q	R	S
1 Set Custom Plans, plus			
1 Set Standard Deck Details	$35	$40	$45

Landscape Plans Price Schedule

Price Group	X	Y	Z
1 set	$35	$45	$55
3 sets	$50	$60	$70
6 sets	$65	$75	$85

Additional Identical Sets....................................$10 each
Reverse Sets (mirror image)..............................$10 each

Index

To use the Index below, refer to the design number listed in numerical order (a helpful page reference is also given). Note the price index letter and refer to the House Blueprint Price Schedule above for the cost of one, four or eight sets of blueprints or the cost of a reproducible sepia. Additional prices are shown for identical and reverse blueprint sets, as well as a very useful Materials List for some of the plans. Also note in the Index below those plans that have matching or complementary Deck Plans or Landscape Plans. Refer to the schedules above for prices of these plans. All plans in this publication are customizable. However, only Home Planners plans can be customized with Home Planners Home Customizer® Package. These plans are indicated below with this symbol: ☏. See page 221 for information. Some plans are also part of our Quote One® estimating service and are indicated by this symbol: 🏠. Many plans offer Materials Lists and are included by this symbol ✓. See page 214 for more information.

To Order: Fill in and send the order form on page 221—or call toll free 1-800-981-1525 or 520-297-8200. FAX: 800-244-6699 or 520-544-3086.

DESIGN	PRICE	PAGE	MATERIAL LIST	CUSTOMIZABLE	QUOTE ONE®	DECK	DECK PRICE	LANDSCAPE	LANDSCAPE PRICE	REGIONS
1113	A	37	✓	☏	🏠	...D113	...R	..L202	...X	1-3,5,6,8
1361	A	167	✓	☏		...D117	...S	..L225	...X	1-3,5,6,8
1956	A	9				...D117	...S			
1957	A	239	✓		🏠	...D100	...Q	..L228	...Y	1-8
2488	A	22	✓	☏	🏠	...D102	...Q			
2493	C	23	✓		🏠					
2622	A	164	✓	☏		...D103	...R	..L200	...X	1-3,5,6,8
2657	B	236		☏	🏠			..L200	...C	1-3,5,6,8
2661	A	48			🏠	...D113	...R	..L202	...X	1-3,5,6,8
2707	A	238		☏		...D117	...S	..L226	...X	1-8
2711	B	72		☏	🏠	...D105	...R	..L229	...Y	1-8
2864	A	214	✓		🏠	...D100	...Q	..L225	...X	1-3,5,6,8
2937	C	73	✓	☏				..L229	...Y	1-8
2974	A	11	✓	☏	🏠			..L223	...Z	1-3,5,6,8
3316	A	6	✓	☏				..L202	...X	1-3,5,6,8
3460	A	146	✓		🏠			..L200	...X	1-3,5,6,8
3562	B	111	✓		🏠	...D110	...R	..L238	...Y	3,4,7,8
3659	B	145	✓		🏠			..L290	...Y	1-8
3718	A	67	✓	☏						
3721	B	36	✓	☏						
3723	B	114	✓	☏						
3734	C	62		☏						
3735	C	63		☏						
3736	C	64		☏						
3737	C	65		☏						
5504	C	232	✓		🏠					
5505	C	232	✓		🏠					
5507	B	199	✓		🏠					
5508	B	199	✓		🏠					
5514	A	240	✓		🏠					
5515	A	240	✓		🏠					
5525	B	39	✓	☏	🏠					
5526	B	39	✓	☏	🏠					
5527	C	38	✓	☏	🏠					
5529	C	38	✓	☏	🏠					
5531	B	147	✓	☏	🏠					
5533	B	147	✓	☏	🏠					
5537	B	177	✓	☏	🏠					
5538	B	177	✓	☏	🏠					
5551	B	151	✓	☏	🏠					
5552	B	151	✓	☏	🏠					
6655	C	18								
6680	D	160								
6682	D	227								
6686	C	53								
6688	D	225								
6691	C	19								
6693	D	161								
6698	D	203								
6700	D	55								
6701	C	54								
7026	B	88	✓							
7216	C	95	✓							
7248	C	86	✓							
7251	C	93	✓							
7253	C	8	✓							
7289	C	194	✓							
7310	C	143	✓							
7328	C	94	✓							
7330	D	195	✓							
7338	C	126	✓							
7375	B	78	✓							

Before You Order . . .

Before filling out the coupon at right or calling us on our Toll-Free Blueprint Hotline, you may want to learn more about our services and products. Here's some information you will find helpful.

Quick Turnaround

We process and ship every blueprint order from our office within two business days. Because of this quick turnaround, we won't send a formal notice acknowledging receipt of your order.

Our Exchange Policy

Since blueprints are printed in response to your order, we cannot honor requests for refunds. However, we will exchange your entire first order for an equal number of blueprints at a price of $50 for the first set and $10 for each additional set; $70 total exchange fee for 4 sets; $100 total exchange fee for 8 sets . . . *plus* the difference in cost if exchanging for a design in a higher price bracket or *less* the difference in cost if exchanging for a design in lower price bracket. One exchange is allowed within a year of purchase date. **(Sepias and reproducibles are not refundable, returnable or exchangeable.)** All sets from the first order must be returned before the exchange can take place. Please add $18 for postage and handling via Regular Service; $30 via Priority Service; $40 via Express Service. Returns and cancellations are subject to a 20% restocking fee, and shipping and handling charges are not refundable.

About Reverse Blueprints

If you want to build in reverse of the plan as shown, we will include any number of reverse blueprints (mirror image) from a 4- or 8-set package for an additional fee of $50. Although lettering and dimensions will appear backward, reverses will be a useful aid if you decide to flop the plan.

Revising, Modifying and Customizing Plans

The wide variety of designs available in this publication allows you to select ideas and concepts for a home to fit your building site and match your family's needs, wants and budget. Like many homeowners who buy these plans, you and your builder, architect or engineer may want to make changes to them. Some minor changes may be made by your builder, but we recommend that most changes be made by a licensed architect or engineer. If you need to make alterations to a design that is customizable, you need only order our Home Customizer® Package to get you started. As set forth below, we cannot assume any responsibility for blueprints which have been changed, whether by you, your builder or by professionals selected by you or referred to you by us, because such individuals are outside our supervision and control.

Architectural and Engineering Seals

Some cities and states are now requiring that a licensed architect or engineer review and "seal" a blueprint, or officially approve it, prior to construction due to concerns over energy costs, safety and other factors. Prior to application for a building permit or the start of actual construction, we strongly advise that you consult your local building official who can tell you if such a review is required.

About the Designers

The architects and designers whose work appears in this publication are among America's leading residential designers. Each plan was designed to meet the requirements of a nationally recognized model building code in effect at the time and place the plan was drawn. Because national building codes change from time to time, plans may not comply with any such code at the time they are sold to a customer. In addition, building officials may not accept these plans as final construction documents of record as the plans may need to be modified and additional drawings and details added to suit local conditions and requirements. We strongly advise that purchasers consult a licensed architect or engineer, and their local building official, before starting any construction related to these plans.

Local Building Codes and Zoning Requirements

At the time of creation, our plans are drawn to specifications published by the Building Officials and Code Administrators (BOCA) International, Inc.; the Southern Building Code Congress (SBCCI) International, Inc.; the International Conference of Building Officials; or the Council of American Building Officials (CABO). Our plans are designed to meet or exceed national building standards. Because of the great differences in geography and climate throughout the United States and Canada, each state, county and municipality has its own building codes, zone requirements, ordinances and building regulations. Your plan may need to be modified to comply with local requirements regarding snow loads, energy codes, soil and seismic conditions and a wide range of other matters. In addition, you may need to obtain permits or inspections from local governments before and in the course of construction. Prior to using blueprints ordered from us, we strongly advise that you consult a licensed architect or engineer—and speak with your local building official—before applying for any permit or beginning construction. We authorize the use of our blueprints on the express condition that you strictly comply with all local building codes, zoning requirements and other applicable laws, regulations, ordinances and requirements. **Notice:** Plans for homes to be built in Nevada must be re-drawn by a Nevada-registered professional. Consult your building official for more information on this subject.

Foundation and Exterior Wall Changes

Most of our plans are drawn with either a full or partial basement foundation. Depending on your specific climate or regional building practices, you may wish to change this basement to a slab or crawlspace. Most professional contractors and builders can easily adapt your plans to alternate foundation types. Likewise, most can easily change 2x4 wall construction to 2x6, or vice versa.

Disclaimer

We and the designers we work with have put substantial care and effort into the creation of our blueprints. However, because we cannot provide on-site consultation, supervision and control over actual construction, and because of the great variance in local building requirements, building practices and soil, seismic, weather and other conditions, WE CANNOT MAKE ANY WARRANTY, EXPRESS OR IMPLIED, WITH RESPECT TO THE CONTENT OR USE OF OUR BLUEPRINTS, INCLUDING BUT NOT LIMITED TO ANY WARRANTY OF MERCHANTABILITY OR OF FITNESS FOR A PARTICULAR PURPOSE.

Terms and Conditions

These designs are protected under the terms of United States Copyright Law and may not be copied or reproduced in any way, by any means, unless you have purchased Sepias or Reproducibles which clearly indicate your right to copy or reproduce. We authorize the use of your chosen design as an aid in the construction of one single family home only. You may not use this design to build a second or multiple dwellings without purchasing another blueprint or blueprints or paying additional design fees.

How Many Blueprints Do You Need?

A single set of blueprints is sufficient to study a home in greater detail. However, if you are planning to obtain cost estimates from a contractor or subcontractors—or if you are planning to build immediately—you will need more sets. Because additional sets are cheaper when ordered in quantity with the original order, make sure you order enough blueprints to satisfy all requirements. The following checklist will help you determine how many you need:

____ Owner

____ Builder (generally requires at least three sets; one as a legal document, one to use during inspections, and at least one to give to subcontractors)

____ Local Building Department (often requires two sets)

____ Mortgage Lender (usually one set for a conventional loan; three sets for FHA or VA loans)

____ TOTAL NUMBER OF SETS

Have You Seen Our Newest Designs?

Home Planners is one of the country's most active home design firms, creating nearly 100 new plans each year. At least 50 of our latest creations are featured in each edition of our New Design Portfolio. You may have received a copy with your latest purchase by mail. If not, or if you purchased this book from a local retailer, just return the coupon below for your FREE copy. Make sure you consider the very latest of what Home Planners has to offer.

Yes! Please send my FREE copy of your latest New Design Portfolio.

Offer good to U.S. shipping address only.

Name _____

Address _____

City_____ State_____ Zip _____

Toll Free 1-800-521-6797

Regular Office Hours:
8:00 a.m. to 8:00 p.m. Eastern Time, Monday through Friday
Our staff will gladly answer any questions during regular office hours. Our answering service can place orders after hours or on weekends.

If we receive your order by 4:00 p.m. Eastern Time, Monday through Friday, we'll process it and ship within two business days. When ordering by phone, please have your credit card ready. We'll also ask you for the Order Form Key Number at the bottom of the coupon.

By FAX: Copy the Order Form on the next page and send it on our FAX line: 1-800-224-6699 or 1-520-544-3086.

Canadian Customers
Order Toll-Free 1-800-561-4169

For faster service and plans that are modified for building in Canada, customers may now call in orders directly to our Canadian supplier of plans and charge the purchase to a credit card. Or, you may complete the order form at right, adding the current exchange rate to all prices and mail in Canadian funds to:

The Plan Centre 60 Baffin Place
Unit 5
Waterloo, Ontario N2V 1Z7

OR: Copy the Order Form and send it via our Canadian FAX line: 1-800-719-3291.

The Home Customizer®

"This house is perfect...if only the family room were two feet wider." Sound familiar? In response to the numerous requests for this type of modification, Home Planners has developed **The Home Customizer® Package**. This exclusive package offers our top-of-the-line materials to make it easy for anyone, anywhere to customize any Home Planners design to fit their needs. Check the index on pages 218-219 for those plans which are customizable.

Some of the changes you can make to any of our plans include:

- exterior elevation changes
- kitchen and bath modifications
- roof, wall and foundation changes
- room additions and more!

The Home Customizer® Package includes everything you'll need to make the necessary changes to your favorite Home Planners design. The package includes:

- instruction book with examples
- architectural scale and clear work film
- erasable red marker and removable correction tape
- ¼"-scale furniture cutouts
- 1 set reproducible, erasable Sepias
- 1 set study blueprints for communicating changes to your design professional
- a copyright release letter so you can make copies as you need them
- referral letter with the name, address and telephone number of the professional in your region who is trained in modifying Home Planners designs efficiently and inexpensively.

The price of the **Home Customizer® Package** ranges from $645 to $885, depending on the price schedule of the design you have chosen. **The Home Customizer® Package** will not only save you 25% to 75% of the cost of drawing the plans from scratch with a custom architect or engineer, it will also give you the flexibility to have your changes and modifications made by our referral network or by the professional of your choice. Now it's even easier and more affordable to have the custom home you've always wanted.

ORDER TOLL FREE!
For information about any of our services or to order call 1-800-521-6797 or 520-297-8200. Browse our website: www.homeplanners.com

For Customer Service, call toll free 1-888-690-1116.

 HOME PLANNERS, LLC
Wholly owned by Hanley-Wood, Inc.
3275 WEST INA ROAD, SUITE 110
TUCSON, ARIZONA 85741

THE BASIC BLUEPRINT PACKAGE
Rush me the following (please refer to the Plans Index and Price Schedule in this section):
_____ Set(s) of blueprints for plan number(s) _____. $_____
_____ Set(s) of sepias for plan number(s) _____. $_____
_____ Home Customizer® Package for plan(s)_____. $_____
_____ Additional identical blueprints (standard or reverse) in same order @ $50 per set. $_____
_____ Reverse blueprints @ $50 fee per order. $_____

IMPORTANT EXTRAS
Rush me the following:
_____ Materials List: $50 (Must be purchased with Blueprint set.) $75 Design Basics. Add $10 for a Schedule E–G plan. $_____
_____ **Quote One®** Summary Cost Report @ $19.95 for 1, $14.95 for each additional, for plans _____ $_____
Building location: City _____ Zip Code _____
_____ **Quote One®** Materials Cost Report @ $110 Schedule A–D; $120 Schedule E, for plan _____ $_____
(Must be purchased with Blueprints set.)
Building location: City _____ Zip Code _____
_____ Specification Outlines @ $10 each. $_____
_____ Detail Sets @ $14.95 each; any two for $22.95; any three for $29.95; all four for $39.95 (save $19.85). $_____
❑ Plumbing ❑ Electrical ❑ Construction ❑ Mechanical (These helpful details provide general construction advice and are not specific to any single plan.)
_____ Plan-A-Home® @ $29.95 each. $_____
DECK BLUEPRINTS
_____ Set(s) of Deck Plan _____. $_____
_____ Additional identical blueprints in same order @ $10 per set. $_____
_____ Reverse blueprints @ $10 per set. $_____
_____ Set of Standard Deck Details @ $14.95 per set. $_____
_____ Set of Complete Building Package (Best Buy!) Includes Custom Deck Plan _____. (See Index and Price Schedule) Plus Standard Deck Details $_____
LANDSCAPE BLUEPRINTS
_____ Set(s) of Landscape Plan _____. $_____
_____ Additional identical blueprints in same order @ $10 per set. $_____
_____ Reverse blueprints @ $10 per set. $_____
Please indicate the appropriate region of the country for Plant & Material List. (See Map on page 217): Region _____

POSTAGE AND HANDLING	1–3 sets	4+ sets
Signature is required for all deliveries. **DELIVERY** No CODs (Requires street address—No P.O. Boxes)		
•Regular Service (Allow 7–10 business days delivery)	❑ $15.00	❑ $18.00
•Priority (Allow 4–5 business days delivery)	❑ $20.00	❑ $30.00
•Express (Allow 3 business days delivery)	❑ $30.00	❑ $40.00
CERTIFIED MAIL If no street address available. (Allow 7–10 days delivery)	❑ $20.00	❑ $30.00
OVERSEAS DELIVERY Note: All delivery times are from date Blueprint Package is shipped.	fax, phone or mail for quote	

POSTAGE (From box above) $_____
SUBTOTAL $_____
SALES TAX (AZ, MI & WA residents, please add appropriate state and local sales tax.) $_____
TOTAL (Subtotal and tax) $_____

YOUR ADDRESS (please print)
Name _____
Street _____
City _____ State _____ Zip _____
Daytime telephone number (_____) _____

FOR CREDIT CARD ORDERS ONLY
Please fill in the information below:
Credit card number _____
Exp. Date: Month/Year _____
Check one ❑ Visa ❑ MasterCard ❑ Discover Card ❑ American Express
Signature _____

Please check appropriate box: ❑ Licensed Builder-Contractor ❑ Homeowner

ORDER TOLL FREE!
1-800-521-6797 or 520-297-8200

Order Form Key
TB62

Helpful Books & Software

Home Planners wants your building experience to be as pleasant and trouble-free as possible. That's why we've expanded our library of Do-It-Yourself titles to help you along. In addition to our beautiful plans books, we've added books to guide you through specific projects as well as the construction process. In fact, these are titles that will be as useful after your dream home is built as they are right now.

ONE-STORY	TWO-STORY	VACATION	MULTI-LEVEL	COUNTRY	MOVE-UP	NARROW-LOT	SMALL HOUSE

1 448 designs for all lifestyles. 860 to 5,400 square feet. 384 pages $9.95

2 460 designs for one-and-a-half and two stories. 1,245 to 7,275 square feet. 384 pages $9.95

3 345 designs for recreation, retirement and leisure. 312 pages $8.95

4 214 designs for split-levels, bi-levels, multi-levels and walkouts. 224 pages $8.95

5 200 country designs from classic to contemporary by 7 winning designers. 224 pages $8.95

6 200 stylish designs for today's growing families from 9 hot designers. 224 pages $8.95

7 200 unique homes less than 60' wide from 7 designers. Up to 3,000 square feet. 224 pages $8.95

8 200 beautiful designs chosen for versatility and affordability. 224 pages $8.95

BUDGET-SMART	EXPANDABLES	ENCYCLOPEDIA	AFFORDABLE	ENCYCLOPEDIA 2	VICTORIAN	ESTATE	LUXURY

9 200 efficient plans from 7 top designers, that you can really afford to build! 224 pages $8.95

10 200 flexible plans that expand with your needs from 7 top designers. 240 pages $8.95

11 500 exceptional plans for all styles and budgets—the best book of its kind! 352 pages $9.95

12 Completely revised and updated, featuring 300 designs for modest budgets. 256 pages $9.95

13 500 completely new plans. Spacious and stylish designs for every budget and taste. 352 pages $9.95

14 160 striking Victorian and Farmhouse designs from three leading designers. 192 pages $12.95

15 Dream big! Twenty-one designers showcase their biggest and best plans. 208 pages. $15.95

16 154 fine luxury plans—loaded with luscious amenities! 192 pages $14.95

COTTAGES	BEST SELLERS	SPECIAL COLLECTION	COUNTRY HOUSES	CLASSIC	CONTEMPORARY	EASY-LIVING	SOUTHERN

17 25 fresh new designs that are as warm as a tropical breeze. A blend of the best aspects of many coastal styles. 64 pages. $19.95

18 Our 50th Anniversary book with 200 of our very best designs in full color! 224 pages $12.95

19 70 Romantic house plans that capture the classic tradition of home design. 160 pages $17.95

20 208 unique home plans that combine traditional style and modern livability. 224 pages $9.95

21 Timeless, elegant designs that always feel like home. Gorgeous plans that are as flexible and up-to-date as their occupants. 240 pages. $9.95

22 The most complete and imaginative collection of contemporary designs available anywhere. 240 pages. $9.95

23 200 efficient and sophisticated plans that are small in size, but big on livability. 224 pages $8.95

24 207 homes rich in Southern styling and comfort. 240 pages $8.95

SUNBELT	WESTERN	ENERGY GUIDE	**Design Software**		**Outdoor Projects**		
			BOOK & CD ROM	3D DESIGN SUITE	OUTDOOR	GARAGES & MORE	DECKS

25 215 designs that capture the spirit of the Southwest. 208 pages $10.95

26 215 designs that capture the spirit and diversity of the Western lifestyle. 208 pages $9.95

27 The most comprehensive energy efficiency and conservation guide available. 280 pages $35.00

28 Both the Home Planners Gold book and matching Windows™ CD ROM with 3D floorplans. $24.95

29 Home design made easy! View designs in 3D, take a virtual reality tour, add decorating details and more. $59.95

30 42 unique outdoor projects. Gazebos, strombellas, bridges, sheds, playsets and more! 96 pages $7.95

31 101 multi-use garages and outdoor structures to enhance any home. 96 pages $7.95

32 25 outstanding single-, double- and multi-level decks you can build. 112 pages $7.95

Landscape Designs

EASY CARE	FRONT & BACK	BACKYARDS	BEDS & BORDERS	BATHROOMS	KITCHENS	HOUSE CONTRACTING	WINDOWS & DOORS

33 41 special landscapes designed for beauty and low maintenance. 160 pages $14.95

34 The first book of do-it-yourself landscapes. 40 front, 15 backyards. 208 pages $14.95

35 40 designs focused solely on creating your own specially themed backyard oasis. 160 pages $14.95

36 Practical advice and maintenance techniques for a wide variety of yard projects. 160 pages. $14.95

37 An innovative guide to organizing, remodeling and decorating your bathroom. 96 pages $10.95

38 An imaginative guide to designing the perfect kitchen. Chock full of bright ideas to make your job easier. 176 pages $14.95

39 Everything you need to know to act as your own general contractor...and save up to 25% off building costs. 134 pages $14.95

40 Installation techniques and tips that make your project easier and more professional looking. 80 pages $7.95

ROOFING	FRAMING	VISUAL HANDBOOK	BASIC WIRING	PATIOS & WALKS	TILE	TRIM & MOLDING

41 Information on the latest tools, materials and techniques for roof installation or repair. 80 pages $7.95

42 For those who want to take a more-hands on approach to their dream. 319 pages $19.95

43 A plain-talk guide to the construction process; financing to final walk-through, this book covers it all. 498 pages $19.95

44 A straight forward guide to one of the most misunderstood systems in the home. 160 pages $12.95

45 Clear step-by-step instructions take you from the basic design stages to the finished project. 80 pages $7.95

46 Every kind of tile for every kind of application. Includes tips on use installation and repair. 176 pages $12.95

47 Step-by-step instructions for installing baseboards, window and door casings and more. 80 pages $7.95

Additional Books Order Form

To order your books, just check the box of the book numbered below and complete the coupon. We will process your order and ship it from our office within 48 hours. Send coupon and check (in U.S. funds).

YES! Please send me the books I've indicated:

☐ 1:VO	$9.95	☐ 25:SW	$10.95
☐ 2:VT	$9.95	☐ 26:WH	$9.95
☐ 3:VH	$8.95	☐ 27:RES	$35.00
☐ 4:VS	$8.95	☐ 28:HPGC	$24.95
☐ 5:FH	$8.95	☐ 29:PLANSUITE	$59.95
☐ 6:MU	$8.95	☐ 30:YG	$7.95
☐ 7:NL	$8.95	☐ 31:GG	$7.95
☐ 8:SM	$8.95	☐ 32:DP	$7.95
☐ 9:BS	$8.95	☐ 33:ECL	$14.95
☐ 10:EX	$8.95	☐ 34:HL	$14.95
☐ 11:EN	$9.95	☐ 35:BYL	$14.95
☐ 12:AF	$9.95	☐ 36:BB	$14.95
☐ 13:E2	$9.95	☐ 37:CDB	$10.95
☐ 14:VDH	$12.95	☐ 38:CKI	$14.95
☐ 15:EDH	$15.95	☐ 39:SBC	$14.95
☐ 16:LD2	$14.95	☐ 40:CGD	$7.95
☐ 17:CTG	$19.95	☐ 41:CGR	$7.95
☐ 18:HPG	$12.95	☐ 42:SRF	$19.95
☐ 19:WEP	$17.95	☐ 43:RVH	$19.95
☐ 20:CN	$9.95	☐ 44:CBW	$12.95
☐ 21:CS	$9.95	☐ 45:CGW	$7.95
☐ 22:CM	$9.95	☐ 46:CWT	$12.95
☐ 23:EL	$8.95	☐ 47:CGT	$7.95
☐ 24:SH	$8.95		

Canadian Customers
Order Toll-Free 1-800-561-4169

Additional Books Subtotal $ _____
ADD Postage and Handling $ 4.00
Sales Tax: (AZ, MI & WA residents, please add appropriate state and local sales tax.) $ _____
YOUR TOTAL (Subtotal, Postage/Handling, Tax) $ _____

YOUR ADDRESS (Please print)

Name _____

Street _____

City _____ State _____ Zip _____

Phone (_____) _____ — _____

YOUR PAYMENT
Check one: ☐ Check ☐ Visa ☐ MasterCard ☐ Discover Card
☐ American Express
Required credit card information:

Credit Card Number _____

Expiration Date (Month/Year) _____ / _____

Signature Required _____

 Home Planners, LLC
Wholly owned by Hanley-Wood, Inc.
3275 W. Ina Road, Suite 110, Dept. BK, Tucson, AZ 85741

TB62

Design 5527, page 38

OVER 3 MILLION BLUEPRINTS SOLD

"We instructed our builder to follow the plans including all of the many details which make this house so elegant…Our home is a fine example of the results one can achieve by purchasing and following the plans which you offer…Everyone who has seen it has assured us that it belongs in 'a picture book.' I truly mean it when I say that my home 'is a DREAM HOUSE.'"

S.P.
Anderson, SC

"We have had a steady stream of visitors, many of whom tell us this is the most beautiful home they've seen. Everyone is amazed at the layout and remarks on how unique it is. Our real estate attorney, who is a Chicago dweller and who deals with highly valued properties, told me this is the only suburban home he has seen that he would want to live in."

W. & P.S.
Flossmoor, IL

"Your blueprints saved us a great deal of money. I acted as the general contractor and we did a lot of the work ourselves. We probably built it for half the cost! We are thinking about more plans for another home. I purchased a competitor's book but my husband wants only your plans!"

K.M.
Grovetown, GA

"We are very happy with the product of our efforts. The neighbors and passersby appreciate what we have created. We have had many people stop by to discuss our house and kindly praise it as being the nicest house in our area of new construction. We have even had one person stop and make us an unsolicited offer to buy the house for much more than we have invested in it."

K. & L.S.
Bolingbrook, IL

"The traffic going past our house is unbelievable. On several occasions, we have heard that it is the 'prettiest house in Batvia.' Also, when meeting someone new and mentioning what street we live on, quite often we're told, 'Oh, you're the one in the yellow house with the wrap-around porch! I love it!'"

A.W.
-Batvia, NY

"I have been involved in the building trades my entire life…Since building our home we have built two other homes for other families. Their plans from local professional architects were not nearly as good as yours. For that reason we are ordering additional plan books from you."

T.F.
Kingston, WA

"The blueprints we received from you were of excellent quality and provided us with exactly what we needed to get our successful home-building project underway. We appreciate your invaluable role in our home-building effort."

T.A.
Concord, TN